Sign

of

Her Heart

formerly

MARY IN HER SCAPULAR PROMISE

by

John Mathias Haffert

preface by
Most Rev. Fulton J. Sheen, Ph.D., LL.D., S.T.D.

printed in the U.S.A.
by

The 101 Foundation, Inc.
P.O. Box 151
Asbury, New Jersey 08802

phone: 908-689 8792
fax: 908-689 1957

ISBN # 1-890137-11-1

MARY IN HER SCAPULAR PROMISE

Beato Alphonso Mariæ · Spiritum · Deo Reddenti · Scapulare Hoc · B · M · V · Impositum XXVII · Annorum · Spatio · Una · Cum · Exuviis · Sepultum · Integrum · Incorruptumque · Uti · Veneratur Repertum ....

A picture shown here of the two-hundred-year-old scapular of St. Alphonsus shows it to be remarkable even had it not been in the tomb for forty years. The cotton picture is even intact, with the thread fastening it to the wool. Yet in the tomb, all beneath and above it turned to dust. It was found as pictured

here . . . on the saint's skeleton. Examination proves that it had no special treatment that could account for this wonder. And since clothing beneath and above it disappeared, and the body itself turned to dust, it is obvious that we are in the presence of a wonder which cannot be naturally explained.

CONTENTS

PREFACE

THE PERFECTIONS of God are so infinite that no single creature could possibly reflect His Power and Goodness. God therefore multiplied creatures that what one failed to reveal the other might declare. The same is true of the Incarnate Son of God, Our Lord and Saviour Jesus Christ. The richness of His Redemptive Blood would not be reflected in only one material way. Rather like the sun, the beauties of whose seven rays are reflected only by shining through the prism, the beauties of Calvary are only adequately revealed to us as they shine through the prism of Christ's Church and split up into the vivifying graces of the seven Sacraments.

Mary, the Mother of that Divine Saviour, is only a creature, human and not divine. But exalted to the high office of being the ciborium of Emmanuel for the nine months she bore about in her virgin flesh the Host Who is the lamb of God, it follows that she has so much dignity that no one title could exhaust it. That is why there is a Litany to her made up of many titles, as so many facets reflecting the various lights of the diamond of her Divine Maternity.

In like manner, the tradition of the Church is full of various titles under which the intercessory power of the Blessed Mother may be invoked. At one time, it is as the Defender of Christianity when the Turks invaded Europe; at another as the Queen of Peace; at another as the Lady of Lourdes. This book is concerned with one of these titles and one of the most glorious of them all: "Mary, Mother of the Scapular of Mount Carmel."

Mr. Haffert, in writing its history, has in a masterly way laid bare the solid foundations upon which this devotion reposes. In doing this he has satisfied the mood and temper of the modern mind which wants a realistic foundation for its idealism. His case is so strikingly presented that to challenge this devotion is to challenge to some extent the tradition and authority of the Church. Since we learn to love ends because we know their beginnings, so we are strengthened in our love of the Blessed Mother by being shown the foundation stones upon which it reposes. More than that, one sees in the Scapular, which is a miniature clothing, a reversal of the penalties and effects of original sin. Before Adam sinned, he was naked but not ashamed. That was because of the integrity of his human nature by which senses were subject to reason and reason to God. His union with God was, as it were, the clothing of his whole being. But once that union was disrupted, he was naked and ashamed. He now had need of clothing. From that day to this, human nature has used either one of two kinds of clothing, depending upon whether they emphasized the nakedness of souls or the nakedness of the body. Those who are totally disinterested in God clothe themselves with jewels and finery to compensate, whether

they know it or not, for their inner spiritual poverty.
Those who love God, and therefore have souls
clothed with the raiments of His grace, need never
care about the richness of the external. We see
something of the symbolism of this in the clothing
of a nun. When the ceremony begins she is dressed
in surpassing beauty and bedecked with jewels. But
once she consecrates herself to God, she clothes herself in the poverty-stricken garments of her community. Being clothed with the richness of Divinity,
why should she concern herself with the superficial
beauty of the world?

There must be something of this symbolism in
Mary's gift of the Scapular which was originally a
habit. "The beauty of the King's daughter is from
within." Mary's gift of clothing is just a simple
garment, sufficient to cover the traces of original sin
in us, but its very simplicity is also a witness to the
fact that her own beautiful mantle covers our souls.
The Scapular bears therefore a double witness: to
Mary's protection against the ravages of the flesh
occasioned by the Fall, and to Mary's influence as
Mediatrix of graces, who covers our souls with the
richness of her Son's Redemption.

Mary has been constituted by her Divine Son as
the intermediary between our needs and His wants;
such was the role she played at the marriage feast
of Cana, when she interceded for the needy guests
to the miraculous power of her Divine Son. It is a
singular fact that in answer to her request Our Lord
addressed her, not as 'Mother,' but as 'Woman,' as
if to imply that once she began interceding for the

humanity whom He was to redeem when "the hour" would come, she entered into a larger relationship than merely that of being His Mother, namely, that of 'Woman,' the new Mother of redeemed men.

On the Cross this title is conferred again when Our Lord addresses her as "Woman! Behold thy son!" She had brought forth her "first born" in the flesh at Bethlehem, now she was to bring forth her first born in the spirit at Calvary, namely John, the beloved disciple. John was the symbol of men, whose motherhood Mary purchased at the foot of the Cross in union with her Divine Son. It is not by a figure of speech, nor by a metaphor that Mary is our Mother, but rather by virtue of the pangs of childbirth. As a woman can never forget the child of her womb, so neither can Mary forget us.

With particular reference to Mary's intercession for our eternal salvation, Mr. Haffert has been inspired to write this book of devotion. It should bring forth a response which the love that went into its writing deserves. And I am sure that if but one soul, who otherwise would not have known Mary and her scapular, comes to know and love her through this book, Mr. Haffert would feel that his work has been well done.

MOST REV. FULTON J. SHEEN,
Auxiliary Bishop of New York.

Feast of St. Simon Stock
May 16, 1940.

ACKNOWLEDGMENTS

THE AUTHOR expresses a debt of gratitude to the Most Rev. FULTON J. SHEEN, D.D., who, with a preface to this book, has virtually stooped from the pulpit of the world to add the universality of his voice to its humble message. Likewise he expresses his gratitude to MOTHER AGNES OF JESUS, Prioress of the Carmelite Convent of Lisieux, for the letter quoted at the end of the book by which she has placed the author's work under the auspices of her little sister, the world-beloved Saint of Carmel. Gratitude is also due to his Excellency, the MOST REV. BARTHOLOMEW J. EUSTACE, D.D., Bishop of Camden, for having read the MS. and made many valuable criticisms; to the MOST REVEREND HILARY M. DOSWALD, O. Carm., Prior General of the Carmelite Order; to the VERY REV. GABRIEL N. PAUSBACK, O. Carm., Assistant General of the Carmelites, who helped particularly with the Second Edition after the most careful study; to the VERY REV. BARTHOLOMEW M. XIBERTA, O. Carm., ex-Assistant General of the Carmelite Order and Carmelite Historian; to DR. CYRIL KEHOE, O. Carm., Professor of Theology at the diocesan seminary, Toronto, Canada; to the REV. MALACHY LYNCH, O. Carm., Prior at Abereswyth, Wales, and founder of the League of Our Lady, for having read the MS. and offered literary suggestions; to JEANNE ELIZABETH KOHL, M.A., of Immaculata College, Immaculata, Pa., for assistance with the proofs; to the REV. M. LAFLANCHE, Vicar General of the diocese of Nimes, France; to the MONASTERY OF THE VISITATION AT PARAY LE MONIAL and to the Jesuits of the same city. Finally, a deep recognition must be voiced to the many Carmelites in America who have assisted in the production of this book and without whose cooperation it could never have appeared. This appreciation is especially due to the REV. JOHN J. HAFFERT, O. Carm., Novice Master in the Carmelite Order more than fourteen years, for having offered invaluable advice after thrice reading the entire manuscript. Likewise a special appreciation is due to the VERY REV. DIONYSIUS L. FLANAGAN, O. Carm., Prior Provincial of the New York Province of Carmelites, for his friendship and support; to the REV. NORBERT PIPER, O. Carm., Master of Professed in the Carmelite Seminary at Niagara Falls, for his assistance; to the Rev. SYLVESTER J. MAHER, O. Carm., Prior at Saint Albert's College, Middletown, N. Y.; to the REV. THOMAS M. KILDUFF, O. D. C., Prior of the Discalced Carmelite Fathers, Washington, D. C., and to the REV. ELISEUS J. COSTA, O. D. C., Sub-Prior; and to many other Carmelites. In appreciation, the author would like to remark that the whole world owes a debt of gratitude to the Carmelites—a debt not only because Our Heavenly Mother gave us the Scapular through them, but also because the great Scapular Devotion would be almost unknown to us were it not for their zeal. The bibliography of the present book is a monument to them; subtract from it the names of Carmelite authors and its seventeen pages dwindle to less than one!

May She of whom this book is written take upon Herself acknowledgment of its author's debts.

Feast of Immaculate Heart
Dec. 8th, 1941.

Special Acknowledgment for the Third Edition

Since the above acknowledgments were written (in 1940) several of those mentioned have passed to their eternal reward and some, like Bishop Sheen, have received greater honors than they had.

Great acknowledgment is now due to the wonderful Catholics of the New World who have developed the great love for the Blessed Virgin which flourished in many old worlds. Since 1940 they have made this book a perennial best-seller and . . . as though merely waiting to be reminded . . . they have hastened to clothe themselves in Our Lady's precious Habit. In 1940, little more than 500,000 Scapulars were used annually in the United States. In 1952, as this book went into its seventieth thousand impression, almost that many were being used in the city of Detroit alone.

Moreover, one more Carmelite name must now be entered into the specific rolls of acknowledgment: Rev. Luis Gonzaga de Oliveira, O. Carm., of Lisbon, Portugal, through whom the author was introduced to the Bishop of Fatima and obtained a personal interview with "Lucia," sole survivor of the three children who saw Our Lady of Fatima. In that interview the seer of Fatima explained that the very last appearance of Our Lady of Fatima was the Mother described in this book . . . Our Lady of the Scapular Promise . . . the Mother who, as Blessed Claude said over a century ago: In giving the Scapular *"Revealed all the tenderness of Her Heart."* And in 1950, commemorating the seventh centennial of the Scapular Vision, Pope Pius XII designated the Scapular as our "Sign of Consecration to the Immaculate Heart of Mary."

INVOCATION

THE AUTHOR would like to place this book in the hands of Mary's "Little Flower." No one may look to see his dedication, but he would like to feel that St. Therese has placed her seal on these pages and made their doctrine, which is her doctrine, a part of her apostolate on earth. May she speak, from between the lines, illuminating the understanding and touching the affections of all its readers. For when its author wrote to her living sisters and explained what Mary in Her Scapular Promise might mean to the world, the unusual answer came back from Saint Therese's "little mother" herself: "We pray wholeheartedly that your immense desires to make Our Lady of Mount Carmel known and loved may be realized and *it is our belief that Saint Therese of the Child Jesus, who so much loves the Blessed Virgin, will aid in their realization.* We can only collaborate in this work by our prayers, but our Saint will know, at the opportune time, to obtain the necessary aids for the work in question."

Therefore, Saint Therese, the work has already been placed in your hands by her whom you called here on earth "my little mother." Beloved Flower of Carmel's Queen, bless those who embrace it and seek to propagate it! Bless the good priest and humble brother who are its inspiration. And since you said that Our Lady of Mount Carmel cured "Her little flower" that she might shed the sweet fragrance then received "in Her Garden of Carmel," so shed that fragrance in Her vast confraternity that its millions of Marian souls may be drawn to follow you to Mary that they, too, humbly and purely as children, may find Jesus! You said that had you been a priest you should have shown how imitable Mary is. But now you exercise your priestly mission from the pulpit of Heaven and the Scapular shows how imitable Mary is. Will you not, therefore, make it your mission to propagate that Sign of Mary and make it known and appreciated everywhere?

Obtain from Our Lady, dear Therese, the grace that everyone may see how Her Scapular preaches an imitable Virgin, more a Mother than a Queen. Since the Vicars of Christ on earth have said that if the world would imitate you the nations would be quickly reformed, and since the Scapular devotion was your secret, impart this secret to the world that the Reign of Jesus through Mary be hastened! Since your union with Mary has alone done so much to save the world, unite all of us who wear the Scapular to that loving Mother and teach us, under Her Mantle, the sweet secrets of Nazareth which you learned there.

The Scapular is today becoming a symbol of your little way. Is not its world propagation, therefore, your mission, Therese? Then, be its signature, sweet Image of Carmel's Queen. By that great power with which the Child Jesus has invested your prayer, be its signature the world over!

"In that celebrated Promise

Mary reveals

All the tenderness of Her Heart." *

BL. CLAUDE DE LA COLOMBIERE

   * *The personal pronoun referring to the Blessed Virgin is capitalized throughout these pages partially out of respect but primarily to specify the reference. The Blessed Virgin is not Divine, but has been made perfect above all creatures to be the Queen of all. This book is about Her, in the light of the Scapular Devotion, rather than just about the devotion in itself.*

CHAPTER ONE

Origin of the Promise

IT IS eight hundred and sixty years before Christ. A striking scene is being enacted in Palestine. The entire Jewish nation is assembled there on the summit of the Scripturally famous Mount Carmel. Dinning within a circle formed by the thousands of Israelites, four hundred and fifty pagan priests are screaming fiendishly about a stone altar upon which they have laid a dressed bullock. Early this memorable morning they began dancing about according to their rite and slashing themselves with their lancets. Their shouts have been rising shrilly, their lancets waving more and more wildly until now, at noon, they mill about in an exhausted frenzy, covered from head to feet in their own blood.

Deafened by the shrieks of the many hysterical, blood-covered priests, the Jewish King, Achab, presses foremost in the tremendous crowd of onlookers. His face is contracted with worry and pain; the faces of his entourage are crestfallen. But to the side, alone, a white-bearded old man stands wreathed in smiles! His eyes glint like fire and quick gestures betray a great nervous strength in his thin and poorly clad body. He is jesting with the priests and taunting them!

Behind this mysterious and horrible scene lies a tense drama.

The Jewish nation has fallen into idolatry and three years and six months before this day, that old man—who was dwelling on this same mountain—walked down the streets of the royal city and up to the palace. He then proclaimed before the king that if the nation did not return to its God it would be divinely punished. Since that very day, when he was sent away from the royal palace unheeded, it has not rained in all Palestine. But now, at the summons of the king, the whole nation is gathered on Mount Carmel. The venerable old man—who is the fiery prophet, Elias—having once more presented himself, commanded the capitulating monarch to "gather unto me all Israel, on Mount Carmel, and with them the pagan prophets who eat at the queen's table: four hundred and fifty prophets of Baal and four hundred prophets of the groves." [1]

Early this unforgettable morning, Elias stood before the vast, wondering throng and cried: "How long do you halt between two sides? If the Lord be God, follow Him! but if Baal, follow him!" No one spoke a word. Not a move was made. So the prophet fairly proposed a contest. The pagan prophets would build an altar and he would build one. Then they would both offer holocausts and pray for miraculous fires to consume their offerings: the God Who sent down the consuming fire would be acknowledged by the nation as the true God. The pagans have been storming their idols for hours while their holocaust only dries in that relentless sun from a sky that has been cloudless so interminably long.

However, it is not so much for the fire-contest between the prophets that we interest ourselves in this strange sight but for the after-event. After he has brought down a miraculous fire and thus proved that "God is God" and after he has seen the whole nation fall to its knees with the cry, "The Lord is God! The Lord is God!", the mysterious prophet turns to the king and says that *now it will rain.* And while the king goes to take dinner at the prophet's bidding, we follow Elias as he proceeds to a place near the side of Carmel. The murmur of the Mediterranean, which laves Carmel's foot in a perpetual homage to her mysteries, seems to rise like the overture of some great event. Preoccupied, the old man sits on the ground and crouches there, his head between his knees, and tells his young servant to go and look out over the sea; six times we see him return only to report to his venerable master: "There is nothing."

What an unusual scene! What if the Israelites, feasting nearby, were to know that this venerable old man is destined to live until the end of the world! . . . What if they knew that in a future century he is to appear with the greatest of their prophets in that one moment of the earthly life of the Incarnate God when He will let fall the veil from His divine splen-

dor! Yes, right over there on that peak facing them
—of Mount Tabor—this old man will appear at a
moment that will astound the world down thru the
ages to a streamlined century of which they do not
even dream. What if they knew that *at this very
moment* that awesome figure is not only about to
present a material salvation to them but is also about
to behold a *prophetic vision of the spiritual Salvation
of all mankind through an Immaculate Virgin* . . .

We see the servant return the sixth time to be
again sent by Elias to "look out over the sea." This
seventh time he hastens back for, rising out of the
sea at the foot of the Mount, he has seen a small
cloud in the shape of a human foot!

In the near tomorrows, sainted Doctors of the true
Church will explain to the world how this little
cloud, rising pure out of its bitter sea and leaving all
impurities behind, is a *figure of an Immaculate Virgin* who will rise pure out of the sea of humankind,
free of its universal impurity of original sin.[2] As soon
as Elias is told of the tiny cloud ascending over the
side of the mystic mountain, we see him rise from
his unusual position. Within an incredibly short
while: "The Heavens grew dark with clouds and
wind and there fell a great rain" (Kings III, ch. 18).

* * * *

Two thousand, one hundred and ten years later,
we see another king expectantly climbing up Mount
Carmel. He is not clothed in a toga-like robe but
in glistening armor with a large Cross blazoned upon
his shield and upon his breastplate. Surely he does

not expect to find a fiery prophet on this Mount; Elias has been taken to Heaven centuries ago, has come in the spirit of John the Baptist to herald the approach of the Son of God, has appeared at the Transfiguration, and has even entered the mystical life of the new Church, a "saint" and a mystery.

No, but this king is the holy Louis IX of France, who will one day be canonized a saint. He is interested in some most holy men who, he has been informed, dwell in the grottos of this Mountain and call themselves "Hermits of Saint Mary of Mount Carmel." [3] Due to the gains of the infidels into Palestine these men are being forced to emigrate to Europe; since their sanctity is a byword, Saint Louis wants some of it for France.

Having ascended Mount Carmel and having met the monks there, Saint Louis is astounded by the account of a most unusual tradition.

The saintly monks say that they are the descendants of the Prophet Elias and call themselves "Hermits of Saint Mary of Mount Carmel" because the fiery prophet, whom they imitate, had beheld, in a foot-shaped cloud that had divinely soared from the sea below them, a prophetic image of the Immaculate Virgin Mary who was to bring forth man's Salvation and to conquer the pride of Satan with Her heel of humility. He had instructed his followers to pray for the advent of this Virgin, saying that the vestigial form of the cloud bore out the divine malediction against the devil: "I shall place enmities between thee and the Woman, thy seed and

Her seed . . . thou shalt lie in wait for Her heel and She shall crush thy head . . . " [4]

They informed Saint Louis that, from the time of Elias until the birth of the Blessed Virgin, the great prophet's successors on Mount Carmel handed down from one to another the great revelation of their Founder, all the while praying for the appearance of that Immaculate Virgin. She had finally come right down in that little town of Nazareth, over at the other side of that plain which lies at the foot of the Mount, where they could look down on its mystery. And then Mary visited them, and the Holy Family, on the return from the seven-year sojourn in Egypt, rested awhile among them. They had erected, here on Mount Carmel, the very first chapel on earth ever to be dedicated to the Mother of God. Furthermore, when the Church was spreading and Mary had gone to join Her Divine Son, because of Her predilection for them they received custody of the Holy House in Nazareth.

"Hermits of Our Lady!" Saint Louis must have thought. "Truly if what these holy men believe is fact, they are indeed the 'Family of the Blessed Virgin.' "

Our Lord Himself, in a colloquy with His beloved Saint Teresa, designated these hermits "The Order of the Virgin"! And if St. Louis was struck with a reverential awe by the holiness of this family of Mary, *what would have been his feelings were he to know what was happening at that very moment,* in another part of the world, *between Our Lady and "Her Order"?*

Some thirty years before Saint Louis came to Mount Carmel to persuade six of the hermits to return with him to France, two English crusaders took a few of the hermits to England. A strange but holy man joined them there in whom they could not help but recognize a great likeness to the fiery prophet whom they ever emulated. He took the name "Simon"; his surname, "Stock," was symbolic of the life he had led prior to their coming: he had been dwelling alone in the fastnesses of an English forest in a tree-trunk hollow even as Elias had dwelt in Carmel's natural caves. Our Lady, in a personal apparition, had told him that Her devotees were coming from Palestine and that he should join their society.[6]

The persecutions, which now were a tremendous force in Palestine and the reason for Saint Louis' presence there, caused so many of the 'Carmelites' to move West that a Vicar General had to be appointed there. Simon Stock received this honor. He found himself at the helm of Mary's bark, in more than usually troublous waters. By the time he was made General of the entire Order, six years later (1245), it became apparent that nothing less than heroic faith was required to pilot the sea fearlessly.

Adapting the heretofore contemplative Order to a mixed life, in a seeming awareness that a marked change was about to take place in the body of Mary's special sons, the saint sent the younger men to the Universities. He thereby alarmed the old men who had led lives of utter solitude on Carmel. However, he recognized that they had been providentially forced from Carmel and, guided by Mary, he braved the ugly dissension that his policy evoked.

But this inward cancer was not the only affliction. Outside the Order, the whole secular clergy was raising a din at the sight of another group joining the ranks of the odious mendicant friars; not only did they persecute the men from Carmel everywhere, but they carried their cries to Rome, demanding the suppression of these "newcomers." Moreover, strange as it may seem, the barred-cloak, which these Palestinians wore, seemed violently to irritate Western sensibilities. Saint Simon thought to change it because the unpopularity of the Elian garb was hindering the growth of his family of Mary; he refrained in deference to the views of the older members who naturally loved their ancient cloak, redolent of Elian traditions.

For the first five years of his generalship, the opposition from within and without grew daily stronger. Hence, in the year of 1251 we find Simon retiring to the Cambridge monastery, weighed down by his ninety years and a trial well beyond the strength of even a far younger man. He seems to be seeking the solitude of his cell even as he had been wont to retire to his tree-trunk, in his youth, to pray. Probably he is thinking to himself, as Saint Teresa of Avila said later, "Can the hand of God be shorter for the Order of His Mother than for other

Orders?"[7] And it is not merely a question of remov-
ing obstacles that confronts the Saint now; it is a
question of preserving the Order's very life.

This sickness of the Order that was "fomented by
Satan," as a contemporary of St. Simon describes,
may put one in mind of a certain "Little Flower's"
childhood sickness. Carmel is Mary's Flower, She its
blossoming vine; now the Flower droops her head.
Let us apply the words of Thérèse:

> "It was an illness in which Satan assuredly had
> a hand . . . He wished in his jealousy to avenge him-
> self on me for the grave mischief my family was to
> do him in the future . . . He little knew, however,
> that the Queen of Heaven was keeping a faithful and
> affectionate watch from above on Her Little Flower,
> and was making ready to still the tempest just as the
> frail and delicate stem was on the point of breaking." [8]

Yes, the Order of Carmel, Mary's Flower, sinks
and droops her head; dissension and persecution,
fomented by Satan who hates Mary and Her seed,
are the raging sicknesses that stretch her upon a bed
of death. Since the worst suffering takes place in the
head of a body, the aged General and Saint is the
most cruelly weighed upon by the multiple afflictions
that beset his Order of Mary. Kneeling in his tiny
cell, he pours forth his soul with deep and longing
sighs in what has been often called "after the *Hail
Mary*, the most beautiful of all Marian prayers":[9]

> "Flower of Carmel,
> Vine blossom-laden,
> Splendor of Heaven,
> Child-bearing maiden,
>   None equals thee!

O Mother benign,
Who no man didst know,
On all Carmel's children
Thy favors bestow,
    Star of the Sea!"

As the Saint lifts his tear-dimmed eyes, the cell is suddenly flooded with a great light. Surrounded by a great concourse of angels, the Queen of Heaven is descending towards him, holding forth the Brown Scapular of the friars and saying: "RECEIVE, MY BELOVED SON, THIS HABIT OF THY ORDER: THIS SHALL BE TO THEE AND TO ALL CARMELITES A PRIVILEGE, THAT WHOSOEVER DIES CLOTHED IN THIS SHALL NEVER SUFFER ETERNAL FIRE." [10]

The purpose, the *raison d'être*, of that long established and special "family of Mary" stands revealed.

"O Mary, who from that hour (that Elias beheld the foot-shaped cloud over Carmel) didst preside over the watches of God's army, without ever failing for a single day: now that the Lord has truly come through Thee, it is no longer the land of Judea alone, but the whole earth that Thou coverest as a cloud, shedding down blessings in abundance. Thine ancient clients —the sons of the prophets—experienced this when, the land of promise becoming unfaithful, they were forced to transplant their customs and traditions to other climes; they found that even into our far West the Cloud of Carmel had poured its fertilizing dew, and that nowhere would its protection be wanting to them . . . Since their tents have been pitched around the hills where the new Sion is built upon Peter, the cloud has shed all around showers of blessings more

*precious than ever, driving back into the abyss the
flames of Hell . . ."* [11]

DOM GUERANGER

*"This most extraordinary gift of the Scapular—
from the Mother of God to Saint Simon Stock—
brings its great usefulness not only to the Carmelite
Family of Mary but also to all the rest of the faithful
who wish, affiliated to that Family, to follow Mary
with a very special devotion."* [12]

PIUS IX

The Queen of Carmel gives the Scapular.

CHAPTER TWO

Meaning of the Promise

PRESENTING the Scapular to Saint Simon for the world, Our Lady makes but one condition to Her promise of Salvation: "Whosoever dies *clothed in this Habit* shall not suffer the fires of hell." She promises that anyone who enters Her family of Carmel, and dies there, shall not be lost.

Seven centuries have passed over that promise and its exact meaning, which is anything but obscure, seems to have troubled hundreds of speakers and writers almost to the point of obsession. "Satan perceived what a great multitude of souls the Scapular was going to snatch from him," remarks a modern writer. "He groaned with rage and swore to avenge himself of this recent, other most terrible blow that the Immaculate had just given him. In his fury he declared war to the death on this sacred Habit, especially attacking the unusual privilege with which it is endowed, and hence one soon saw arising from all parts, even from the bosom of the Church, a cloud of specious objections against the remarkable promise attached to Mary's Scapular. Some denied its existence; others saw in it a direct contradiction to the divine teaching; it was combatted, mal-interpreted, and even denatured." [1] So probably the first thing we will ask ourselves on hearing Mary's remarkable words is: "What did Our Lady mean?" First, Mary does *not* mean by Her promise that anyone dying even in mortal sin will be saved. *Death in mortal sin* and *damnation* are one and the same thing. Mary's promise naturally rewords itself: "Whosoever dies clothed in this Habit *shall not die in mortal sin.*" To make this clear, the Church often inserts the word "piously" into the promise: *Quicumque in hoc "pie" moriens, aeternum non patietur incendium.* [2]

Catholic theologians and authorities like Vermeersch, Saint Robert Bellarmine, Beringer, Benedict XIV, etc., explain the promise to mean that anyone dying in Mary's family will receive from Her, at the hour of death, either the grace of perseverance in the state of grace or the grace of final contrition.

To die in the membership of Mary's family is the one condition. Now, in order to so die, having been validly enrolled in the Confraternity by a Carmelite or a duly authorized priest, one must die clothed in the sign of membership. This Sign of membership may be the large Scapular of the religious Habit, the small Scapular, or the Scapular Medal; all have been recognized by the Sovereign Pontiffs as valid signs of that membership which the Mother of God rewards by an absolute assurance of final contrition and perseverance.

Hence the main requisite is valid enrollment. One must voluntarily join Mary's great Confraternity through the hands of an authorized priest. A priest obtains his faculties from the Carmelite Order or from the Holy See. When he enrolls anyone, unless he has the special privilege of enrolling without the obligation of inscribing the names, he *must* see that the name of the one whom he enrolls is duly inscribed in the Confraternity register. If he does not, the one invested is deprived of many benefits of the Scapular.[3] There are a few instances when the names need not be entered on the register. Missionaries have the power, at times, to enroll many people at one time by the recitation of one single formula. In this case, technically known as *magnus concursus fidelium,* those enrolled are really members of the Confraternity without the inscription of the names because the Holy See has so willed. Pope Pius X granted to soldiers at war the unusual privilege of enrolling themselves. In such a case, however, the Scapular, or Scapular medal, must have been previously blessed and, while clothing himself, the soldier must recite some prayer to the Blessed Virgin, be it only three Hail Marys.

Many have not understood Mary's Promise exactly. On hearing the importance of enrollment and inscription of names, a doubt arises in their minds as to whether they may have been validly invested. Due to the bounty of the Popes, however, there need be no such worry. Pius X, on January the twentieth, nineteen hundred and fourteen, officially validated, with his Sovereign power, the admission of any of the faithful into the Confraternity that had been invalid *for any cause whatsoever.* Pius XI renewed that validation in 1924, 1928 and 1939.[4] Anyone enrolled before April, 1939, is therefore sure that he is a member of Mary's family.

As the reader will understand more fully later, the whole meaning of the Scapular Promise derives from the fact that *the wearing of the Scapular* is a *true devotion in its primitive sense of dedication to Mary.* Hence, that the Scapular-wearer have his name on the confraternity register is not enough to obtain the benefits of the Scapular. True devotion to Mary always has three notes: homage, confidence and love; and to be a sign of Salvation those three notes must be practiced *perseveringly.* When we invest ourselves in the Scapular we practice the homage of becoming members of the Queen's battalion, we profess confidence in Her promises, and we become Her special children of love. But in order to be assured of Salvation, we must persevere in those sentiments and it is only by wearing the Sign of membership until death that we can continually show the Mother of God that we venerate Her, believe in Her, and love Her. Hence, it is not enough to be a member of Mary's family; we must profess our membership. Only he is sure of Mary's great promise who has validly entered the Society gathered 'neath Her mantle and dies actually clothed in the Sign of that membership.

Much discussion has arisen in recent years as to just what is validly a Sign of Membership in the

Carmelite Confraternity. There are undoubtedly three valid signs; but just how must they be worn and when may one or the other be worn?

The large habit of the Carmelite Order offers no difficulty.

The small habit, known commonly as the "Brown Scapular," is likewise clearly defined. It differs from the large habit only in size. After he is enrolled, therefore, a member of the Confraternity can renew his own Scapular even as a religious, once invested, can make his own habit. It must, however, be like the large one. It must be of woven wool, of a color somewhere between brown and black (preferably brown, of course), and of rectangular shape. It must be so made that it can hang over the shoulders and thus rest at once against the front and back of the body. New Scapulars need not be blessed once the wearer has been enrolled; they derive their excellence from the fact that they are a Sign of that membership which Mary rewards with an assurance of Salvation; they become such a sign the moment that a duly enrolled member of the Confraternity assumes them.

In 1910, Pope Pius X made an astounding legislation. He declared that the cloth Scapular, after the enrollment, could be replaced by a medal which bore on one side an image of the Sacred Heart and on the other an image of Our Lady.[5] The missionaries in torrid zones had besought him to authoritatively make such a mutation of the Sign of membership because cloth Scapulars were so inconvenient for the natives. With no outer clothing to protect those two little pieces of cloth joined by strings, the Scapulars soon became ragged and knotted; due to the heat and frequent uncleanliness of the natives, they also became nesting places for vermin; smelly, curled and unsightly. Surely what Our Lady had made a Sign of membership in Europe was not appropriate in the tropics. So the Vicar of Christ changed it, as Mary undoubtedly wished. And if ever an act was providential, it was this very legislation! Four years later the World War broke out and literally millions would have had to face death without Mary's assurance of Salvation had it not been for the Scapular Medal. Not only did it become difficult to obtain the cloth Scapulars in that terrible war but something more drastic happened. In the filth of the trenches the Scapulars, which the soldiers would never take off, became nests for vermin and soldiers were officially deprived of them! But the medal was then to be had ...

It is apparent that the Holy Father did not change the Sign of Mary's Confraternity in order to truckle to the fashions of the day. During the several days in which His Holiness was deliberating about conceding the Scapular Medal, one of the Cardinals approached him with what he thought to be a very strong objection. "Your Holiness," he said, "to grant the Medal would seem an admission to objectors that the Blessed Virgin never appeared to Saint Simon Stock." [6] Probably the Cardinal did not understand the real meaning of the Scapular Promise but the Pope simply turned and said brusquely: "But *I* believe in the Scapular Vision!" And, as the Vicar of Christ, in granting the Medal he said: "I desire *most vehemently* that the cloth Scapulars be worn as heretofore." [7]

Many did not see, or at least professed not to see, that the Sovereign Pontiff only willed the Medal to take the place of the Scapular in case of necessity or for very serious reasons. The Medal became widespread, not without some injury to the devotion. However, the actions of the successors of Pius X leave no doubt that we should not wear the Medal in place of the Scapular *without sufficient reason,* and since no official pronouncement has been made, one who does wear the Medal without sufficient reason runs the danger of not receiving the Promise. Mary cannot be pleased with one who changes Her gift out of vanity or fear to make open profession of his affiliation to Her. Moreover, the cloth Scapular has seven centuries of sacred tradition behind it. It has become redolent of the fragrance of Our Heavenly Mother. Not only was it by that Habit that She originally took unto Herself "special children of love," [8] as the Church sings in the Preface of Her special Mass for July 16th, but it has been the vehicle of numerous miracles. Those two bits of cloth have extinguished tremendous fires and then have been taken intact from the glowing embers! They have been found miraculously preserved in the tombs of Saints where everything else had turned to dust! Often people miraculously preserved from a watery grave have found their little habits perfectly dry, the added miraculous touch of a Mother who not only protects us but wants to show us that She does so, because She loves us as Her special children. The Medal has never seen any of these things; it is sure that, as a substitute for the Habit, it can mean *as much* as the cloth Scapular only to one who cannot wear the cloth Scapular.

But Pope Pius XI has made it possible for everyone to wear the cloth Scapular. By a decree of May 8, 1925, this great Pontiff approved what is known as the "protected Scapular." Instead of just the two pieces of brown cloth joined by string or cord, one may wear the two pieces of cloth *joined by chains and enclosed in cases.*[9]

There are, consequently, few remaining reasons for Americans or Europeans to be without the cloth Scapular. To prevent being conspicuous, one may sew or pin the Scapular to an undergarment so that it cannot rise and show about the neck. To prevent irritation of sensitive skin one may resort to some sort of covering over the Scapular, perhaps of oil-silk or of cellophane. Moreover, as was stated previously, not only may the Scapular be encased but the strings may be white or blue, satin or cotton . . . of any color and of any material. Consequently it should certainly be no more difficult to wear the small Scapular than it is to wear any other undergarment.

The first successor of Pius X, His Holiness Pope Benedict XV, declared on July 8, 1916: "In order that one may see that it is Our desire that the Brown Scapular be worn, We concede to it a grace that the Scapular Medal shall not enjoy." And the Pontiff proceeded to grant an indulgence of five hundred days for *each time the Scapular is kissed.* [10]

After the Scapular Medal legislation, Cardinal Mercier wrote: "It is so popular among us to wear the Scapular that we should see with the greatest disgust that, without any foundation, so laudable a custom might be lost; let us use the medal *only* when we have some real inconvenience in wearing the Scapular." [11] And Father Vermeersch, S. J., said: "I would prefer that, in order to honor the principal Scapular which is that of Carmel, the Brown Scapular be worn in the accustomed form and the medal only as a substitute for the other Scapulars in order that one may not have to wear too many." [12] Hence it would be wise never to use the Scapular Medal *in place* of the Brown Scapular but only *together with* the Brown Scapular as a substitute for the less important Scapulars.

We have summarily analysed, therefore, the meaning of those first words of the Promise: "Whosoever dies *clothed in this Habit.*" Our Lady made a Promise of Salvation to all who die in Her Family of Carmel; so to die, one has to be validly enrolled in the Habit of that family and perseveringly wear it.

Now we turn to understand a little more fully the most astounding promise itself, viz., that those who die in Mary's family *shall not suffer the fires of Hell.*

As was said in the beginning of this chapter, Our

Lady's Promise does not mean a removal of God's sanction of the moral law, i. e., that regardless of what we do we shall not be eternally punished. Saints and Pontiffs often warn us of the foolhardiness of abusing Mary's Promise. At the same time that he joyfully professed: "I learned to love the Scapular Virgin in the arms of my mother," Pope Pius XI warned all the faithful that "although it is very true that the Blessed Virgin loves all who love Her, nevertheless those who wish to have the Blessed Mother as a helper at the hour of death, must in life merit such a signal favor by abstaining from sin and laboring in Her honor." [13] One can take it as certain that if he continually sins because of Mary's Scapular Promise, *he shall not die in the Scapular.* To lead a sinful life while trusting in the Scapular Promise is to commit a sin the horror of which borders on sacrilege; its punishment will not only be eternal but far worse than if one had led a sinful life without making the Mother of God an excuse for crucifying Her Son . . .

There are times when a person is tempted to some great sin, such as impurity or theft, that the suggestion comes: "Why not do it? You wear the Scapular and after this moment is passed you will still have no fear about your eternal salvation." It is Satan using the Scapular Promise to draw a soul to sin, a worse sin than the objective act itself. Like all sin, it can become a habit. A typical and warningful example is found in a certain well-testified Scapular miracle. A man openly excused a wicked life by boasting that he wore the Scapular; he claimed surety of salvation while he disedified his neighbors by abominable excesses. In this presumptuous belief he persevered until death overtook him. Then those whom he had disedified became witnesses to an event that has not been uncommon in the years that men have sought to realize Mary's promise. As death approached, the poor wretch thought that the Scapular was *the cause of his agony.* He cried out painfully that it was *burning* him. In a last supreme effort, tearing it off, he flung it from him . . . and went to meet a Divine Judge . . .[14]

Mary's promise is the masterpiece of Her motherly love. It was made to be a source of hope and confidence to us. In the supreme moment of our lives—the moment when we feel this earth slipping away with all that it has meant to us while a strange life yawns at our feet into eternity, we need a mother. Probably it was at the foot of the Cross, the moment when Her Divine Son made Her our Mother in a gesture of death-parting, that Mary thought to assure us of a Mother's love at our dying moment. Soldiers cast lots over the earthly garments She had made for Her crucified Redeemer; She would make a heavenly garment for Her Blood-purchased redeemed.

"Whosoever dies clothed in this Scapular shall not suffer the fires of hell." . . . Savaria remarks that it is these words, so very extraordinary, that comprehend the full value of the Brown Scapular. "One cannot descend too far into their depths," he says.

"It is only by penetrating beyond the sensible that one comes to know the spiritual treasures which this Heavenly Garment conceals. Especially today, with the power of Satan threatening to shake the very foundations of the world, we need a rational knowledge of our devotions and above all of Her who crushes the head of the infernal serpent." [15]

Yes, we need Mary today with Her Satan-crushing prayer. Her great promise must be understood because we also need the union that it has established. We need "Her family," both as corporate members of a militant Church against Satan and as individual warriors with a private battle. Pope Benedict XV, addressing the seminarians of Rome one July 16th, said: "Let all of you have a common language and a common armor: the language, the sentences of the Gospel; the common armor, the Scapular of the Virgin of Carmel, which you all ought to wear and which enjoys the singular privilege of protection even after death." [16]

Hence it is only natural that we seek to have a rational knowledge of the Scapular Promise. And although the words of Our Lady's Promise are clear, how sure are we that She spoke them? And how can it be that for wearing two pieces of cloth, She saves us? What is the meaning of that denomination of the Scapular, which one hears so often, *Mary's Sacrament?* Is the wearing of Mary's Sign really a devotion? Is it really an armor that should be as common in the Church as the language of the Gospel? Does it really assure *salvation* and, then, *aid us even after death?*

These are a few apparent questions that probably flock to the reader's mind upon understanding the meaning of Mary's words and hearing that they have some very deep significance.. And as he looks further at the Scapular, further questions will arise until he will, most probably, find himself mute before the overwhelming magnificence of Mary's gift.

> *"In admitting me into Her Family of Carmel, Mary promises me three great favors. She will protect me in danger, She will help me to die well, and She will promptly aid me after death. It is She Herself who has assumed all these obligations in my regard."* [17]
>
> FR. CHAIGNON, S. J.

> *"We believe that all those who have the happiness of wearing the Scapular while dying, obtain Grace before God and are preserved from the fire of hell, because we believe that Mary, to keep Her promise, draws forth for them from the divine treasures of which She is the depository, the graces necessary for their perseverance in justice or their sincere conversion. And thus fortified, and reconciled with God through the Sacraments of perfect contrition, the associates of the Scapular, dying in this Holy Habit, do not fall under the blows of an inexorable justice."* [18]
>
> R. P. MAUREL, S. J.

CHAPTER THREE

Historicity of the Promise

THAT THE Mother of God appeared to Saint Simon Stock, promising that anyone who died in Her Scapular would not suffer eternal fire, is as certain as the fact that George Washington defeated Cornwallis, in 1781, at Yorktown. There are documentary proofs; the Catholic Church has propagated the devotion for seven centuries; and more miracles have been worked through the Brown Scapular than through almost any other Sign this world has ever had.[1] While one miracle—one operation above the power of nature—is God's word, innumerable miracles are decidedly a bit of divine emphasis. Hence we might say that one has *more* ground for believing in the Scapular Promises than for believing in the defeat of Cornwallis or the signing of the Declaration of Independence. Besides *documents,* we have the word of God and His Church.

Since elsewhere the authority of God and of the Church will show itself in support of the Scapular Vision, the reader is invited to consider, here, the documented history. Nor is this invitation extended

25

because the reader might not be sympathetic to miracles and to universal Catholic sentiment.

A short time ago, the Scapular was presented to a man who was at the point of death. Gazing at it in mingled pain and frustration, he sobbed: "Oh, if only I could believe in that!" [2] But he had not learned the facts of the Scapular in life. Faced with death, he could not believe even while his whole being cried out for the sweet, Marian assurance it brings.

Reading the documented history of the Vision to Saint Simon Stock, which lessens the demands on our faith, we cannot fail to acquire a greater reverence and a deeper appreciation of that historical descent of a Mother from Heaven to earth, where She lovingly folded Her children beneath Her mantle to assure their salvation.

It must be pointed out in the very beginning, however, that obviously a tremendous force has been at work to destroy historical monuments of the Scapular Vision and even to hide, under a cloud of controversy, those documents that have proved indestructible. The printing press was not invented until two hundred years after the Vision and therefore almost all the first-hand records of the Vision were unique documents. These documents were, so far as we know, archived in the Carmelite libraries at Bordeaux (where Saint Simon Stock died and where his body now lies, and at London). [3] After the Black Plague, less than a hundred years after the Vision, *the Bordeaux library was burned* by city officials, to prevent the possible spread of contagion. In the beginnings of the Anglican schism, the heretical Henry VIII *ordered the London library razed to the ground*. Moreover, it seems never to have occurred to the Catholic World of those first four centuries after the Vision that seven centuries later we might like to see some documents. Most of the information we have is either indirect or left to us by chance. Perhaps, however, that is the explanation of its power.

After the Vision (July 16, 1251), the Scapular Devotion spread throughout the universal Church, being richly indulgenced by the Popes and being the vehicle of miracles, *until the middle of the seventeenth century*. At that time, a bitter enemy of the Holy See and especially of Religious Orders (the Gallican, Launoy), dipped his pen into the red ink of negative argument to smudge the Scapular. "It is a legend," he declared, "there is no documentary evidence of it until two hundred years after the alleged vision." [4] Unfortunately, where were the documents? No one had thought of such things and the London and Bordeaux libraries were gone . . .

The Church answered by putting Launoy's book on the Roman Index of Prohibited Books and by adding more indulgences to the Scapular. Others responded like the great Jesuit General, Father Aquaviva, who ordered his whole Order to propagate the devotion with fervor as one of its very missions.[5] Father Papebroech, S. J., when accused of siding with Launoy considered the accusation *a calumny* because "the Scapular is a devotion approved by the Sovereign Pontiffs and by celestial favors." [6] Benedict XIV, one of the most learned theologians of all time, not only argued against Launoy but expressed the opinion that only a contemner of religion could deny the authenticity of the Scapular Vision.[7]

But Launoy's book, although placed on the Roman Index and banned as utterly un-Catholic, continued to be quoted. The negative arguments against the Scapular persisted and, to our amazement, solid documentary evidence offered in refutation was belittled, its whole force gradually smothered in a cloud of doubt stirred from disputes over *one* document that was probably spurious.[8] It was not until recently that the historicity of the Scapular has been undeniably established not only on circumstantial evidence but even on a documentary basis.

The scattered ashes of perished documents could hardly be resurrected, but the record of the vision in one book—written, by a man of unquestionable character who was sure of his facts, in the century after the vision—is authentic.

In 1389, the General of the Carmelite Order, John Grossi, wrote the book known as "The Viridarium." [9] A Catalogue of the Carmelite Saints, it gives the following integral account of the Scapular Vision:

"The ninth Saint of the Order is Saint Simon of England, the sixth General, who besought the Most Glorious Mother of God that She grant some privilege to the Carmelites, who rejoiced in being named especially 'the Order of the Virgin.' He repeated in a most devout manner:

> Flos Carmeli,
> Vitis florigera,
> Splendor Coeli,
> Virgo puerpera,
>   Singularis!
>
> Mater mitis,
> Sed viri nescia,
> Carmelitis
> Da privilegia
>   Stella Maris!

And, accompanied by a multitude of Angels, the Blessed Virgin appeared to him, holding in Her hands the Scapular of the Order and said: THIS SHALL BE TO YOU AND TO ALL CARMELITES A PRIVILEGE, THAT ANYONE WHO DIES CLOTHED IN THIS SHALL NOT SUFFER ETERNAL FIRE: and if wearing it they die, they shall be saved. The said Simon, whilst on a visitation of the Province of Vasconia, died in the Province of Bordeaux . . ."

The author was a great and holy man, famous in the whole Church because of his activity to end the Great Western Schism and deemed worthy to be unanimously elected General by both factions of the Order after the Schism. Scholarly as well as holy, John Grossi's word is sacred. And not only is his word sacred as regards his own integrity of character; it is sacred also in that *he knew* what a momentous event he was recording; he consulted the very companions of those who had lived with, and had talked to, Saint Simon; he had access to all the libraries in the Order. Would he record the Scapular

Vision without verifying it? No, and he tells us so
explicitly, declaring that he writes nothing in his
Viridarium that is not from *ancient documents*.
Hence the Scapular Vision rests historically at least
on a document of which the author *knew* what he
was writing, *could* and *did verify his facts*, and *who
would not deceive us*.

Despite the wonder that any documentary proof
for the Scapular exists upon consideration of the first
four hundred years that followed the bestowal of the
Scapular, *it would be impossible, in several pages, to
submit all the proof which bears out the fact
recorded by General Grossi;* too much has been
written on this subject in recent years to be fully
summarized. There are twenty-nine other documents which we might consider, but at greater length
than John Grossi's Viridarium.[10] There are likewise
many substantiating proofs of a quasi-documentary
character.

After the Vision, an almost miraculous change
took place in the Carmelite Order. The book in
which this effect first finds record is in itself a great
historical monument. A few years after Saint Simon's death, a contemporary who lived in Palestine
wrote the work entitled: *De Multiplicatione Religionis Carmelitarum per Provincias Syriae et Europae:
et de perditione Monasteriorum Terrae Sanctae.*
Therein he recorded the terrible persecutions and
dissensions that wracked the Order of Carmel before
Our Lady's Apparition. He opined that they were
"fomented by Satan." [11] Finally, he stated that the

Blessed Virgin appeared to the Prior General (Saint Simon) and that, after the Vision, the Pope not only approved the Order but commanded that Ecclesiastical censures be used against anyone who further molested its members.

This utter reversal of attitude toward the Order is eloquent. In 1252, King Henry III issued letters of royal protection to the newly transplanted Order; [12] the Sovereign Pontiff issued letters to all the Archbishops and Bishops whom his letters should reach, exhorting them to treat with more charity and consideration his beloved brothers, the Hermits of Saint Mary of Mount Carmel; they were to receive grants of land and suitable monasteries and Ecclesiastical censures were to be used against those who would persist in molesting them in future. [13]

Fifteen years after Saint Simon's death, January 10th, 1276, Pope Gregory X was laid to rest at Arezzo. In 1830 his remains were disinterred to be newly placed in a silver reliquary. There, in the old tomb, a small Scapular was lying over the pontiff's shoulders, incorrupt. It is now in perfect preservation, one of the great treasures of the celebrated Arezzo museum.

This is the first small Scapular in history. As befitted a Pope, it was made of purple silk with exquisite gold embroidery (now turned to a brownish silver). In shape it is the same as the small Scapular worn today, six and a half hundred years later. However, its ribbons give it a greater resemblance to the large Scapular of the Religious Habit; they are not straight, as are most strings on Scapulars of today, but somewhat rounded inside at the top of the Scapular like the large Scapular of the Religious Habit.

This Scapular of Pope Gregory X does not lend positive evidence to the Scapular Vision, because there is no certainty that it was a sign of affiliation to the Order of Carmel. However, a record of those times tells us that Gregory X became affiliated to the Carmelite Order before ascending the papal throne and that he wore the Carmelite Habit as a sign of affiliation.[14] Moreover, this Scapular, seven centuries old, is the first small Scapular in history. Since the Carmelite Scapular may be the first one ever to have been used in an abbreviated form by confreres of an Order, this small Scapular of Gregory X, made of *purple silk,* rightfully merits the honor of introducing us to a very important aspect of the history of the "Brown" Scapular.

In the first days after the Scapular Vision, the material construction of the Scapular—color, material, weave, etc.—did not make much difference. Our Lady had merely said that She promised salvation to anyone who wore the *Carmelite Habit.* All the requisites enumerated in the previous chapter are Church regulations, promulgated centuries after the Vision by the Holy See as definitive regulations for the gaining of Her indulgences. Thus we find the General Chapter of Carmelites decreeing, in 1469, that the lay brothers should wear a *white* Scapular.[15] Although this legislation lasted but two years it shows that in the first Scapular centuries one did not understand Mary's Promise as dependent essentially on wearing a certain definite sign. Rather was the essential condition of the Promise understood to be membership in the Order of the Virgin, a condition which naturally implied that one wear *whatever was officially recognized as the Habit of the Order.* Today, many were surprised when Pope Pius X, to meet a necessity, officially decreed that in place of the cloth Scapular one might wear a Scapular medal; in those days, an understanding of the Scapular Promise rendered authoritative mutations a matter of course.

Although Our Lady gave Saint Simon a large garment, the small Scapular is of great historical importance also. It seems that the large garment given by Mary was divided, *because of the small Scapular* with which many thousands of confreres hastened to clothe themselves, into two garments.

The phenomenal spread of the small Scapular —as recorded by many historians—is in itself tantalizingly eloquent.[25] It gives us at least sufficient taste of the activity of Saint Simon Stock to make us realize our misfortune in not having had more information preserved to us.

However, there is further eloquence in the fact that the Carmelites declared, in their great General Chapter of Montpelier, July, 1287, that "The outer garment, which is commonly named the mantle, is not an integral part of the religious habit nor essential to the Carmelite state." This shows that those first Carmelites to enjoy Mary's gift were so over-whelmed that they almost completely shelved their devotion to that ancient mantle of their founder Elias in complete honor and respect for the habit so exalted by Mary. They ordered that when the white cloak was worn, thereafter it was "to be so parted in the middle that the Scapular shine plainly through." [26] And the white cloak was *a symbol of Carmel's antiquity.* The Scapular was a garment more or less common to all Orders.

To appreciate this shelving of the cloak in favor of the Scapular, one must know of the tremendous controversies that raged among the mendicant Orders concerning their individuality and their antiquity. Violent tongue and pen battles over the settlement of which mendicant Order was most ancient almost filled the century after the Scapular Vision, yet those first more Marian than Elian Carmelites decreed that their white mantle should be "So parted in the middle that the Scapular shine plainly through." (See note below.)

N. B. When the Blessed Virgin appeared to Saint Simon and told him to receive the "Habit of his Order," the habit had only three parts of cloth: the tunic, the capuche and the cloak.[16] The cloak was worn only when the religious were in choir, or out of the monastery, or performing some dignified function. However, it was the principal part of the Habit. Elias had let fall his mantle to Eliseus, imparting to that noble successor his "double spirit." [17] Hence that brown and white striped mantle was dear to the Hermits of Mount Carmel, redolent of their Elian and Palestinian origin.

We see, therefore, that although those libraries were burned into which the Carmelites of those first Scapular years had entrusted their most valuable documents, their Constitutions and Chapter pronouncements divulge some of their secrets. Copies

Since the barred cloak was not worn at all times, the usual Habit was simply the tunic, with its belt, and the capuche. Now, only this latter article of clothing, i.e., the *capuche*, was called "the habit." The tunic was, and is today, the ordinary dress of any religious: at investiture, a candidate enters the church *to be invested*, already *wearing the tunic;* the habit of the Order is then placed over it.

It was this "capuche," therefore, which the Blessed Virgin held in Her hand when She appeared to Saint Simon.

Although called "a capuche," i.e., a *hood*, this every-day-garb was more like *a Scapular*. It hung over the shoulders, down the front and back, to form an apron-like garment over the tunic. Besides being called "capuche," it was often designated as the "supertunic." However, it differed essentially from the tunic in that it had the hood attached to it; hence, despite its size, it was commonly known by the short name, "capuche."

Naturally, when the Confraternity was established according to Our Lady's words that "whosoever" died in that Habit would not be lost, it was apparent that the full supertunic, or capuche, would have to be modified if laymen were to wear it continuously. At the Confraternity meetings, which were almost a religious function to Scapular wearers, the full supertunic was worn.[18] However, just the essential "Scapular" element was kept as the sign of affiliation in ordinary life.

After the Vision, the every-day habit, i.e., the "capuche," became the essential part of the Carmelite Habit. The ancient and formerly distinctive cloak began to be almost ignored.[19] Gradually, too, since the abbreviated Habit worn by the growing thousands of confreres was a Scapular without any hood attached to it, the old name of "capuche" began to fall into desuetude. The hood was finally separated from the Scapular

of the Constitutions had to be had in all the monasteries and extant copies show that some great power
had been invested in the Scapular. The Constitutions of 1357 (editions of Constitutions are usually
reprints of former copies) say that "The Scapular,
which was formerly called the capuche, is to be con-

and made a garment in itself. Thus the present Carmelite
Habit of *four* cloth pieces (instead of three) evolved: the
tunic, the Scapular, the capuche and the cloak. The present
capuche is a cape that goes all the way around the upper part
of the body, extending half-way down the back, and the hood
(the only real "capuche" element) is attached to it. The
present Scapular is simply one long and straight garment, the
width of the body, which goes over the head like the small
Scapular and hangs full in front and back. Today, too, not
only is the Scapular the "Habit of the Order," but the small
Scapular in some countries is simply known as "the little
Habit." [20]

Exactly when the Carmelite Habit came to be constituted
of four pieces instead of three, we do not know. Ten years
after the death of Saint Simon, in the time of Pope Gregory X,
the "Habit of Profession" was called "the Scapular," but even
though changing in name it seems that it was still with the
hood attached in 1324. The Constitutions of that year say:
"The brother to be professed enters the church clothed in a
tunic without *Scapular and white cloak* (three pieces mentioned in all); having sprinkled the garments (the Scapular
and cloak) with holy water, the Prior then clothes the brother
in the Habit, saying: 'Receive this Habit in remission of your
sins and for the increase of our holy institute' . . . after which
he proceeds to clothe the brother in the white cloak . . ." [21]

Riboti informs us, in his book: *De Institutione et pe-
culiaribus gestis religiosorum Carmelitarum,* that the Scapular,
known before the Vision as either the capuche or the supertunic, was an imitation of the garment worn by the Doctors of
the Old Law merely bereft of its great borders and tassels.[22]
As we know, that garment of the Old Testament was often

sidered to be the *special habit* of the Order"; the
Constitutions of 1324 ordered that anyone going to
bed in just his tunic, "without the Scapular," was
to be severely punished; in 1369, they pronounced
any Carmelite excommunicated who should say
Mass without his Scapular. And *Religious Orders
do not throw their antiquity to the wind, and ful-
minate excommunications against their members,
either for little or for uncertain things.*

The most ancient minutes of a Confraternity
meeting that have come down to us are those of a
meeting which took place at Florence, Italy, in 1280
(the Vision occurred in 1251). At this meeting the
forty members wore the *capuche,* or supertunic, and
the purpose of their session was: "To render glory
to God and to His Glorious Mother, the Blessed Virgin Mary." [27] By these meetings they entered more

---

called a "superhumeral" (over-the-shoulders); hence the
name "Scapular" just naturally fell to the small habit of the
Confraternity which had no hood attached to it, and to the
"supertunic" itself. The Carmelite *Ordinale,* after the Vision,
says that: "The brother to be interred is to be clothed in his
grey tunic and Scapular, the hood or capuche covering his
face." [23] Hence, although they were not physically separate
under Saint Simon Stock, due undoubtedly to the rise of the
small Scapular, they were morally so. The fact that the hood
was attached to the supertunic was incidental to that large garment and, in fact, had been added sometime after the Scapular
was first adopted in imitation of the garment of the Doctors of
the Old Law. The Venerable Catherine Emmerick, who resaw
the Scapular Vision, says that Our Lady gave Saint Simon
"an article of dress in which was a square opening for the head
to pass through," and she adds that "it was like the vestment of
the High Priest that Zacharias showed to Saint Joseph." [24]

into the devotion of the Scapular; they felt more closely allied to Mary's family and nearer to Her.

Undoubtedly, the Confraternity was established by Saint Simon Stock. A year after his death, Urban IV granted favors to its members,[28] and such a society is usually rather well established before it is honored with papal favors.

Now, it is most remarkable that this Confraternity is held to be the *first one ever established in the Church.*[29] Perhaps it is not remarkable in light of the fact that the Brown Scapular is accepted as the first of all the small Scapulars, and their model. But it is most remarkable that the first Confraternity, which is an association of laymen to a Religious Order, should arise in that Order which only just before the affiliation of lay-members had almost broken upon the question of being completely contemplative or not! However, the explanation of this phenomenon is found in those words of the Blessed Virgin, recounted by the Most Reverend John Grossi, "*Whosoever* dies in this Habit shall not suffer eternal fire."

Hence, the Apparition of the Blessed Virgin to Saint Simon Stock is historically quite certain. This is well, because to have the historicity of a devotion established is to prevent the very sceptical—in the case of the Scapular, possible "contemners of religion"—from causing harm to the devotion by diverting attention from its intrinsic worth to an unestablished historicity. Most writers on the Scapular devotion simply invite belief in Mary's Promise on its being unspeakably favored by the Church and miraculously authorized by God Himself.[30]

However, fault can be found even with truth. It is a standing pleasantry that a critic once evaluated a picture as "rather too unrealistic" and was rather disconcerted when "the picture" started to move in the frame and politely thanked him in quite a too realistic voice. Anything can be ridiculed, even that which is most real and beautiful. Thanks to John Grossi, to other ancient writers, and to the early Carmelite Constitutions, the Scapular Vision is historically beyond question. But someone is sure to feel the inclination to attack it from other points of view; Satan not only fears but hates it. But as Father Clarke, S. J., remarked, it is to be remembered: "Any attack on the Scapular is an indirect attack on the Mother of God." [31] Just a few years ago some Catholic periodicals carried the unusual report of a heretic struck with insanity as he was in the act of ridiculing the Scapular.[32] He was reaching out his hand to tear it and stopped, his hand in mid-air, unable to finish his blasphemy nor even to tell those about him what had happened. Surely *a Catholic* should never ridicule Mary's Scapular—a devotion of unexcelled ecclesiastical approbation and a vehicle of miracles. He should seek every opportunity to defend its historicity and to explain its value.

When the confused Thomas fell at the feet of the King of Kings mumbling "My Lord and My God!", Our Lord said: "Because thou hast seen Me, Thomas, thou hast believed: blessed are they that have not seen, and have believed" (John, xx, 29). And to the millions of simple souls who would not be without the Brown Scapular because of sheer trust in the Church and of reverence for Mary, Our Lady must voice a similar commendation. However, on beholding the evidence of Her appearance to Saint Simon—vestiges of which She has kept in History despite the efforts of Satan to efface them—we cannot help but fall on our knees with our hearts giving forth the cry: "My Queen and my Mother."

"Will you say that you do not believe? Truly, you are to be pitied! . . . Ah, but begone from us with your pretended unbelief! It is a long time since we learned the certain marks of folly; and, if we had not learned them, you would teach them to us!" [33]
MONSIGNOR GAUME

"The positive evidence in favor of the apparition establishes its authenticity by proof so irrefragable, that nothing but ignorance or a determined bias could fail to be convinced by them . . . And what the Ecclesia docens *(the Church teaching) accepts and approves, what Catholic instinct, unfailing touchstone of truth in things spiritual, pronounces to be in accordance with the ways of God's Providence, and what an ever increasing experience comfirms and ratifies, cannot be rejected without the greatest peril, except where invincible ignorance excuses."* [34]
R. F. CLARKE, S. J.

CHAPTER FOUR

How the Promise is Kept

THE AUTHOR vividly remembers the day that he heard the parting word of an old priest who had just spent several hours going over the theological background of the Scapular Promise. It was in the semi-darkness of a seminary room that was atmosphered by piles of often consulted books in a background of more dusty tomes. The old Doctor, who had been teaching Theology in a large diocesan seminary for more than a quarter of a century, slowly rose to his feet. "Young man," he said earnestly, "what I have outlined to you in these few hours is a formulation that took me forty-two years . . . "

What he had outlined has, in its clarity, opened new vistas of thought and shed abundant light upon most vital truths. And in the comprehension of those truths lies a comprehension of the Scapular Promise and why it is kept . . .

Almost everyone has heard that all Grace comes to man through Mary. How many know the explanation of it? Acquainted with the picture on the miraculous medal, of the Blessed Virgin with rays of light streaming from Her hands in representation of the flow of Grace, are there some who think that this is how grace flows through Mary, through Her hands? To really understand the answer, the reader is invited to see (1) what Grace is, (2) how it comes to man at all and, then, (3) how Mary is positioned in its flow.

THE DIVINE PLAN

To understand what Grace is we might consider the difference between man's power of moving a corpse and God's power.

Man can lift a corpse and move its arms; he cannot make it lift itself and move its own arms. However, God, Who controls the inward springs of life, can so touch the dead body that what was a corpse begins *to move itself* and *becomes a living thing*.

Now, Grace is the life of the soul. It is that awakening touch of the Divinity upon inward springs which gives to the soul the power of spiritually moving itself, of responding to the love of its God. When the soul is in mortal sin and grace is gone, the soul is dead. Only God can give it life again because *He alone is the Source of Grace*.

All Grace comes, therefore, from the Holy Trinity. The Triune God—Father, Son and Holy Ghost—is the One Source of Grace. From this Triune Source, Grace is communicated to man through the Man-God, Christ: He descended from the Trinity, through Mary, to make us participators in the Divine Nature. He brought our souls to life. Scripture says that while He was on earth "Grace went out from Him." If He touched a man, Grace flowed through

His human nature from His Trinity with the Father and the Holy Ghost. But, since before He ascended into Heaven He established the seven sacraments, we still receive Grace through Him. Those sacraments are like physical extensions of Himself, the hands of His mystical Body in the dispensation of Grace from His Trinity with the Holy Ghost and the Father.

The Divine Plan can thus be summarized: Grace, the spiritual life of the soul, flows to man, from the Trinity, through Christ.

MARY IN THE DIVINE PLAN

But do not the Saints and Doctors of the Church say that *all Grace comes through Mary?* The Divine Plan seems quite complete without Her: God is the only Efficient Cause of Grace and Christ is its Channel . . .

Well, if someone asks another to perform a certain action, the one who asks is by his request or persuasion the indirect cause of the thing which is then accomplished at his bidding. Thus if the reader were asked by a friend to close this book and he did so, his friend would be the indirect and secondary cause of the book being closed. So, in the Divine Plan just outlined above, although the direct and efficient cause of Grace is God, Mary, in Her way, is the indirect cause. She asks Her Divine Son to dispense the life and the impulse of Grace, and it is at Her bidding that He chooses to do so. Hence we say that all Grace flows through Mary because, in

His exaltation of His holy Mother, God has deigned to make *Her prayer* an indirect cause of Grace.

Material examples of deeply spiritual truths cannot but be jarring on our appreciation of their sublimity. However, an example is but a means of rising to the simplicity of the abstract. To show how all Grace flows through Mary, we might liken the human nature of Our Lord to a conduit of Divine Life in which a spring-fitted valve *has to be continually held open* to allow the continued flow of that life. Mary is that valve and it is Her prayer which must take place to allow the flow of Grace. Thus does She continually cooperate with Her Divine Son in His eternal mission. In this Office She is called "Mediatrix of All Grace."

But we must not forget that Mary is totally dependent on Her Divine Son. From Him She receives all that She possesses. If Her prayers are a necessary condition for the flow of Grace, it is only because He has so willed it. Hence there can be no question of who is more merciful, Jesus or Mary. Mary is nothing without Him and Her mercy is but a sweet manifestation of His mercy; He not only died to save us but even gave us this most perfect, most lovable, and most glorious Mother.

On the other hand, although Mary *would be* nothing without Jesus, Jesus has made Her *by participation* (i. e., by the Grace of which Mary is "full") *what He is by nature* (somewhat as a reflector can be made as bright as the light which it reflects).

Hence Mary is, in a dependent way, all-powerful. No one can think of any non-contradictory possibility which Her prayers cannot resolve. Neither can anyone measure the depths of Her heart; Her maternal love is beyond the cognitive power of human intellects.

We see, then, that the Blessed Virgin is different from all other inhabitants of Heaven. Rising above saints and angels, as the Immaculate Mother of God and of Eve's redeemed children, She enters into the very plan of God's relation to His creatures. Pope Leo XIII described Her mediation in our regard as *a function divinely assigned to Her,* like the natural duty of mothers toward their children.[1] As Mother of God, from Her exalted position in union with Her Divine Son, She beholds the souls of each and everyone of us; in Her place as Mother of mankind, seeing each and every one of our needs, She asks Her Divine Son to give us Grace. Her prayer is an infallible power that continually pours Grace at the doors of our souls, where we may accept or reject it.

Now, let us especially notice that Mary is not in the Divine Plan to draw souls to Herself. She is there to draw them to Her Divine Son, the Source of Eternal Life. In this function of Mary we recognize a great truth: Not only is Mary the way by which God has come to us but She is also the way by which He wills us to come to Him. This is why Pope Pius X expostulated: "Can anyone fail to see that there is no more direct or surer way (than Mary) to unite all mankind in Christ and to obtain through

Him the perfect adoption of sons that we may be holy and immaculate in the eyes of God?" [2]

Hence we see the tremendous significance of the fact that this Blessed Virgin, this Mediatrix of All Grace, has promised salvation to anyone who wears *Her Sign of Alliance*. It is with awe that we picture to ourselves Her descent to Saint Simon Stock, surrounded by the pomp of Her Heavenly Court, to clothe us in Her garment, to proclaim Her Motherhood even as at Lourdes She has proclaimed Her Immaculate Conception. Moreover, *we see the explanation of the Scapular*.

In considering Mary from any angle, we are struck with particular force by two prerogatives: Her power and Her love—the one omnipotent, the other fathomless. It is because of Her love that She made the Scapular Promise and it is by Her prayer-power that She keeps it.

THEOLOGY OF THE SCAPULAR

It is everything but a dogma of our Catholic Faith that anyone who practices true devotion to Mary perseveringly will infallibly be saved. Moreover, not only is true devotion to Mary, perseveringly practiced, a Sign of Predestination, remarks a certain theologian, but "even sinners can have true devotion to Her." [3]

True devotion to Mary consists in only three things: homage, confidence, and love. Anyone who comes to death with the surety that he has *faithfully praised, trusted and loved Mary*, can be also sure that *he will not be eternally lost*. Such is the doctrine of the Church because, says Saint Alphonsus, one who is thus a true devotee of Mary is protected at death by Her over whom Satan has never had empire and who vanquishes and crushes him by Her mere presence.[4] Quoting and explaining Saint Bernard, Saint Alphonsus says further: "If we follow Mary we shall never err from the paths of Salvation. *Imploring Her thou wilt not despair* (St. Bernard). Each time that we invoke Her aid, we shall be inspired with perfect confidence. *If She supports thee thou canst not fail;* if She protects thee thou hast nothing to fear, for thou canst not be lost: with Her for thy guide, thou wilt not be weary: for thy salvation will be worked with ease."

Now, when we take the Scapular, says Saint Alphonsus, we render *homage* to the Mother of God: "Just as men take pride in having others wear their livery, so the most holy Mary is pleased when Her servants wear Her Scapular as a mark that they have dedicated themselves to Her service and are members of the Family of the Mother of God." [5] Moreover, we show that we believe in Her power to save us and in Her promises; that is *confidence.* Finally, in making ourselves in a special way Her children, thus rendering to Her the homage of membership in Her family and confiding in Her power and affection, we show that *we love Her,* that we desire to have Her for a Mother.

Containing the three elements of a true Marian devotion, the wearing of the Scapular is by its very nature a Sign of Salvation.

It might seem, as a consequence, that our Heavenly Mother has not really done anything very remarkable in making the Scapular Promise. However,
what is more remarkable than a true devotion to
Her *that is by its nature perpetual?* What is more
wonderful than an absolute assurance at death that
*we have always loved the Blessed Virgin, always had
confidence in Her and always rendered homage at
Her shrine of devotion?* And yet, such an assurance
is the Scapular. Indeed, there is no sweeter nor more
complete assurance at the death of "everyman" than
the presence upon him of this Sign of true devotion
to Heaven's Queen.

The reader has probably begun to recognize the
Scapular Devotion not only as *a* true devotion to
Mary but as the *best* one. In no other devotion has
Mary unconditionally promised Salvation, or made
us special children "brought forth by Her and nourished at Her breasts" (Greg. XIII),[6] or given such a
Sign of perpetual homage that it even makes us
members of Her first and most dear family. It is little
wonder that Blessed Claude de la Colombière said:

> *"I would reproach myself were I to weaken your
> confidence in those other practices of devotion to
> Mary which are approved by the Church. They are
> all salutary and cannot fail to touch Her maternal
> heart. But if She graciously accords Her favor to
> those who avail themselves of those devotions, how
> much more propitious will She not be to all who
> clothe themselves in Her holy livery?"* [7]

Now, let us notice a unique and glorious character
of this childlike, simple devotion: that it is *wordless.*
The wearing of the Scapular gives rise to a mystical

union between the soul and Mary where not a word is spoken. "I am the City of Refuge," says Saint John Damascene in Mary's name, "for all who fly to Me." And Saint Alphonsus comments: "It is sufficient to have recourse to Her, for whoever has the good fortune to enter this city need not speak to be saved. *Assemble yourselves and let us enter the fenced city and let us be silent there* (Jeremias VIII, 14), to speak in the words of Jeremias . . . It will suffice to enter this city and be silent because Mary will speak and ask all that we require. For this reason a devout author (Bl. Fernandez) exhorts all sinners to take refuge under the Mantle of Mary, exclaiming: 'Fly, O Adam and Eve and all you their children who have outraged God; fly and take refuge in the bosom of this good Mother; know you not that She is our only city of refuge?' " [8]

By way of parenthesis, let us remark that Saint Alphonsus says: "It will suffice to keep silent"; he wishes to indicate that it is profitable to do more than fly under Mary's mantle, viz., not only to show our confidence, homage and love *by just being there,* but to practice that fourth and perfecting element of Marian devotion: imitation. By rendering homage to Mary we give Her our minds; by confidence we give our wills; by love we give our hearts. Such is *true* but *not perfect devotion.* To be perfect we must sell all and follow Mary; we must give Her our whole selves by imitation.[9] Later the reader will see how the Scapular renders this perfection of devotion to Our Lady very easy; he is now concerned with what is sufficient and we return to the consideration of Mary's Promise only in so far as it is a means of salvation.

"I made that in the Heavens there should rise light that never faileth" (Ecclus, 24, 6), says Scripture, and Cardinal Hugo comments in Mary's name: "I have caused as many lights to shine eternally in Heaven as I have clients." Now, if we wonder *how* Mary does this, we have the explanation again from Saint Alphonsus: *"By Her powerful intercession* She led them thither." [10] When heeding the cry of Her children, voiced in the infancy of the Church by Saint Ephrem: "O most holy Virgin, receive us under Thy protection if Thou wilt see us saved for we have no hope of salvation but through Thy means," the Blessed Virgin came down and actually spread a mantle over us. In thus making us Her clients and promising to cause us to shine in Heaven, She made the Scapular the *Sign of Her intercession.*

Thus the Scapular, a visible sign of Mary's invisible mediation, has come to be called Her sacrament in the dispensation of Grace to special devotees. This arises from the fact that the Scapular *unites us to Mary,* where we cannot be lost. In giving us the Scapular, Our Lady does not force us to come under Her Mantle; She merely spreads it out and *invites* us to come within its folds where, as a member of Her family and as a privileged son, each one of us shall be saved. Hence the alliance is two-sided: Mary on Her part offers to be our Mother, we offer to be Her children; *moral union* is the result. Anyone who actually thinks of Mary with love, confidence and homage, is morally united to Her and, by the Scapular, this union is continual. Probably the greatest excellence of the Scapular derives just from this unbroken union effected between us and Mary, between the redeemed and the universal Mediatrix. It is the Sign of a bi-lateral contract and, on Her side, Mary assures us of Her intercession.

When we say that Mary is continually present to Her Scapular wearers by what is called "moral union," we simply mean that She is united to them by intention. When I think of someone whom I love while he thinks of me, he and I are united by common intention. If I wear the Scapular, Mary is continually thinking of me and loving me as Her special child and I, in turn, am thinking of Her and loving Her as my dearest Mother. I may not be *actually* thinking of Her, at the moment, but the Scapular proclaims that I think of Her and love Her at least by *intention*.

An understanding of the nature of a *virtual intention* is all-important to an understanding of the continual moral union with Mary that results from the Scapular Devotion. It is the virtual intention, of which the Scapular we wear gives testimony, that renders a *perpetual* moral union possible.

To understand the force of the virtual intention, let us take the example (though the reality would be most undesirable) of a priest who puts on the vestments in order to baptize a child and, as he is about to leave the vestry, receives such very distressing news that he enters the baptistry to perform the ceremony totally distracted, even to the point of not adverting to the fact that he is administering the Sacrament. Is the child validly baptized? Yes, because although the priest had not at the moment an actual intention, nevertheless he did nothing to exclude the actual intention which he had when putting on the vestments. Thus he may be said to have had, throughout the ceremony, a virtual intention. In vesting himself he made the actual intention of administering Baptism, and the very vestments he wore during the ceremony showed that the Baptism was willed by him. So, too, the Scapular shows that we will to be united to Mary even when we do not advert to its presence. Consequently, Mary is always present to Scapular wearers in a special way: protecting, guiding, adorning, lavishing a Mother's love.

Hence the Scapular is a bond of union between Mary and the soul. The one who wears the Scapular enjoys Mary's presence by Her contract and his. The Scapular is but the symbol of that contract. And since Satan can do nothing against Mary, the Immaculate Conception, he can do nothing against us when She protects us. That is why one who practices true devotion to Her, and more particularly one who wears the Scapular, cannot be lost.

As a sort of consequence of all this, do we not see that Mary's Scapular alliance—contracted by a Promise on the one hand, and an acceptance on the other—has the power of drawing all mankind to union under Mary's mantle? Two things united to a third are united to each other. In entering the Scapular Confraternity we enter into union not only with Mary but with everyone similarly united to Her. Thus, here on earth, a tremendous Marian force is latent in the Scapular Confraternity wherein millions and millions of souls are each, to some degree at least, united to the Blessed Virgin.

It is indeed true that we cannot sound the depths of the Scapular Promise. We see it constituting a true Marian devotion. We see it spreading Mary's Mantle over the earth, under which we can enter and be allied in a special way to the invincible Queen of Heaven. We see it creating a great spiritual force among millions of souls, in a Confraternity of Mary which it will suffice to enter and be silent, "for Mary will speak and ask all that we require."

"The faithful so unanimously agree that devotion to the Mother of God is a mark of predestination that, independently of the reasons upon which this opinion is based, I think a concordance so general should cause it to be regarded as a truth of our holy religion . . . And because all the forms of our love for the Blessed Virgin, all its various modes of expression cannot be equally agreeable to Her and therefore do not assist us in the same degree to Heaven, I aver without a moment's hesitation that the Scapular is the most favored of all." [11]

Bl. Claude de la Colombiere, S. J.

"We must not look on the Scapular as a talisman operating by some magic virtue of its own, but rather as a manifestation of devotion which derives all its benevolence from the Blessed Virgin and is the HOMAGE of respectful AFFECTION, of FILIAL CONFIDENCE, and CONTINUAL supplication." [12]

A. J. Vermeersch, S. J.

CHAPTER FIVE

Mary's Sacrament

COMPOSED OF spirit and flesh, we men find that our minds cannot act, in their present state, except through the body. If the cells of the brain are destroyed, the intellectual soul is helpless. Even for the origin of its most exalted activities, the spiritual intellect needs its material instrument—the brain. That is why, in the *spiritual* life, we thirst for *material* signs.[1] We linger at Lourdes because of the supernatural atmosphere and the spiritual associations of its surroundings, or we feast our eyes on the Host in the monstrance because we know that underneath that white dot, in its setting of gold, is the Body of Christ.

Having created us, God knew well our need of signs: the *Word* became *flesh*. God bowed to human nature and clothed His Divinity to come to us. Nor was it enough for Him to have lived as a human model; He immolated Himself visibly for us and then, in instituting the Church that was to perpetuate the flow of Graces opened on Calvary's altar, He instituted seven "visible signs of invisible Grace."

Somewhat as Our Lord has done in giving us Salvation and communicating to us His Divine Life,

Mary has done in assuring us Salvation and communicating to us Her protection. She has instituted *a visible sign of Her invisible mediation.*

For more than four centuries, the Scapular has been known as "Mary's sacrament." Vastly different from those seven magnificent institutions of Christ which effect Grace *ex opere operato* (having Grace, as it were, in the vessels of their own material form), as instituted by the Mediatrix of all Grace, it is a source of Eternal Life only in an indirect way: "It derives all its excellence *from the prayers of Mary*" (Vermeersch).[2] But are not the prayers of Mary the channel of Grace?

So, just as is one bound to adore the Infinite Wisdom of God in acting so completely in accordance with our nature in order to give us a participation in His own Nature, we are forced to lovingly admire the great goodness of Mary as She makes an exterior sign the vehicle of Her great Promise. It is solely from the fact that it was made over a tangible sign that the Promise brings Mary to us: it is because we wear that sign that we practice *perpetual devotion* of homage, confidence and love.

If we go back in spirit to the time when there was no Scapular Promise, we can appreciate Mary's Gift. We can hear the cry of Saint Ephrem: "O Mary! take us under Thy mantle!" or the longing sigh of a St. Bernard: "O Mary! if we are Thy devotees, we cannot be lost!" Would not we ourselves exclaim: "Oh! if only I could come to death with some sign that I had perseveringly practiced homage, confi-

dence and love towards Mary! The Church assures
me that then I could not be lost!" The centuries
were crying: "Holy Mary, Mother of God, pray for
us sinners *now and at the hour of our death!*"

On July 16th, 1251, Mary showed Herself to be
a Mother. Realizing our human longings for a sign
of having persevered in a true devotion to Her, She
came down to us with a garment: "Whosoever dies
in this shall not suffer eternal fire." She bound Herself to pray for us. She instituted a true devotion to
Herself, so simple that its perfection is amazing.

We merely put the Scapular on, but then Mary
must pray for us. By taking it we enroll ourselves
under Her standard, clothe ourselves in Her livery,
thus rendering to Her the homage of service and
praise; we show Her that we have confidence in Her
power and intercession; uniting ourselves to Her,
entering into Her special alliance of son and mother,
we show Her a filial love.[3] "And although other
pious practices are attached to certain times and certain places," says Father Chaignon, S. J., "the
devotion of the Scapular belongs to all times and to
all places: thanks to my little Habit, wherever I am,
whatever I am doing, Mary never sees me without
seeing on my body an evidence of my devotion to
Her." [4]

Thus the Scapular is not only an assurance of Salvation after death; it is even now a powerful means
of Grace. In instituting such a simple but complete
devotion, Mary continually binds Herself, as it were,
to intercede for us. Truly, then, is the Scapular Her

Sacrament: it is a visible pledge of Her intercession, the very channel of Grace. She has complete dominion over Grace, says Saint Bernard, so that "She dispenses to whom She wills, when She wills, and in so much as She wills," [5] and She has given us a Promise-bearing Sign which marks us Her devotees, Her beloved children to whom She chooses to dispense Grace; such is the import of Her Promise to make those, who wear Her Scapular, saints.

"It is not enough to say that the Habit of the Blessed Virgin is a mark of predestination," says Blessed Claude. That Habit is *more* than a sign of true devotion to Mary. "Because of *the alliance,* which Mary contracts with us and which we contract with Her," he adds, "no other devotion renders our salvation so certain." [6] Father Houdry, S. J., corroborates this statement and further explains the reason which Blessed Claude gives for the claim that the Scapular does more than mark us as predestinate. "The Scapular is one of the greatest means of salvation," says Father Houdry, "because Mary has attached a promise of Salvation to the Scapular and *hence a special protection,* which means that She gives us a very powerful means for working out our salvation. It only remains for us to make them infallible." [7]

A most powerful aid to salvation, the Scapular is in a category of its own. "It is a devotion of *faith* and *feeling* that is always indicative of one's spiritual state," says a devout Augustinian writer.[8] Hence it is truly the devotion which approaches nearest to those great institutions of Our Lord, the Sacraments. It seems, in a sense, to be more than a mere Sacramental. Aids to salvation instituted *by the Church* are the "sacramentals" and they derive their value from the prayers of the Church. The Scapular, in that it derives its excellence from the *prayers* of Mary, is similar to the sacramentals. However, it may be placed in a unique category because, neither instituted by Christ like the Sacraments, nor by the Church like the sacramentals, it was instituted *by Mary,* the Mediatrix of all Grace. "There is a certain connection," says Father Clarke, S. J., "between the presence of Grace in the soul and the presence of the Scapular, and between the absence of Grace and the absence of the Scapular." [9]

It is of vital interest to see how the Scapular acts as Mary's sacrament.

When the young couple at Cana were on the point of serious embarrassment, Mary turned unasked to say to Jesus: "They have no wine." [10] And why, but because this couple had invited Her? (Jesus came along, of course, although they did not then know Who He was.) Being so loving and so kind of heart, it was only natural for Mary to notice their trouble and use Her great power of impetration. And when we mystically invite Mary into our hearts by accepting Her Scapular, She comes. A moment arrives that our devotion fails; we begin to grow cold. But Mary sees this. Unasked She turns to Her Divine Son and says: "The wine of devotion is failing." Perhaps Our Lord might reply: "But My time is not yet come: this soul has not turned to Me and, in fact, is now turning from Me and refusing to recognize My love." However, Our Lady will whisper in our hearts: "Read this book," or "Visit the Blessed Sacrament," or "Make this little act of self-denial." She will have us prepare for Our Lord's action because She knows that even though we have been unfaithful, Jesus will, because of love for His Mother, change the water of faithlessness, joyful that thus again He can act in our souls, whereas before our inconstancy prevented Him. This is, in fact, why He gave us Mary, His Mother. And that is why Mary, His Mother, gave us the Scapular.

Pope Leo XI recognized one aspect of the sacramental quality of the Scapular when he said, on its being accidentally removed from him at the moment of his papal investiture: "Leave me Mary, *lest Mary leave me!*" [11] So did the Curè of Ars (Saint John Vianney) when he called the Scapular one's *safeguard against temptation.*[12] So also did Blessed Claude de la Colombière when he declared that *"No other devotion* renders our salvation so certain." [13] The Scapular of Our Lady of Mount Carmel, says Savaria, "is the masterpiece, the *chef-d'oeuvre,* of the love of the Most Holy Virgin for mankind; it is the touching mystery of Her powerful intervention in applying the Infinite Merits of Her Divine Son." [14]

The abuse of Our Lord's Sacraments constitutes the horrible crime of sacrilege. So, too, the abuse of Mary's Scapular is a great crime. It would be utter folly for anyone to think he could take advantage of

Mary's Promise to wear the Scapular as an excuse for sin! If need be, a miracle would be worked to deprive him of the Scapular at death, and one refrains from imagining the horror of that state of damnation into which a sinner must be cast when God must work a miracle to allow it. Better indeed would it be for that man had he not been born . . .

But abuse of the Scapular Promise is a thing almost unheard of. Much more general is the *lack of appreciation* of the heavenly treasures which Mary's Sign conceals. Just as many receive the Sacraments almost with indifference, millions wear the Scapular and rarely think of it as more than an assurance of Salvation. Its wearing rarely becomes more in their lives than the simplest degree of a true Marian devotion.

The wearing of the Scapular is always a potent means of Grace. German Catholics express this with their one word for the Scapular: *Gnadenkleid*, i. e., Grace-garment. It is always a powerful means of Grace because it always assures us of Mary's prayers. However, its degree of efficacy depends on us.

Although anyone who wears the Scapular devoutly practices a true devotion to Mary—a devotion of homage, confidence and love—still that true devotion may be very slight. The homage may be there, and the confidence, but what about the love? Is that Scapular-wearer a person who thinks nothing of offending Mary's Son? If so, the true devotion is on the decline. The minimum of love for Mary—little more than a desire for Her protection that arises from his desire to escape Hell—is bound to disappear if the careless sinner does not better his ways so that, finally, he will forget to wear Her Sign of affiliation. One who is devout, on the other hand, will reap the unfailing consequence of perseverance in wearing the Scapular: he will grow in Divine Life, if in the state of Grace, or he will be restored to Divine Life, if in sin. Mary, by Her all-powerful prayer, obtains for him those actual graces which impel him to use the Sacraments of the Church. But for the one who *enters into the Scapular Devotion,* for the one who not only wears the Scapular but frequently adverts to his alliance with Mary, the power of "Mary's sacrament" becomes tremendous! She is a Mother who will not be outdone in generosity and the Scapular is in itself the greatest sign of that generosity.

How unfortunate it would be were we to carry about with us this fathomless treasure without delving into its coffers to take possession of the gold of homage, confidence, and love that glistens there! How unfortunate it would be if we never reminded the Dispensatrix of All Grace that She has contracted an alliance with us . . . or if we never gave entrance to those sentiments of recognition and love, which Her Scapular almost forces to our hearts.

One of the greatest means of Salvation, the Scapular is probably the *best* means of practicing the virtue of religion through Mary. Not to take advantage of this Sign, with its *hidden graces* of Mary's presence and constant motherliness, is to turn our

backs on the easy acquisition of all heavenly treasures. For, in the Scapular, do we not find Mary?
And Saint Alphonsus finds Scripture saying: "Whoever finds Mary finds every good thing, obtains all
graces and all virtues; by Her powerful intercession
She obtains all that is necessary to enrich them with
Divine Grace: with Me are riches . . . and glorious
riches . . . that I may enrich them that love Me"
(Prov. viii, 21).[15]

An anxious soul needs no urging to benefit by
Mary's sacrament. Entering into its three sentiments, she knows that soon shall she realize the
words of Scripture: "Now all good things have come
to me together with Her" (Wisdom, vii, 11). "The
Blessed Virgin is the Mother and dispenser of all
good things," said Saint Alphonsus, "and hence the
whole world, and more particularly each individual
who lives in it as a devout client of this great Queen,
may say with truth that with devotion to Mary, both
he and the world have received everything good and
perfect." [16] And the Scapular is a visible ornament,
assuring us of Mary's invisible, all-powerful mediation. The Church applies to the Scapular the words
of Scripture: *Ornament* and *strength* are Her garment . . . and She shall laugh in the latter day"
(Prov. xxxi, 25).

> *"I wanted to know if Mary really and truly inter-*
> *ested Herself in me. And in the Scapular She has*
> *given me the most tangible assurance; I have only to*
> *open my eyes: She has attached Her protection to*
> *this Scapular: 'Whosoever dies clothed in this shall*
> *not suffer eternal fire!'"* [17]
>
> BLESSED CLAUDE.

"Our Lady of Mount Carmel, wishing to contract an alliance with Her children on earth, gave them the Scapular as testimony of this alliance. It is the exterior guarantee, the sensible testimony which She places in their hands, that they may never forget the union which they have contracted with Her. This alliance is stable and permanent by its very nature because it is founded on the bounty of Our Mother in Heaven, which never changes." [18]

REV. J. T. SAVARIA.

"In the same way that Jesus wished that something visible would reveal in the Sacraments the invisible effects of His Grace, so also has Mary wished that the more particular protection which She accords to all those who serve Her with fidelity would be marked by an exterior sign, the Scapular." [19]

R. P. LASELVE, O. F. M.

Scapular of Saint Alphonsus,
front view.

CHAPTER SIX

Scapular Prayer

and

Communication of Benefits

WITHOUT SAYING to Mary that we venerate Her, that we have confidence in Her, that we love Her, by simply wearing the Scapular we tell Her all these things every minute of the day. The Scapular is a prayer.

Now, when we think devoutly of the Scapular and renew its sentiments in our hearts, that prayer, becomes more intense than passionate volumes.

Let us consider the case of a young man who leaves his home in Syria to study for the priesthood at Paris. He will be gone for several years and his mother feels the sacrifice to be almost beyond her strength. At the moment of departure, she takes a locket that contains her picture and strings it about the neck of her son, begging him to wear it as a symbol of her and a reminder that he must never do anything that would make her ashamed of him. And years later, this son returns, a priest. The train is pulling into the station and there, bathed in tears of joy, stands his mother. They are still too far apart for a word. Lifting the locket from his breast, gazing at his mother with love-laden eyes, the young priest presses it to his lips . . . .

Not a word is spoken, but the intense embrace of such an action speaks volumes.

Such, too, is the mystical prayer made possible by Our Lady's Sign. She has placed the Scapular about our necks to remind us that we have a Mother in Heaven waiting, and watching, and loving us more than our earthly mothers could love us. And when we make that Sign of Her an incentive to virtue, a means of intensifying our oral prayers or those of affection, Her heart goes out to us and union with Her is deepened immeasurably. Hence Pope Benedict XV—the celebrated "World-War Pontiff"—granted five hundred days' indulgence for the kissing of the Scapular, every time that it is kissed.

Often, on our journey to Heaven, we may mystically embrace our Mother even though too far off to see Her, too far away to be ravished by Her actual presence and made exceptionally glorious, as the Little Flower says, by the radiance of such a Queen. Moreover, our wordless Scapular Prayer can take many forms. It may lead to any other kind of prayer such as ejaculatory prayer or the fervent recitation of the "Hail Mary" or the "Our Father," even though it is in itself, according to the authorities on the spiritual life, a practice of the highest form of prayer. And who will measure the value of this prayer with the Mother who has promised: "Whosoever dies clothed in this (i.e., practicing the very minimum of the prayer) shall not suffer eternal fire"?

Although a little lengthy, the following example from Deschamps' *"The New Eve"* will show the value of the Scapular from many points of view but especially as a Sign of mystical union with the Mother of God and of the intense prayer that may result from it.

When a somewhat worldly young girl once went to Confession—which she was in the habit of doing at rare intervals—the priest asked her if she practiced any devotion in honor of Mary. After a few moments of silence she replied: "Nothing, Father, but the *Hail Mary* in my daily prayers."

"Would you be willing to do something more?" the priest asked.

"Yes, Father. If it would not be too difficult."

"Very well. Take the Scapular."

"I do not know what that is."

"It is the livery of all true children of Mary. All true children of Mary cherish it as a souvenir of their beloved Mother, a sign of the love they have for Her, and they wear it although it is unseen by the world. To wear the Scapular is to perform a lasting act of piety, and yet nothing is less difficult. It is always easy to love our Mother."

"Give it to me," the young woman warmly exclaimed. "I will gladly wear it!"

Some weeks later she returned to this confessor to express her gratitude. That act of devotion toward the Blessed Virgin, the wearing of the Scapular, had proved to be a bright first link in a long chain of graces which were to effect an entire transformation in her spiritual life.

Some years elapsed after this conversation when the same priest, one morning about nine o'clock, set out from his rectory with a ponderous volume under his arm. He was wont to flee from the busy city and to seek the silence of an adjacent forest, and thus enjoy without interruption his favorite study, philosophy. Strange to say, however, this morning he could not concentrate upon his book. It was not that thoughts foreign to the subject intruded themselves. It was simply an interior feeling for which he could not account. He felt powerfully drawn to return to his church. Finally, conquered by the attraction, he closed his book and retraced his steps until he reached the church door and entered. The attraction becoming each moment more powerful, he knelt down; perhaps it were more exact to say that he was impelled, by some secret power, to fall to his knees before the most Blessed Sacrament. There, instead of making a visit to the Saviour hidden beneath the mystic veils, he received one! A light, until then unknown to the eyes of his soul, revealed divine truths to him more vividly than ever before. The spirit of God transfixed his heart like a sword.

Was it joy? Was it sorrow? Was it love? Was it pain? It was a mingling of all, but the priest would not have exchanged one of those tears for all the delights of the world. The divine visitation lasted for a long while. Gradually returning to himself he

recited again and again: "My God! . . . What hast
Thou done to me? I was not seeking Thee, yet didst
Thou come. Whence is it, O Lord, that I have been
thus highly favored?"

The following day he received a letter wherein he
read: "Yesterday Miss X made her solemn vows.
The silence of her holy retreat still lingers to too
great an extent for her to write to you herself, but
she requested me to say that immediately after her
oblation, she recited a *Hail Mary,* HER HAND
UPON HER SCAPULAR, and fervently implored
the Divine Mother thus: 'Dear Mother, beg Jesus,
Thy beloved Son, to give back to my director the
good which he so abundantly gave to me.' " [1]

A prayer uttered to Mary through the mystical
Scapular embrace is as perfect as a prayer can be.
Our Lord taught us to say the "Our Father"; Mary
has handed us the Scapular. When we use it as a
prayer, Our Lady draws us, and those for whom we
pray, to the Sacred Heart in the tabernacle.

The unusualness of Mary's Sign, as a perfect
wordless prayer, lies in its simplicity. Simplicity is, in
fact, the most striking feature of the Scapular from
any point of view: the Mother of God has combined
utmost magnificence with surprising, almost unbelievable simplicity. "Mary gives us the richest present," remarks Father Houdry, "and this present, in
the eyes of those who have not faith, is almost nothing. What has more simplicity than this little Scapular of rough cloth? Yet what has greater magnificence than the promises which are attached to it?

Mary gives it as a Sign of Salvation and Grace; She promises those who wear it that they will never be condemned to the fires of Hell. Could anything be more magnificent?" [2]

So the Scapular, as though its very make-up were a prayer, seems an echo of Mary's Magnificat. Mary said in Her great canticle: "He that is mighty hath done *great things* to Me . . . He hath regarded *the lowliness* of His Handmaid." [3] And in wearing the Scapular the Magnificat wells up from our hearts in a vibrating melody of mystical union with Heaven's Queen, pouring its notes like diamond jets around the Heaven-throne of God.

> "*Every day witnesses the fulfillment of Her prophetic words of the Magnificat: 'Behold from henceforth all generations shall call me blessed.' Ever new and fresh garlands does faithful Christiandom place at the feet of the ever Blessed Virgin! And among these is that devotion as simple as it is powerful . . . a devotion which more or less culminates the veneration of the ever Blessed Virgin.*" [4]
>
> FR. RAPHAEL FUHR, O. S. F.

COMMUNICATION OF BENEFITS

A final aspect of Scapular Theology is the communication of benefits among members of the Confraternity of the Scapular. Those who wear the Scapular have a deeper and fuller participation than non-wearers of the Scapular in all the prayers, Masses and works of satisfaction of other members of the Confraternity of the whole Church.

In the Church there is a spiritual solidarity that binds together the faithful on earth, the souls in

Purgatory, and the saints in Heaven. This solidarity implies a variety of inter-relations: "Within the Church Militant, not only the participation in the same faith, sacraments, and government, but also the mutual exchange of examples, prayers, merits, and satisfactions; between the Church on earth on the one hand, and purgatory and heaven on the other, suffrages, invocation, intercession, veneration." [5] The explanation of this participation of the spiritual goods, which is called the "communion of saints," is to be found in the fact that since we are all children of God and participate in the life and merits of Christ, our own merits and satisfactions are shared among ourselves through the bond of charity.

Those who are united by the Scapular have a bond which, besides making them children of God, binds them together as *special* children of Mary. They have a bond over and above that of seeking the common end of being sanctified through the merits of Christ; they have the special end of honoring the Queen of Heaven in a particular manner. Moreover, they wear a common sign which unites them in a special manner to Mary and consequently to each other in Her. A German writer remarks, in comparing the Scapular bond to that of marriage: "As long as two are united to a third, they are also united to each other. So long, then, as the soul of a father and the soul of a mother are bound by the Holy Scapular to Mary, they are also united, by a heavenly bond, one to another, and this union is stronger than even that of marriage because *not even death* can break it, but only serves to give hope that both shall find each other beyond in the bliss of Heaven." [6]

Among Scapular wearers, therefore, there is a special communication of benefits—a deeper and fuller communication, additional to that which arises from membership in the Mystical Body.

The value of this is tremendous. The Scapular is itself a prayer, therefore each one who wears it is a *partner* in a mighty volume of praise! It is no longer a single melody but a grand concert, from millions of souls, that arises at every moment to delight Mary's Son. Moreover, the Scapular wearer has an intimate share in the spiritual goods of millions of saints. Not only is he united to the members of the Carmelite Order and to every wearer of the Scapular, he is even a partner of each of them in the very end of their institution. And imagine the consequent value, for example, that would derive from being an intimate of the "Little Flower" whose Scapular, on earth, was indissolubly interlocked with Her love for Mary, "more a Mother than a Queen." [7] But the Scapular wearer is an intimate not only of Saint Therese but of all the Saints of Carmel and, to a special degree, of Saint Joseph, the spouse of the Blessed Virgin who has a special love for Carmelites —the chosen ones of his queenly consort. And then there are all the other Saints, such as Saint Alphonsus and Saint John Don Bosco, upon whose remains the Scapular was found incorrupt, and multitudes, if not almost all others, canonized in the last six centuries. On earth, there are hundreds of saints wearing the Scapular, hidden in the noise of cities as well as in the quiet of cloisters. There are myriads of holy laymen and religious who seek, together as members of Mary's Scapular Family, the glory promised them. And with all these, each Scapular wearer is a partner, sharing in all spiritual goods. How consoling it will be, and valuable, to have this intimacy with millions of Marian souls when we are in purgatory . . . How much it will and does mean to us in eternal values . . .

But this communication of benefits *within* Mary's family is not all. Popes Clement VII and Clement X declared [8] that Scapular wearers participate *in a special manner* in the fruit not only of the spiritual works of the Carmelites, to whom they are united as a Confraternity, but *also in all the good done throughout the whole Church.*

The reason for this proclamation was probably twofold: (1) the Popes saw that since all Christians are children of Mary, those who are Her special children should have a deeper participation in the works of the others; (2) it was desirable to *draw the whole Church into the close unity of Mary's family,* where membership is rewarded with an assurance of salvation.

In recognition of this latter value, Vermeersch said: "This community of benefits (obtained in the Scapular Confraternity) should excite our gratitude to the kind Providence of God and to Christ, Who is always so full of generosity to His Spouse, the

Church; but does not the Scapular contain other useful lessons? Does it not invite us to *draw closer* the bonds which should make brothers of all Christians?" [9]

Truly it would seem that Mary has omitted nothing in instituting Her simple and magnificent devotion. The Holy Ghost says for Her in Sacred Scripture: "I have led you into the land of Carmel that you may eat its fruit and all the good things thereof" (Jer. II, 7). Grouped into Carmel by that bountiful Virgin, beneath Her Mantle we partake in a special manner of all the good works of Her vast and holy society and even of those performed by all Her other children anywhere in the world.

> *"I have led you into the land of Carmel that you might eat its fruit and all the good things thereof, i.e., for the most difficult labor of the journey I have given you the abundance of all things, which Carmel signifies."* [10]
>
> SAINT JEROME.

CHAPTER SEVEN

The Promise Extended Into Purgatory

UNTIL IT is explained, the Scapular Promise seems unbelievable. Ever since Our Lady appeared to Saint Simon Stock on July 16, 1251, many—yes, thousands—have found it almost impossible to believe that for *so little* a practice as belonging to Her Confraternity, one could be rewarded with *salvation*.

It seems that Our Lady returned to Heaven and considered, as it were, the great favor She had conferred. She saw the amazement of thousands at so small an action as wearing two pieces of cloth being favored by Her with so tremendous a Promise. So She returned again to earth, and this time *to make a Promise still more astounding!*

In the year after Saint Peter Thomas was informed by Her that "the Order of Carmel is destined to exist until the end of the world," the Queen of Heaven conferred a favor through the habit of Her family which has caused the great Pope Benedict XV to exclaim: "Let all of you have a common language and a common armor: the language, the sentences of the gospel; the armor, the *Scapular of Mary* which all ought to wear and *which enjoys the singular privilege of protection even after death.*" [1]

74

This singular privilege is known as "The Sabbatine" (or *Saturday*) Privilege and is based on a bull said to have been issued on March 3rd, 1322, by Pope John XXII. Today, because of the very circumstances described previously in Chapter Three on the Historicity of the Scapular Promise, we have no certain, accurate copy of the "Sabbatine Bull." But the privilege is frequently understood to mean that those who wear the Scapular and fulfill two other conditions (which, according to the only copy of the bull in existence, were made by the Blessed Virgin in an apparition to Pope John XXII) will be *freed from Purgatory on the first Saturday after death.*

However, all that the Church has ever said officially in explanation of this, on several occasions, is that those who fulfill the conditions of the Sabbatine Privilege will be released from Purgatory, through the intercession of Our Lady, *soon* after death, and *especially on Saturday.*

This official statement was issued by Pope Paul V. At a time when both the origin and nature of the Sabbatine Privilege were under serious question, the Pope said:

"It is permitted to preach . . . that the Blessed Virgin will aid the souls of the Brothers and Sisters of the Confraternity of the Blessed Virgin of Mount Carmel after their death by Her continual intercession, by Her suffrages and merits and by Her special protection, especially on the day of Saturday which is the day especially dedicated by the Church to the same Blessed Virgin Mary, if they have worn the habit (the Scapular) during life, observed chastity according to their state, and recited the little office . . . or, not knowing how to recite the office, will have observed the fast days of the Church and abstained from meat on Wednesdays and Saturdays (unless either of these days should coincide with the Feast of Christmas)." [2a]

This "special Protection after death" is the greatest of all the benefits of the Scapular Devotion, excepting the essential benefit of the close bond which the Scapular devotion creates between our hearts and the Immaculate Heart of Mary.

We recall again the words which Pope Benedict XV addressed to the Seminarians of Rome: ". . . The Scapular of Mary . . . enjoys *the singular privilege* of protection even after death."

In his letter of March 18th, 1922, commemorating the sixth centenary of the Sabbatine Privilege, Pope Pius XI said:

"It surely ought to be sufficient merely to exhort all the members of the Confraternity to persevere in the holy exercises which have been prescribed for the gaining of the indulgences to which they are entitled and particularly for the gaining of that indulgence which is the principal and *the greatest of them all,* namely that called the Sabbatine." [2b] (Italics our own.)

Any persevering devotion to Our Lady is held to be a sign of salvation.

But here, attached to the wearing of the Scapular (with fulfillment of two other conditions) is *assur-*

ance of speedy liberation from Purgatory, SOON AFTER DEATH.

One can recall the shock felt around the world in our own day when Our Lady of Fatima revealed that a friend of the children of Fatima—who had died a short time before the Fatima apparitions—would be in Purgatory until the end of time.

In an interview with one of the children of Fatima (Lucia) in 1946, the writer asked about this, and Lucia replied:

"Is it so unbelievable that a soul could be in Purgatory until the end of time, when for one mortal sin a soul can be in Hell for all eternity?" [2c]

Eye has not seen nor ear heard the tremendous suffering that word implies. Little is known about it, beyond its necessary existence, but some theologians are of the opinion that the worst pain we could possibly suffer on earth . . . taken all together . . . cannot be compared to the least of the purgatorial pains.

Comte Paul Biver, in his Life of Father Lamy (1853-1931), quotes the following from Father Lamy's writings:

"The Blessed Virgin hates Purgatory," Father Lamy wrote. "It is a sorry place. I like very much to pray for the souls in Purgatory, but the Blessed Virgin thought that I did not ask enough for them and She said to me: 'I am pouring graces upon those souls' (graces that I did not dare to ask), and then She spoke to me of the Sabbatine Privilege."

On July 16th, 1924, at the end of a conversation with a friend Father Lamy said: "As for Mary, Her kindness gets Her everywhere."

"Still, not in hell, Father," his friend reminded him with a smile.

"Once Our Lady said to me," Father Lamy replied, "that a soul falling into hell and calling upon Her is helped. Today is the feast of the Scapular. The Blessed Virgin said again to me one day that those who have recited their seven Paters, Aves and Glorias (This was, at the time, a popular commutation of the Little Office for gaining the Sabbatine Privilege.—Ed.) shall be drawn out of Purgatory by Her the Saturday after their death.

"How precious then is the Brown Scapular," the saintly priest continued, "which brings deliverance from such places of pain, for Purgatory is extremely painful! Our Lady told me that She thought it better to stay behind fifteen years dragging one's weight on earth than to spend a quarter of an hour in Purgatory."

Referring to this last statement at another time, Father Lamy said:

"I was asking Our Lady that I might leave this world, telling Her that to attain this I should prefer to spend a quarter of an hour in Purgatory. But Our Lady answered that it was better to stay fifteen years on earth for that would be less intense a trial. For some," he continued, "Purgatory is painful by the keenness of their torment, for others by its duration. The result is the same for souls. They suffer deeply."

On another occasion Father Lamy said: "The Blessed Virgin told me that many Christian men and women escape hell through Her intercession. She often promotes repentance when the soul is being reft from the body. At that moment of extreme distress She obtains for them a feeling of love of God and repentance."

And on still another occasion Father Lamy said: "She talked to me and gave me a plan for my own daily life, up to and including the end of evening prayer which was not always recited well. She reminded me of the Sabbatine Privilege. 'You must do what is demanded (to obtain this Privilege),' she told me."

We resort to comparisons with earthly pain . . . such as burning . . . because the type of pain endured in Purgatory is so essentially different from any pain we can endure on earth that it is only by comparisons that we can convey any feeling of what Purgatory might be like. To say, with Saint Thomas Aquinas, that Purgatory is the soul's temporary privation of freedom and of the possession of God after death means next to nothing to us for whose souls it is the natural and normal state, here on earth, to be allocated. Therefore those who understand the spiritual suffering of Purgatory merely tell us, as did Saint Mary Magdalen de Pazzi: "The pains suffered by all the martyrs are as a pleasant garden in comparison with the sufferings of the souls in Purgatory." [8]

Saint Cyril said that, as for himself, he would rather suffer all the pains that have beset man from the time of Adam together with all that will beset him until the end of the world, rather than spend *one day* in purgatory. For since nothing impure can enter

Heaven, one must go to Purgatory and, there, only tremendous suffering can satisfy the temporal punishment due offenses against an Infinite Goodness. Saint Bridget beheld a soul in purgatory tortured inexplicably for having been vain and having thought more of frivolous diversion than of things spiritual.[4] Saint Mary Magdalen de Pazzi reports that a saintly religious was detained sixteen days in purgatory for three trifling faults and that she would have been there longer had it not been that she had been very faithful to her rule.[5] A certain layman, although he was a good Christian, was fifty-nine years in purgatory because of his love of comfort; another, thirty-five years for the same reason; a third, who was too fond of gambling, was in purgatory for sixty-four years.[6] And Saint Augustine says that the torments of purgatory surpass all that a man can suffer on earth [7] . . .

But Mary, who through Her intercession has complete dominion over purgatory,[11] has come to Her special children to assure them that She will not suffer them to remain long in its fires, and will liberate them especially on the day consecrated to Her Honor by the Church. With Saint Bonaventure, we hear Her saying in the words of Scripture: "I have penetrated the depths of the abyss, that is, the depths of purgatory, to help those holy souls." [9] Saint Bernardine had said that the Blessed Virgin always liberates Her special devotees from the torments of purgatory and Saint Denis the Carthusian and Saint Peter Damian had written that on the feasts of the Assumption, Christmas and Easter: "Our Lady descends into purgatory and takes many souls from it." [10] But Our Lady has declared that She will not wait for the great Feasts to liberate Her devotees of the Scapular. Regardless of the punishment merited, provided they have observed chastity and practiced an act of piety regulated by their confessors, She will obtain for them the complete remission of their debt and their complete purification soon after their death and, especially on Saturday, escort them to eternal bliss.

When Saint Teresa was astonished at seeing a certain Carmelite carried straight to Heaven *without even going to purgatory,* she was given to understand that he had been faithful to his rule and avoided purgatory because of Bulls granted to the Carmelite order. [11] Saint John of the Cross rejoiced to die on Saturday because of this "Sabbatine" Privilege. "Everyone should strive for it," said Pope Pius XI.

But there are many who miss this great Privilege. "Although many wear My Scapular," Our Lady complained to the Ven. Dominic of Jesus and Mary, "only a few fulfill the conditions for the Sabbatine Privilege." [12] Similarly, at her death the saintly Carmelite, Frances of the Blessed Sacrament, exclaimed: "There are only a few who receive the Privilege because only a few fulfill the conditions." [13] "Is it true that wearers of the Scapular are actually freed from purgatory on the Saturday after their deaths?" was one of the questions put to her father by Sister Seraphina in the celebrated communications with his

suffering soul which caused international comment.
"Yes," was the answer, *"when they have truly ful-
filled all the obligations."* [14]

And yet the privilege is very easily obtained. *One
must observe chastity according to his state in life.*
But this must be done, privilege or no privilege, and
if one should have the misfortune of falling into
grievous sin, it is the opinion of authorities that as
soon as he *repents* and *resolves never to sin again,* his
right to the privilege begins anew. The other condition for obtaining the Sabbatine Indulgence often
varies. Our Lady required the daily *recitation of the
Office* [15] or, if recitation of it should be impossible,
the keeping of the fasts of the Church together with
abstinence from meat on Wednesdays and Saturdays.
However, if one cannot observe even this condition,
then any other work may be substituted by a confessor, either inside or outside the confessional. (It
is to be noted, however, that only a confessor with
the *special faculty* . . . which faculty is often obtained together with the faculty of enrolling in the
Scapular but which does not follow from the latter
. . . can commute the saying of the Little Office to
Abstinence from meat on Wednesdays and Saturdays. It is only this latter condition which can be
commuted by all confessors.) Hence, were the
reader told by a confessor with the proper faculties
that all he had to do in order to enjoy the Sabbatine
Privilege was to fervently kiss his Scapular every
day (besides wearing the Scapular and observing
chastity according to his state), upon doing so with

the right intention the reader would have the assurance of being freed from purgatory soon after his death.[16]

It is a semi-triumph for Satan to cause souls to suffer in purgatory as the result of unrequited sin. Mary sees them, Her children, in unspeakable suffering; the Heart of Her Son, which longs to give bliss to these predestined ones whom He has ransomed at the price of His Blood, is deterred for a time from being finally united to them. Hence Satan celebrates a victory. How crushing it must be to him, an incarnation of pride, to be vanquished by so simple a Marian devotion as the Scapular! And where the promise of Salvation rendered him powerless against souls who died in the Scapular, now a further promise almost completely curtails his power. To keep souls in purgatory which do not enjoy the Sabbatine Privilege he can use his wiles to prevent suffrages from being offered for them, but, before Mary's new Scapular Promise, he is impotent. How true it is that the Immaculate crushes his head, the seat of pride, with Her heel! We are again forcibly reminded of the cloud that appeared to Elias over Mount Carmel, the prophetic vision that gave rise to the title of the Scapular Queen, "Our Lady of Mount Carmel." For even as that little foot-shaped cloud brought material salvation and cooled the burning earth, so does Mary, through Her humble garment of Carmel, bring spiritual salvation and cool the fires of purgatory.

Naturally Satan did not allow the Sabbatine Privilege to spread in the Church without a great struggle. In the opposition that has met it from every quarter it is not difficult to discern his forces at work. A privilege that is authoritatively confirmed by the Holy See, for which Popes have almost begged us to enter the Scapular Confraternity, should be utterly beyond question. A Pope granted it and Popes have ratified it; John XXII, Alexander V, Nicholas V, Sixtus IV, Clement VII, Paul III, Saint Pius V, Clement VIII, Leo XI, Paul V, Urban VIII, Alexander VII, Benedict XIV, Pius VI, Pius X, Benedict XV, Pius XI.[17] But even though everyone knows that the indulgence comes through the Church, it has been mysteriously clouded by a discussion as to the authenticity of *our present copy of the original bull!* [18] As in the case of the Scapular Vision, we see a document being attacked and defended again and again, as though with the fall of that document the Sabbatine Privilege would cease to exist. The easiest way to dispel such a cloud is to point out to the querulous that if the Blessed Virgin did not grant the indulgence, what they refuse to attribute to Her they cannot refuse to attribute to the Popes.

Now, it seems that there is more in the Sabbatine Privilege than first appears.

In what is probably the greatest of all Marian books, the author of which has been declared a Doctor of the Universal Church, the unusual opinion is voiced that if a Scapular wearer does a little more than Mary requires as conditional for obtaining the

Sabbatine Privilege, he *will never go to Purgatory at all.*[19]

The book is *The Glories of Mary,* by Saint Alphonsus Ligouri.

After the death of St. Alphonsus, there was a clamor for his canonization. When his body was solemnly exhumed, upon removal of the inner coffin covering his remains, a most remarkable sight met the eyes of the examiners; there, in the coffin, where the body and episcopal robes had decomposed, *the Scapular lay incorrupt.* Was it Mary's testimony to that most unusual statement, in Saint Alphonsus' famous book, concerning the Sabbatine Privilege of Her Scapular?

It is noteworthy that many devotees of the Scapular Queen hope and pray for the grace of dying on Saturday, and receive their request. An edifying incident occurred some years ago when, despite the opinion of her doctor that she should die on Wednesday, a certain lady earnestly protested that ever since she had sought the Sabbatine Privilege she had begged Mary not to let her die until Saturday, and she felt certain that she would not die until that day. To the doctor's surprise, she did not.[20] Saint John of the Cross died in 1591 saying: "The Mother of God and of Carmel hastens to purgatory with grace, on Saturday, and delivers those souls who have worn Her Scapular. Blessed be such a Lady who wills that, on this day of Saturday, I shall depart from this life!" [21] Saint Alphonsus asks: "Can we not hope for the same grace if we also do a little more than Mary asked? [22]   Saint Alphonsus himself did more, and with the result that the Mother of God *came to his death bed,* personally to bear his beloved soul straight to Her Divine Son. As was said, although all else perished in his tomb, Mary's Scapular remained incorrupt . . .

The Virgin of the Scapular is so full of love for Her children, so unspeakably good and completely condescending, that She is not content with being at their side in death, but She aids them after death. It is little wonder that Pope Leo XIII, as he saw death approaching, called his familiars to his bed and said: "Let us make a novena to Our Lady of the Scapular and I shall be ready to die!" [23]

> *"For the gate of the inner court which looks to the east shall be shut for six days, but on the Sabbath it shall be opened."—Offertory of the Mass on the Scapular Feast.*

But Our Blessed Mother is so desirous of making us saints that she has placed the reward of the Sabbatine Privilege upon a simple formula—the simple method of spirituality promulgated by Pope John XXII over six hundred years ago, recalled to the world by Our Lady at Fatima, and sealed with the promise that if enough persons follow this formula Russia will change and there will be peace. Also, those who follow this simple formula perseveringly will be rewarded, not only by her special aid at the hour of death, but by *speedy release from Purgatory* "especially on Saturday" (decree of Pope Paul V).

Pope John XXII

CHAPTER EIGHT

The Church Adds Lustre
to the Promise

THE CHURCH has a treasury into whose coffers Our Lord has poured the Infinite Merits of His Precious Blood. When she sees something of unusual worth, she dispenses from that treasury with prodigal liberality.

Hence it is that Pope has vied with Pope in pouring the spiritual treasures of the Church upon the Scapular. It is literally true that Pontiffs have tried to outdo each other in indulgencing the practice of wearing Our Lady's livery. They have sought thus to encourage the faithful to wear the Scapular and, recognizing the value that union with Mary through the Scapular gives to acts of piety, they have indulgenced many practices of piety as performed by a Scapular wearer. Just to give an example of the holy rivalry of the Popes in indulgencing the Scapular, one might cite the indulgence granted to the faithful who would call the wearers of Mary's Habit "Brothers of Our Lady of Mount Carmel." Originally the faithful received the equivalent of three hundred days of canonical penance by a grant of Urban VI for giving Scapular wearers this title; Pope Nicholas V doubled it; Clement X added seven years and

seven quarantines; finally it became thirteen years
and thirteen quarantines. Sixtus IV granted to members of the Scapular Confraternity all the privileges,
indulgences, graces, and favors which are granted
to the Cord of Saint Francis, to the Rosary of Our
Blessed Lady, or to any confraternity whatsoever, "so
that they do enjoy them as much as if they were
really members of these sodalities, by reason of their
communication in privileges with the order of Carmelites." Some of the Popes went so far in indulgencing the Scapular that the bounds of practicality
were exceeded and many indulgences had to be
recalled by Popes other than those who granted
them; we even have instances in which the Pope
who granted the indulgences, since they invaded the
rights of others, was forced to revoke them himself.

One of the most magnificent of the indulgences
heaped upon the Scapular was granted by a modern
Pope, Leo XIII: "To increase more and more
among the faithful the devotion and piety towards
the Most Blessed Virgin of Mount Carmel, whence
flow the richest and most wholesome fruits for the
soul." On May 16, 1892, he granted a *plenary indulgence,* applicable to the souls in purgatory, to all
who visit a Carmelite church on the Scapular Feast
as often as they repeat the visit! [1]

This indulgence turned the eyes of the world to
Our Lady of the Scapular. One saw such articles
appearing as "The Church's Treasury Opened on
Behalf of the Carmelites" [2] and with such statements
as: "No other devotion can rival the Scapular, either
as regards its popularity, its extension, or its assur-

ance"; or again: "It may safely be said that, after
the Catholic Church, the Confraternity of Our Lady
of Mount Carmel is the largest society in the
world."

To appreciate how the Church enriches the Scapular and how we can reap those riches, it is well to
consider the meaning of indulgences. We can hardly
sufficiently appreciate the fact that they are the
remission of the temporal punishment due to our
sins, that they place in our hands the spiritual where-
withal for settling debts that would often otherwise
be settled only in the pains of purgatory.

In the early days of the Church, temporal punishment for sin was satisfied this side of purgatory by
heavy penance, e. g., a hundred days on bread and
water. And when a Pope granted an indulgence,
opening the merits of the Church-Treasury to be
used in place of the merits acquired only by those
long penances, the faithful knew their value. Today,
however, even though that value has not changed
we often fail to recognize it. Few appreciate the fact
that in giving indulgences the Church is drawing on
"the fulness of the Blood of Christ." In his bull
"Unigenitus" (Jan. 27, 1343), Clement VI said:
"Upon the altar of the Cross, Christ shed of His
Blood, not merely a drop (though this would have
sufficed, by reason of the union with the Word, to redeem the whole human race) but a copious torrent
. . . thereby laying up an *infinite treasure* for mankind. This treasure He neither wrapped in a napkin
nor hid in a field, but entrusted to Blessed Peter, the
key bearer, and his successors, that they might, for

just and reasonable causes, distribute it to the faithful in full or in partial remission of the temporal punishment due to sin." [3]

Through the Sacrament of Confession, the Church remits the eternal and part of the temporal punishment due to sin and God ratifies that remission in Heaven; through indulgences she remits more temporal punishment, and that too is ratified in Heaven: "Whatsoever you shall loose on earth shall be loosed also in Heaven" (Matt. xviii, 18).

There are several kinds of these remittances of temporal punishment and conditions for gaining them vary. The one usual condition is that we be *in the state of Grace.* To gain a partial indulgence, all that we need besides being in the state of Grace is the fulfillment of the act to which the indulgence is attached. To gain a plenary indulgence, however, we must also go to confession and receive Holy Communion within eight days of the act to which the indulgence is attached and pray for the intention of the Holy Father. The recitation of one Our Father, Hail Mary, and Glory for the intention of the Holy Father will satisfy the latter condition, except for the *toties quoties* plenary indulgences, to be gained as at each repeated visit to the church on July 16, for which we must say six Our Fathers, Hail Marys, and Glorys for the intention of His Holiness.

Before considering the different kinds of indulgences attached to the Scapular, let us note again that an indulgence of so many days means that the person who gains the indulgence is remitted that amount of purgatorial punishment which would have been remitted in the sight of God by the performance of so many days or years of canonical penance. Such a value is tremendous. Furthermore, just as Our Blessed Lady has extended the efficacy of the Scapular beyond the grave through the Sabbatine Privilege, so the Church has enriched the Scapular with many indulgences that can be applied to the suffering souls in Purgatory. Thus, we must not think that, because of the Sabbatine Privilege, the efforts of the Church to enhance the Scapular (by indulgences which shorten purgatory) are of less value because of what Our Lady has already done. One of the most meritorious acts which we can perform on earth is to aid the souls in purgatory, freeing them. Saint Francis de Sales, a great Scapular devotee, remarked: "With charity toward the dead we practice *all the works of mercy!*" [4] For it is a work that is at once an act of supreme charity to the suffering souls (and to God and His Holy Mother) and one that greatly increases our own store of eternal merit. We *who will enjoy the Sabbatine Privilege* ought especially to imitate our Heavenly Mother by having mercy on the suffering souls in purgatory. The Church enables us, with the Scapular, to apply to them quantities of merits that equal, *in God's eyes,* thousands of years of such mortifications as, for instance, continual fasting on bread and water, or *daily* chastisement with *rope disciplines,* or going thousands of times to sacrifice our lives in holy wars against infidels. It is no wonder that the late Most Reverend Elias Magennis, Prior General of the Carmelite Order and a great authority on the Scapu-

lar, remarked that even in preference to a knowledge
of miracles, which show the value of the Scapular,
"it is far more important to the great body of faithful to know that plenary indulgences can be gained
often, through being a member of the Scapular Confraternity." [5]

Those who have been enrolled as members of the
Carmelite Scapular Confraternity by legitimately
delegated Priests, and who carry on their person the
Holy Scapular in the prescribed manner, can gain
the following Indulgences and enjoy the following
Privileges and Indults: [6]

First, they can gain *Plenary Indulgences* on the
following days:

1. On the day they are enrolled in the Scapular.

2. On the Feast of Our Lady of Mount Carmel, July
the sixteenth, or any other day chosen for the celebration
of the Feast according to the custom of the place in which
they live.

3. As often as they visit a Carmelite church or public
oratory on that same Feast of Our Lady of Mount Carmel. The indulgence is also gained on visiting *any* church
or public oratory wherein a Scapular Confraternity is
legitimately erected. On each visit prayers must be said
for the intentions of the Holy Father: six Our Fathers,
six Hail Marys, and six Glorys. (This is known as the
Toties Quoties indulgence of July 16th.)

4. On one Sunday in each month, on condition that the
wearer of the Scapular be present at the procession of the
members of the Confraternity. It is not necessary that one
should actually join in the procession. It is sufficient to be
present in the Church at the time.

5. On the Feast of Pentecost.

6. On the day on which there is a Commemoration of
all the Defunct of the Carmelite Order. This is usually

the fifteenth of November, or, if that day falls on Sunday, the day following.

7. At the hour of death, upon invocation of the Holy Name.

Anyone who visits a Carmelite church, on the following days, can gain a plenary indulgence upon the fulfillment of the usual conditions:

1. The Feast of the Circumcision of Our Lord.

2. The Feast of the Most Holy Name of Jesus.

3. The Feast of St. Peter Thomas (January 16).

4. The Feast of the Purification of the Blessed Virgin (February 2).

5. The Feast of St. Andrew Corsini (February 4).

6. The Feast of St. Avertanus (February 25).

7. The Feast of St. Cyril, Confessor and Doctor (March 6).

8. The Feast of St. Joseph, Protector of the Order (March 19). The indulgence may be gained on any day of the Novena in preparation for the Feast, or on any day of the Octave following.

9. The Feast of Blessed Baptist of Mantua (March 20).

10. The Feast of Gabriel the Archangel (March 24).

11. The Feast of the Annunciation of the Blessed Virgin (March 25).

12. The Feast of Saint Berthold (March 29).

13. The Feast of St. Albert, Bishop and Confessor (September 16).

14. On the Thursday of Holy Week.

15. Feast of the Resurrection of Our Lord.

16. The Feast of St. Angelus, Martyr (May 5).

17. The Feast of St. Simon Stock (May 16).

18. The Feast of St. Mary Magdalen of Pazzi (May 25).

19. The Feast of the Patronage of St. Joseph (Third Wednesday after Easter), or on any day within the Octave of the Feast.

20. The Feast of the Ascension of Our Lord.

21. On the same day, another plenary indulgence for the Stations.

22. The Feast of the Blessed Trinity.

23. The Feast of Corpus Christi, or any day within the Octave.

24. The Feast of the Most Sacred Heart of Jesus.

25. The Feast of the Visitation of the Blessed Virgin (July 2).

26. The Feast of the Solemn Commemoration of Our Lady of Mount Carmel (July 16), or any day within the Octave. On the day itself, as we have said, there is a *Toties Quoties* indulgence for visiting Carmelite churches, etc.

27. The Feast of St. Elias the Prophet, Founder of the Order (July 20).

28. The Feast of St. Theresa and companions, Martyrs (July 24).

29. The Feast of St. Anne, Mother of the Blessed Virgin (July 26).

30. The Feast of St. Albert, Confessor (August 7).

31. The Feast of the Assumption of the Blessed Virgin (August 15).

32. The Feast of St. Joachim, Father of the Blessed Virgin (August 16).

33. The Feast of the Transverberation of the Heart of St. Theresa (August 27).

34. The Feast of the Dedication of the Churches of the Order.

35. The Feast of St. Brocard (September 2).

36. The Feast of the Nativity of the Blessed Virgin (September 8).

37. The Feast of St. Theresa (October 15), or any day within Octave.

38. The Feast of All Saints of the Order (November 14).

39. The Feast of the Presentation of the Blessed Virgin (November 21).

40. The Feast of St. John of the Cross, Doctor (November 24).

41. The Feast of the Blessed Dionysius and Redemptus, Martyrs (November 29).

42. The Feast of the Immaculate Conception of the Blessed Virgin (December 8).

43. The Feast of Blessed Francus (December 11).

44. Whenever the Feast of the Patron Saint, to whom the church is dedicated, is celebrated.

45. On any one day in the year (the choice of day is left completely to the discretion of the member).

46. The Feast of the Nativity of Our Divine Lord.

One who wears the Scapular can also gain the following *partial indulgences:*

1. An indulgence of *five years and five quarantines:*

(a) Once a month, if on the day chosen the member of the Confraternity, having gone to confession, shall have received Holy Communion and prayed for the Pope's intention.

(b) On each occasion the wearer of the Scapular accompanies a priest carrying the Blessed Sacrament in a solemn manner.

2. On every universal Feast of the Blessed Virgin on which the member received Holy Communion in the church or oratory of the confraternity, he receives an indulgence of three years and three quarantines.

3. On each day that he abstains from meat in order to obtain the Sabbatine Privilege, i. e., whenever he observes Wednesday or Saturday as a day of abstinence, an indulgence of three hundred days.

4. For every act of charity and every act of piety, he receives an indulgence of one hundred days.

5. On every Wednesday or Saturday that the Scapular wearer visits a Confraternity church, he receives an indulgence of seven years and seven quarantines.

6. Every day of the year that the Scapular wearer visits a Confraternity church he receives an indulgence of three hundred days. (Except Wednesdays and Saturdays, when he receives an indulgence of seven years and seven quarantines.)

7. Every time he kisses his Scapular he receives an indulgence of five hundred days. (Benedict XV, July 8, 1916).

Anyone may gain an indulgence of *ten years and ten quarantines* for visiting a Carmelite Church on the following days:

1. The Feast of the Nativity of Our Divine Lord.
2. The Feast of the Resurrection of Our Lord.
3. The Feast of Pentecost.
4. The Feast of the Most Blessed Trinity.
5. The Feast of Corpus Christi.
6. The Feast of the Immaculate Conception of the Blessed Virgin.
7. The Feast of the Nativity of the Blessed Virgin.
8. The Feast of the Presentation of the Blessed Virgin.
9. The Feast of the Annunciation of the Blessed Virgin.
10. The Feast of the Visitation of the Blessed Virgin.
11. The Feast of the Purification of the Blessed Virgin.
12. The Feast of the Assumption of the Blessed Virgin.
13. The Feast of Michael the Archangel.
14. The Feast of the Holy Apostles Peter and Paul.
15. The Feast of All Saints.
16. The Feast of the Nativity of St. John the Baptist.
17. The Feast of the Titular Saint of the church.
18. The Feast of the Finding of the Holy Cross.
19. The Feast of the Exaltation of the Holy Cross.
20. On all Sundays and Saturdays of the year, and on the Mondays, Wednesdays and Fridays of the Lenten Season.

Besides being able to obtain all these indulgences, one who wears the Scapular enjoys the following privileges:

1. The Sabbatine Privilege, first granted by Pope John XXII, approved and confirmed by Clement VII (in *Ex Clemente* 12 Aug., 1530), by Saint Pius V (in *Superna dispositione* 18 Feb., 1566), by Gregory XIII (in *Ut Laudes* 18 Sept., 1577), and by others as also by the

Roman and Universal Inquisition under Paul V on January 20, 1613, by a decree of the following tenor: "It is lawful for the Carmelites to preach that Christians may believe with piety in the help promised to the souls of the brethren and the members of the Confraternity of the Blessed Virgin Mary of Mount Carmel, namely, that the Blessed Virgin will assist by Her continual intercession, suffrages and merits and also by Her special protection, especially on Saturday (which day has been consecrated to Her by the Church), the souls of the brothers and members of the Confraternity departing this life in charity who shall have worn the Habit, and shall have observed chastity according to their particular state of life, and also have recited the Little Office (or, if unable to read, have kept the fasts of the Church, and have abstained from the use of meat on Wednesdays and Saturdays, unless the Feast of the Nativity of Our Divine Lord should fall on one of those days).

2. All the Masses that are celebrated for the repose of the souls of members of the Confraternity shall enjoy the same privileges as they would if celebrated on a Privileged Altar.

3. Each of the members can, at the hour of death, obtain the General Absolution and Plenary Indulgence; and this, too, from any *priest* assisting him at that hour.

It is at once apparent that some of these important favors would be gained only by those living near a Carmelite church, or some church or oratory having a legitimately established Confraternity. However, in order to extend these blessings to every wearer of the Scapular, the following provisions of Papal legislation, known as "Indults," have been made:

1. All those living at a distance from any church or oratory, to which a visit must be paid in order to gain any of the above-named indulgences, can, by visiting *their own parish church,* on the days indicated, fulfill this requisite condition and so obtain the same indulgence.

This substitution is allowed only when the distance exceeds a mile.

2. Members of the Confraternity who are unable, for any reason, to be present at the Procession of the members on the appointed Sunday, can gain the same Plenary Indulgence by visiting the Confraternity church or oratory on the same day.

3. Where there is no Confraternity church or, having a Confraternity church, no procession—it is sufficient, for gaining the indulgence, to visit any church or oratory on the Third Sunday of the month.

From the "Indults," one can see how the Church has made it easy, in every way, for the members of the Scapular Confraternity, wherever they may be, to gain all the spiritual favors of the Scapular. Is it not worth recalling again that all the indulgences are *applicable to the souls in purgatory?* "Through the generosity of the Church," the Most Reverend Father Magennis remarked, "we thus have—apart from the two promises of Our Blessed Lady to all who worthily wear Her Scapular—a rich field of spiritual favors from which we may reap an abundant harvest not only for ourselves but also for those suffering souls who, whilst on earth, were united to us by the bonds of love and friendship and fraternal charity." [7]

To gain an indulgence, one must have the intention of doing so. If, upon rising in the morning, a Scapular wearer makes the general intention to gain every indulgence available during the day, he will receive numerous graces from the treasury of the Church. Might not much of this be placed in the hands of Mary to be distributed—as only She knows how to distribute it—for the interests of the Sacred

Heart? When we go to Mary, clothed in Her Scapular, let us not forget that God's Church has placed a superabundance of spiritual riches within our reach.

> *"The Scapular of Our Lady has become one of the richest fountains of Grace which the Church, in her liberality, has opened to us."* [8]
>
> A. A. LAMBING, D. D., LL. D.

Note: Although most indulgences were recalled after Vatican II, we see fit to leave this chapter intact, even with a complete listing of the indulgences attached to the Scapular devotion to show the degree to which Holy Mother Church sanctioned it by indulgences over a period of seven centuries.

Since Vatican II, interpreting Paragraph 67 of LUMEN GENTIUM in his message to the XI International Marian Congress in 1963, Pope Paul VI singled out the Rosary and the Scapular as the two pre-eminent devotions in the Catholic Church to be fostered and encouraged according to the prescription of the Council in that paragraph of the Constitution on the Church.

CHAPTER NINE

Souls

FATHER MILLERIOT, of the Society of Jesus, used often to recount a certain incident that is illustrative of the meaning of Mary's Promise to a missionary.

A certain woman, who had received some favors from the celebrated Jesuit, violated the principles of honor. When, out of dread and shame, she determined upon taking her life, she made known her terrible intention to Father Milleriot. The Jesuit used every argument to dissuade her. Utterly blinded by shame and fear, however, the woman was so possessed by the temptation that the missioner's words had no effect. Finally, he administered his reserved coup.

"At least," he said in a lowered voice, "at least you will do one little thing for me. Let me give you the Scapular and then promise me that you will not take it off."

For a moment, the sinner hesitated. Then she replied: "I will promise you, Father. I could not refuse one who has been so kind to me."

As she left, wearing the livery of Our Lady, Father Milleriot smiled inwardly and said: "My friend, I have you now. Try as you may to take your life, you shall not succeed." [1]

Haunted by the temptation, the poor woman actually did go to the Seine and throw herself into its waters. She was rescued. The next day, she tried again. Again someone saw her fall into the water and again she was unwillingly dragged from the river. This time a severe illness followed. As she lay between life and death, still wearing that miraculous Scapular, grace touched her soul and she realized the horror of what she had been about to do. Father Milleriot found, after her recovery, that in the place of an abandoned sinner was a repentant saint. He signified this great victory over Satan by simply stating the case: "She remained a devout and fervent client of the Blessed Virgin throughout the rest of her life." [2]

What glory Mary gives to Her priests by Her universal assurance of Salvation! It is the assurance of the Queen of Souls that anyone who dies, clothed in a certain sign, shall not die in mortal sin. An elderly pastor in Vienna recently wrote: "So steadfastly do I believe in the fulfillment of the Promise that in every parish that I erected the Scapular Confraternity I always told the faithful: If your pastor knew that all his parishioners wore the Scapular and died in it, he would be certain that you would meet again in Heaven, without a single exception." [3] Another exemplary pastor says: "Since I have given myself to propagate and spread the Scapular in my parish, I have observed that no one dies without the Sacraments." [4] Mary has made it possible for priests to repeat at death those very words which proclaimed Her Divine Son the Perfect Pastor:

"Those whom Thou gavest me have I kept, and none of them is lost" (John, xvii, 12). Moreover this missionary value of the Scapular does not accrue solely to priests!

The greatest work one can accomplish on this earth is the salvation of souls. Nothing is more precious, nothing more dear to the heart of God, than a human soul. One might become the president of his country, the hero of nations, and it would be as nothing in comparison with the glory of procuring the salvation of a single soul.

During the World War, there was a curve in a certain trench of the Allies into which the enemy could fire. The forces of the central powers had a machine gun positioned so that the bullets struck right into the curve; with steady spurts they kept the trench continually divided by a wall of death. When Father William Doyle, the famous war chaplain, heard that a wounded soldier was dying at the other end of the trench, he was working his way through the trench with the Blessed Sacrament when he came to the death spot. Machine-gun bullets were licking the wall in front of him. He stopped. The hot thought coursed through his brain that a man was dying somewhere farther on and possibly was in need of absolution. *Possibly* the soul of a soldier was at stake. Hesitating not another moment, to be sure of that soul Father Doyle plunged forward through what seemed a certain death.

Such is the value of a human soul and, here, the Scapular enables the ordinary every-day man, whose unconsecrated hands are neither priestly nor pastoral, infallibly to assure the salvation of *numerous* fellow men simply by inducing them to the easiest religious practice imaginable!

The following facts, which appeared some years ago in *The Irish Catholic,* although treating of a young priest, might have been your experience or mine. They are illustrative of this power at our disposal in the Scapular.

"Doctor Francis Zaldia, former President of the Republic of Colombia, was an eminent lawyer very much opposed to the Catholic Church. He always belonged to the liberal party, which in that country, as in most countries, is hostile to the Church. To him, partly, the expulsion of the Jesuits has to be ascribed. Nevertheless, he had a son who was edu- cated very carefully and finished his studies at the American College at Rome. The young Colombian studied for the priesthood and was particularly de- voted to the most holy Virgin. Although he prayed to Our Lady incessantly for the conversion of his father, all his efforts seemed in vain.

"After the young cleric had been ordained a priest, he returned to his native country. A few years after his son's return, the old ex-President became hope- lessly sick, but gave no indication that he wished to die as a Christian; on the contrary he awaited death unconcernedly. This almost exasperated the priestly son who stood near the dying father's bed. Making a final effort, the young priest said painfully: 'Dear Father, what human skill could do has been done. Do you not want any spiritual assistance whatever? Please, take this Scapular!' The dying president, accepting the offered Scapular, soon made his confession and declared that he wished to die a son of Mother Church!" [5]

The Scapular is easy to take and yet spiritually transforming after it is taken. That is how we discover Mary in its Promise. She is so easily loved and, *by the very fact that She is loved,* She unites us to God!

Just as Mary's Motherhood is not limited only to Catholics but is extended to all men, so the missionary value of the Scapular extends not only to Catholics. Many miracles of conversion have been wrought in favor of good non-Catholics who, living according to their proper moral code, have been induced to practice the Scapular devotion out of reverence for God's Mother. What is the Scapular Promise but a corroboration of that truth which the Catholic Church has taught for centuries, that a soul dying with devotion to the Mother of God cannot possibly die in mortal sin?

The flowing hours of our lives might be likened to an escalator, upon which God has placed us. The eyes of our souls may be turned straight up to God, or partially to God, partially to the side, or down. God is at the top and the degree to which we keep ourselves turned to Him is the degree to which we render Him glory; if we reach the end facing Him directly, we immediately see Him face to face for all eternity; if we reach there facing Him but partially, we fall into purgatory until we are acclimated to behold His infinite Beauty directly; and if we come to the end with *our backs to God,* having deliberately refused to look at Him during life, we stay that way forever; we have died in mortal sin and have thereby damned ourselves.

But a person who dies with devotion to the Mother of God could not have his back *completely* turned to Her Son; such a thing is incompatible. Nor is this merely true for those baptized in the Church. Anyone who dies with sentiments of homage, confidence, and love for the Blessed Virgin, must die with at least some like sentiments of confidence and love towards God of whom Mary is a reflection. Hence, we can lead non-Catholics to God through the Scapular just as we can lead Catholics to Him, *if* we can persuade non-Catholics to be thus devout to the Blessed Virgin. Thus we may be able to get a non-Catholic to wear the Scapular who desires to possess the faith but cannot bow to certain dogmas; it will assure him of Mary's intercession. Perhaps others can be enticed by the lovableness of so sweet a Mother to practice devotion to Her, and at very least so simple a devotion as that of wearing the Scapular. God revealed to Saint Gertrude that He has made Mary so lovable that She may be a Divine enticement to souls.[6] A non-Catholic, faced with miracles wrought through the Scapular and the very logic of so sweet a practice, may be led to it and thus be assured of dying in the state of Grace.

There are many examples of the Scapular Promise working its wonders in the souls of non-Catholics. A very recent one occurred at the Bellevue Hospital in New York. The prior of the house of studies of a religious Order, a very close friend of the present

author, solemnly testifies to an incident which inaugurated his administration of the Sacrament of
Extreme Unction there. He had just come back
from Rome and was at once appointed to duty at
the Bellevue. The morning came when, for the first
time, the older priest left him alone to take care of
any sick-calls. He was hoping against hope there
would not be any. But one came. Nervously he prepared for it and was then led into a certain ward to
the bed of a patient who, *he believed,* had called for
a priest. Approaching the bed he asked the dying
man if he wished to make his confession. "I am not
a Catholic," came the surprising reply!

Confused, the young priest went to the nurse and
said, "Nurse, there must be some mistake; this man
says that he is not a Catholic!"

"Well, he is wearing the Scapular, Father," the
nurse rejoined.

The priest returned to the bed. "If you are not a
Catholic," he inquired, "why are you wearing the
Scapular?"

"Because some Catholic sisters, who begged alms
near our factory, asked me to wear it," came the
slow answer.

"Well, would you like to be a Catholic?" asked
the priest.

"Father," came the unusual answer, "there is
nothing I would like better!" And he died, newly
baptized, a few days later.

The Venerable Francis Yepès, the brother of Saint
John of the Cross, used to practice his lay-apostolate
by getting many to wear the Scapular. He not only

made that Sign of Mary a means of bringing himself closer to his Mother but he used it to give Her souls to save.

"One night," Father Velasco—his biographer—tells us, "while he was praying for the conversion of sinners, infernal spirits came to assail him with the most frightful temptations. Finally, seeing the uselessness of their efforts they cried to him in rage: "What have we done to you that you torment us so cruelly? Why do you persuade so many persons to wear and to venerate the Scapular of Carmel? Wait until you fall into our power! You shall pay dearly for it!' But the venerable tertiary did not allow himself to be intimidated and quietly finished his prayer."

Hence the Scapular is a sword in the hands of the lay apostles as well as in the hands of priests, and it is at once *a means of victory* and an *assurance* of success.

In the foreign missions, this value of the Scapular in procuring and assuring the salvation of souls seems to have been more evident and more appreciated than here at home where we think less often of the value of saving souls at all. Missionaries seem to have sensed this value of Mary's Promise and they have carried that Sign of Salvation to the four corners of the earth. The Scapular Medal was first given because of a missionary's explanation to the Holy Father of the unsightliness and inconvenience of the cloth Scapulars as worn by natives in tropical zones. Often have missionaries been the witnesses of most unusual miracles wrought through the Scapular and it is largely to them that one can ascribe the "catholicity" of this, Mary's greatest devotion. Saint Peter Claver, in his unsurpassed labors for the conquest of souls, used the Scapular as *an instrument of Divine Providence.*[8] In an apotheosis he is pictured at the moment of his death with the Crucifix in his hand and the Scapular on his breast, and around his bed are many negroes with the Scapular hanging about their necks, kissing the feet and hands of the sainted missionary.

In pioneer days when American Indians had been somewhat Christianized by missionaries while more selfish white men came to be their hated enemies, a most unusual sight greeted investigators at the battle-site after Custer's celebrated stand. Strewn with massacred soldiers, the field presented a most harrowing scene of butchery. But among the lifeless, bloody forms, one body had been signally respected. It was that of Colonel Keogh, an Irishman of deep Catholic faith, which was propped against a tree. The garments over the Colonel's breast had been torn open; there, carefully and neatly disposed by savage hands, was the Scapular of Our Lady of Mount Carmel. The American correspondent of *L'Univers* commented that "without doubt the Sacred Badge awakened recollections of the teachings of some devoted missionary; one could see that several of the savages had assisted in bearing the body of an enemy, only a few moments before an object of detestation, to a sheltered spot; there placing it in a reclining position, the head leaning against a tree, they had carefully arranged the Badge, so loved by the deceased, upon his breast." [9]

Universal, Marian, this little vehicle of a great Promise has been realized to have a tremendous value in the greatest of all human-divine works: the salvation of souls.

God made His Mother the great missionary at the foot of the Cross on Calvary. To understand the wherefore of Her Scapular's being an instrument of Divine Providence in the salvation of souls, we have to go back to that terrible mount. It is there that we learn the meaning of the human soul and the meaning of Mary's universal motherhood.

To grasp the whole significance of the Passion, however, we need only pause at the tenth station: *Jesus is stripped of His garments.* For that station was the moment of supreme sacrifice. The Son of God was about to lay down his life. Oh! what a horrible sight met the gaze of His Mother as the soldiers roughly tore off His vestment: a body mangled from head to foot! That vestment, made by Her hands, became a summation of the complete Passion: the soldiers removed *the crown of thorns* to get it off, and then replaced it; having hardened in the *scourge-wounds,* as the cloth was roughly pulled away it cruelly tore those wounds open anew; once fresh from Mary's hands, it was now dust-covered and its shoulders worn and blood-soaked from the painful *carrying of the cross; He was being stripped to be crucified.* This was a most terrible moment. Anyone can appreciate the fact who has experienced those crowded seconds that prelude some great sacrifice or suffering.

Jesus did not suffer this anguish alone. His Mother, She who had so lovingly clothed Him in that cloak made by Her own hands, felt all those ghastly wounds opened in Her Immaculate Heart. We are told by the Saints how Our Lord, due to the perfection of His Body, suffered unspeakably more pain from each wound than we, whose sensibility to pain has been dulled, can ever realize. *But Mary knew.* To one who knows of the love of Mary for Jesus, is it not enough to say that "Mary stood beneath the Cross, and Mary knew!"?

But look at that bloody garment over which the soldiers are fulfilling a prophecy as they roll their dice. Does it mean anything to us? It means that we are saved! It means that for us the Son of God has mounted the Cross! He has taken off His garment to go into the Valley of Death. Nay, it means more than our Salvation; it means that the Son of God, Whose Sacred Heart is about to be opened with a spear, loves us so much that He *unnecessarily* suffered a cruel scourging, a thorn-crowning, a stripping, all to prove to us that He loves us more than our self-interested hearts can comprehend. Do we not see those *clots of Precious Blood* upon the seamless robe His Mother made?

But what is Our Lord saying from the Cross? Even those tossing the dice pause to look up. The Crucified turns His tormented head to gaze down at the Woman (ah! who can describe Her as She stands and gazes at Him!) and He says to Her: "Woman, behold thy son; son, behold thy Mother."

What strange words are these! Is not He, the Crucified God, Mary's only Son? Is it not She who made that seamless garment which, as it lies on the ground, speaks so eloquently of a Bloody confirmation of Love? Surely this nailed Christ is Her only Son, possessing Her whole heart! But then, suddenly we hear the heart-rending cry: "I thirst!" We understand. One is standing there who is achieving the mission of co-Redemptrix and receiving that of Universal Mediatrix. "Mother, all the souls so dearly purchased at the price of this suffering are the object of My desire. You love Me so dearly that I commission you to bring them to Me that thus My pierced Heart may receive them. Satan has no dominion over you; I make them your children; save them by your prayers! Mother! I thirst for souls!"

When Mary ascended into Heaven, how She must have longed to have men turn to Her that She might thus save them! How She must have longed to see men realize that they needed but to turn to Her, and Her prayers would vanquish Satan! By means of a family brought forth in a prophecy and finally nourished in all the mysteries of its fulfillment, She stooped from Heaven and gathered us into it— beneath Her mantle and next to Her Most Pure Heart. "Receive, My beloved son, this Scapular of My family. Whosoever dies therein shall not suffer eternal fire!"

Like the hand of an invincible missionary, Our Lady's Scapular reaches through the world, van-

quishing Satan everywhere. What a glory it is for us,
Her children, to be enabled by it to become partners
with Her in satisfying the thirst of Her Divine Son,
assuring the Salvation of many souls by simply getting them to wear the Scapular which She has given
us! Is it any wonder that Saint Conrad, recently
canonized by Pope Pius XI, should have distributed
the Scapular to as many visitors as possible, during
his forty years as porter of a Capuchian monastery?
Or that sisters, such as those instrumental in the
death-bed conversion of the factory worker we described, should spread the Scapular everywhere? Or
that laymen, such as Venerable Francis Yepès, should
seize the Scapular as an instrument placed in their
hands by Mary to achieve the greatest work on earth
—the work Christ was about when He taught in
Palestine and died on a Cross? or that priests, such
as several of the author's acquaintance, should always carry the Scapular with them in case of sick-
calls? or that pastors should preach the Scapular
until reasonably sure that all the souls entrusted to
them shall die under Mary's Promise? The garment
Mary made for the Redeemer became a symbol of
Salvation and the garment She has made for the
redeemed has become an assurance of Salvation,
through Her Promise. It seems that thus the Mediatrix of all Grace comes from the foot of the Cross
to give us, Her children, participation in the very
mission which She received there beneath the Cross
of Her Son. He said: "Mother, behold thy son!"
She has said: "My beloved children, receive this
Scapular of our family; WHOSOEVER *dies clothed*

in this SHALL NOT SUFFER THE FIRES OF HELL."

"One purpose for which the Blessed Virgin was created Mother of God is that She may obtain the Salvation of many who, on account of weakness and wickedness, could not be saved according to the rigor of divine justice but might be so with the help of this merciful Mother's powerful intercession." [10]

ST. JOHN CHRYSOSTOM

"As amongst all the blessed spirits there is not one that loves God more than Mary, so we neither have nor can have anyone who, after God, loves us as much as this loving Mother; and if we concentrate all the love that mothers bear their children, husbands, and wives one another, all the love of angels and saints for their clients, it does not equal the love of Mary towards a single soul." [11]

ST. ALPHONSUS LIGOURI

"As the devil goes about seeking whom he may devour, so, on the other hand, Mary goes about seeking whom She may save and to whom She may give life." [12]

ST. BERNARDINE

"Let us enkindle in ourselves a holy zeal for propagating, and causing to be observed with all possible perfection, this devotion which is so dear to Mary and so salutary for man. Through the Scapular, let us give Our Lady of Mount Carmel some new children, and to Heaven, therefore, some new citizens who will express their acknowledgment for all eternity." [13]

RAPHAEL OF ST. JOSEPH, O. D. C.

CHAPTER TEN

A Heavenly Garment

THE READER has probably come to a certain conclusion about the Scapular. He probably feels that the number of values in these two pieces of cloth bewilders him and that there must be an explanation for them deeper than the simple fact that the wearing of the Scapular is a true devotion to Mary.

This conclusion is both logical and accurate. There is indeed more in the wearing of the Scapular than in the practice of a true devotion. *Mary is morally there.*

In presenting to us Her Scapular, Mary gave us Herself. In the Preface of a special Mass, the Church sings on the Scapular Feast: "Through the Holy Scapular She has taken to Herself sons of choice": *Per sacrum Scapulare filios dilectionis assumpsit.* And a mother belongs to Her children. When she gives them birth she becomes their mother, when she becomes their mother she becomes their nurse and protector, and thus she belongs to them. Thus, too, in the very act of taking us under Her mantle to pledge our salvation we see Mary giving Herself, opening Her arms out for us.

The whole meaning of the Scapular derives from this, Mary's gift of Herself to us in the words of its promise. When She descends, surrounded by the pomp of Heaven, to say that whosoever dies under Her mantle shall be saved, does She not clearly mean that while She has brought us all forth to Divine Life in the pains of Her Son's Crucifixion She has come down mystically to retake us into Her womb that She may bring us forth at death to an eternal life?

The deep significance of being special children of Mary is something which every Marian book since the dawn of our Christian era would like to describe. But since all the books about Mary that have ever been written are professedly not adequate to express the value of having the Queen of Heaven for a nursing mother, of being united to Her by bonds that are stronger than death and as permanent as Her own promises, how could this book possibly set about to describe it? Should one insert Saint Alphonsus' *Glories of Mary,* the library which its quotations indicate, together with the eleven large volumes of Jourdain's *Sommes des Grandeurs de Marie?* No, for although the books on Mary are today so numerous that they form an actual literature,[1] all of them are inadequate to discover Mary to us.

However, though an exposition of its excellence is beyond us, we can at least state the fact: Mary has made Herself a Mother to Her Scapular-children to such an extent that they will not be lost if they persevere in their devotion. Once She appeared to Blessed Angela de Arena, clothed in the Carmelite Habit and surrounded by Saints who were particularly devoted to Her during life. There were no Car-

melites there. "Dear Mother, where are your Carmelites?" exclaimed Blessed Angela. And Mary,
quickly pulling back the edges of the white cloak
which hung over Her breast, showed her a bunch of
roses, saying: "Here are My Carmelites." [2]

Hence, in the whole exposition of the Scapular
Promise—its origin, its meaning and historicity, its
donor—Mary—in the Divine Plan, how it unites us
to Mary, how it gives rise to "Her Sacrament," the
Sabbatine Privilege, mystical prayer, union—the
reader beholds an exposition of Mary giving Herself
to us by means of that Promise. Probably by now he
is almost astounded at never having realized what a
real Mother Our Lord gave us on Calvary or that
there could be such greatness in a devotion to which
he rarely gave a thought. He is probably totally
unprepared for *more*. However, in an appendix to
his Commentary on the Acts of the Apostles, Sylveira
reminds us that *"In the holy Scapular, the supreme
Queen of Carmel administers to us a Heavenly Garment, gives us a Sign of Victory over our enemies,
and leads us to the Blessed Eucharist!"* [8] These three
aspects of the Scapular Devotion still remain to com-
mand our wonder.

*　*　*　*

A few years ago, two pilgrims conversing with
Brother André, the miracle-man of Montreal,
snipped off the tassels of his cincture and carried
them away as prized treasures. We all prize relics,
especially if they are those of currently popular
saints or ones to whom we have a special devotion.
And it is probably in recognition of this devotion

which we have to relics of those in the other world which impels the Mother of God to give Her children, as it were, a relic of Herself.

Authoritative writers and Saints speak of the Scapular as "Mary's garment." Now, they do not mean by this that it is Mary's garment solely because it is the sign of Her Promise. They mean that ordinary cloth, when assumed by us as the vehicle of Her Promise, can be said to be *Her garb,* because it has come to us from Her sacred hands and is hallowed by its intimate association with Her.

Objects that have been associated with saints become sacred in that they seem to make a saint more real to us and to give us a special claim to his intercession. We use them at prayer and touch them to the sick with assurance. Those relics which are the vehicles of most miracles and favors are the most desired and most cherished. Thus, the relics of the "Little Flower of Carmel" are today venerated throughout the whole Church and highly prized.

A relic given by the Queen of Heaven has naturally been the vehicle of more miracles than any other relic the world has ever possessed. It is a relic so unique that each and every one of Mary's children can possess it, and it has been hallowed by seven centuries of continuous wonders in every part of the world. Miracles similar to those worked by Our Lord in His public life, Our Lady has wrought in the Scapular. And besides such wonders—the raising of the dead, the restoring of lost senses, delivering from demoniacal possession, etc.—there are wonders proper to the Scapular itself, such as remaining intact after being flung into a raging fire or remaining incorrupt in the decay of tombs. In a work that drew forth high praise from the Sovereign Pontiff, M. D'Arville, an apostolic prothonotary, sketched some of the great Scapular favors that were worked solely before large crowds of people and then exclaimed: "What a host of prodigies present themselves to my gaze! Not favors attested by one or two persons, whose testimony might be held in doubt, but by many witnesses—by whole nations who cannot be suspected of having acted in concert to impose on the whole world . . ." And at the risk of poor form, we call upon the full pen-picture of the power in Mary's Garment as copied, from more ancient writers, in the rough and heavy lines of this Frenchman's vigorous style. In its achievement, the picture is classical.

"One beholds all Provence ravaged by a terrible pestilence," he begins, "and Marseilles, alone, putting its trust in the Scapular is saved. Then it consecrates the memory of that signal favor by a monument worthy of the greatness of Mary and the piety of its inhabitants.

"In Spain, the heavens are closed up, as in the days of Elias; there is a dearth as in the days of Joseph. Mary is appealed to, Her Habit is carried in procession. The sky, before of brass, melts into water, and the people find granaries more abundant than those of Egypt.

"At the siege of the island of Malta, in 1565, and at that of the city of Gueldres, in 1597, nations were seen armed against nations, breathing naught but blood and carnage. Mary is invoked, the Scapular is borne in procession. At sight of that new standard the people are disarmed, the torch of war is extinguished, and the charms of peace appear once more.

"All nature, all the elements, seem to respect the virtue of that Holy Habit. Maladies before unknown, defying the skill of the physicians, depopulate the cities and towns of the province of Anjou. The Scapular appears; the mortality ceases. The powers of the air have formed a frightful tempest, which threatens to devastate, far and wide, the plains of Savoy and Sardinia. By virtue of that celestial Habit, the unchained winds, the hail, the lightning and thunder are instantly dispelled. The sea dares to cross the boundaries that the finger of God has marked out for it. The Scapular is the dyke opposed to it. The pride of the waves is instantly broken, and they retire within their usual limits.

"But if from the wonders operated by virtue of the Holy Scapular, in favor of cities, provinces, and entire kingdoms, we pass to the marvels wrought in favor of individuals, it would require all the tongues that Saint Jerome wished to possess that he might celebrate the virtues of Mary. In truth, *the earth is but one vast stage upon which Heaven seems to delight in manifesting the power of this Habit of the Mother of God.* Conflagrations extinguished! shipwrecks avoided! bullets flattened out! swords blunted! blind restored to sight! cripples and paralytics cured! dead brought back to life." [4]

When Elias ascended into Heaven, he let fall his mantle. Overflowing with gratitude, Saint Eliseus hastened to pick it up; it was a relic of his master, the founder of Mary's Carmel. And that action seems to have almost been prophetical of Mary, the true foundress of Carmel, who was to come later, when Her family needed Her, and let fall Her mantle of Salvation.

With Elias' cloak, Eliseus struck the waters of the Jordan and they divided to make way for him. Mary's mantle has been raised against every kind of obstruction from fire and storm to the attacks of dumb animals, from physical attacks to those of temptation, and all have melted before it.

From the time of the miraculously empowered mantle of Elias, several garments are famous in sacred history. Who does not know the story of St. Martin's mantle? Or of the garment made out of palm leaves by Saint Paul, the first hermit, which was inherited by the great Saint Anthony and worn during the days of Pasch and Pentecost? One might also recall the example of Saint Francis de Paul's mantle which served him as a bark for crossing the sea, of the veil of Saint Agatha which was so powerful in stopping fires, or of the miraculous tunic of Saint Nicholas of Tolentino. Indeed, there are but few illustrious Saints in the Church whose garments have not been the instruments of brilliant and numerous wonders. Now, could one compare any of those garments to the garment of Our Lady of Mount Carmel? "It is no wonder," says a writer in Jourdain's Summa, "that the *Scapular* has been the instrument of wonders a thousand times more numerous." [5]

In 1656 a noteworthy event occurred at St.

Aulaye, in France, at the occasion of a mission there. It came to be recorded because the missionary fathers related it to the celebrated Father Lejeune. It was their testimony that at ten o'clock, one evening during the mission, a house was discovered to be in flames. Each moment added new fuel to the fury of the flames. A missionary recalled that a similar fire that had raged at Perigueux, about twenty years before, was subdued when the Scapular was tossed into it, and he resolved to invoke the aid of Our Lady of Mount Carmel. Quickly, he called a boy whose faith and piety could not fail to be pleasing to the Queen of Heaven, and said: "Take your Scapular, cast it into the fire, and we will see that the fire will be extinguished through Our Lady's power as evinced by Her Garment." The young man felt so secure of the missioner's word that he immediately dashed off and, rushing through the crowd which parted to make way for him, he shouted lustily: "Pray to the Blessed Virgin! I am going to put out the fire!" Running near the soaring conflagration, he tossed his little Scapular into it. At that instant, the whole crowd saw the fire rise like a whirlwind in an immense brazier, then slowly, slowly fall, to finally die away. The next day the Scapular was found in the debris *perfectly intact and uninjured,* though the pungent odor of smoke remained upon it.[6]

In Italy, Our Lady's garb was used to halt a flood. In the sight of the whole town of Rovereto, in 1647, the Prior of the Carmelite Convent cast a Scapular on the surging waters that had already destroyed the cattle and tolled several lives, and at the touch of Mary's Habit, the water receded.[7]

One of the most remarkable incidents to bring out the meaning of the Scapular, not as a condition for gaining a Promise but merely as Our Lady's Habit, is the calming of a raging sea by the almost unseen action of a cabin-boy who tossed his Scapular into the seething waters. It was publicized in 1902 in an American Review and the author of the account had gone to great pains to verify it.[8]

In the year 1845, the *King of the Ocean* left the London docks with a full complement of passengers for Australia.

Amongst the passengers was a devout English Protestant clergyman, the Reverend James Fisher, and his wife and their two children, James and Amelia, aged respectively about nine and seven.

The weather was good until the ship arrived some five hundred miles west of Cape Agulhas, where the trade winds generally keep revel with the fierce under-currents in that part of the Indian Ocean. The sun had scarcely sunk beneath the western waters when a wild tornado swept the ocean from the northwest. The waves were lashed into fury, the sails torn, and all the wooden structures on deck were only as reeds before the angry winds and waves of that memorable night. The passengers were sent below; the captain and crew, who had lashed themselves to the deck rigging, were unable to act. Moans of despair and cries for mercy, mingled with prayers, were heard alike from passengers and crew. Wave on wave washed over the apparently doomed boat, and nothing, short of the intervention of Divine Providence, could save her from a watery grave.

The Reverend Mr. Fisher, with his family and others, struggled to deck and asked all to join in prayer for mercy and forgiveness, as their doom seemed inevitable; but the prayers and cries for help seemed only to be mocked by the hissing and moaning of the infuriated elements.

Among the crew was a young Irish sailor, a native of County Louth, named John McAuliffe, who opened his vest and took from his neck a pair of Scapulars. He waved them in the form of a cross and then threw them into the ocean.

Soon the waters abated their fury. The howling tempest calmed, as it were to a zephyr, but a wavelet washed over the side of the boat and cast near the sailor boy the Scapulars he had thrown into the seething foam some minutes before!

All was now calm. Captain and sailors set about re-rigging their boat and steered her safely into Botany harbor.

The only ones who happened to notice the sailor boy's action, and the return of the Scapular to the drenched deck, were the Fishers. They now approached the boy with deep reverence, and begged him to let them know what those simple pieces of brown braid and cloth, marked B. V. M., might signify. When told, they then and there promised to join the Faith which has for its protectress and powerful advocate the Virgin of Carmel. When they landed at Sydney, they repaired to the little wooden chapel of St. Mary, on the site of which now stands a

magnificent church, and were duly received into the
Church by the then Father Paulding, afterwards
Archbishop.

A friend of the present author, in Vienna, is con-
templating the publication of some thousand Scapular wonders; the author himself has gathered a
variety great enough to produce a book. Hence, this
short chapter cannot essay to do more than give the
reader a general awareness of the Scapular as a sort
of Marian "relic." However, we cannot refrain
from citing a final example which is so pointedly
indicative of Mary's Scapular as a "Heavenly Garment." Saint John don Bosco was buried in the
Scapular in 1888 and in 1929 the Scapular was
found under the rotted garments and remains of
that great apostle and incomparable educator of
youth, in perfect preservation.[9]

"No devotion has been confirmed with so many
authentic miracles as the Scapular," says Blessed
Claude de la Colombière.[10] One need not consider
himself unfortunate if he cannot go to Lourdes for
its waters, nor to La Salette and other distant shrines
for their heavenly power and favors. Mary has
given us a relic of Herself that is more powerful than
all these, now hallowed by seven centuries of wonders in every corner of the earth. It is a tiny garment
we can all wear, *from God's Mother.*

> *"As Saint Basil of Seleucia remarks: if God
> granted to some who were only His servants such
> power that their shadows healed the sick, placed in
> the public streets for this very purpose, how much
> greater must be the power that He has granted to*

Her who was not only His handmaid but His Mother?" [11]

ST. ALPHONSUS

"For us who wear the Scapular, of what noble personage is it the livery? It is the livery of Mary, the Queen of the Universe, the Sovereign of more than the World. What an honor to belong to the Scapular Confraternity! It is so great an honor that we should be able to wear this Heavenly Sign openly, on our breasts, and not only under our garments. The Scapular is honored in the other life also, where the goods and glory of this world are nothing." [12]

R. P. MESCHLER, S. J.

St. Teresa of Avila spoke to Our Lord of the Blessed Virgin as: ". . . Thy most holy Mother, whose merits we share and whose Habit we wear, unworthy though we be by reason of our sins." [13]

"I will lead you into my Family of Carmel where you will wear MY HABIT." [14]—*Our Lady to Blessed Anne of St. Bartholomew.*

CHAPTER ELEVEN

A Sign of Victory

In Her apparition to Saint Simon Stock, the Scapular Queen was heard by the whole world to make a triple promise: "Behold a Sign of Peace, a Safeguard in Danger, a Pledge of My Eternal Alliance." These words have been spontaneously quoted for at least five centuries as actually being words pronounced by Our Lady. With Her miracles, Mary does seem actually to pronounce them: with the Scapular held out to us, She performs wonders that flow like a mystic voice continuing the conversation begun with Saint Simon Stock. "I will procure peace for you," She seems to say, "I will safeguard you in danger and render Satan powerless before you."

Looking with faith beneath the physical Scapular miracles, one cannot but realize that there must be tremendous spiritual miracles worked by the Scapular incessantly. The Blessed Virgin gave it to us primarily for our spiritual salvation. Surely, then, the very reason for which She works such numerous miracles against our *visible* enemies is but Her desire to remind us that Her Sign is truly a *safeguard against our invisible ones*. When the Pharisees thought, "Who is this who speaketh blasphemy?

Who can forgive sins but God alone?" Our Lord turned to them and said: "What is easier to say, thy sins are forgiven thee or to say, arise and walk?" And then the King of Kings cured the poor man "and immediately rising up before them, he took up the bed on which he lay and went to his own house, glorifying God." Does not the Queen do the same in Her apostolate with the Scapular?

When we see that at the Sign of the Scapular, disease dries up in our bodies, we should recall that Mary is pointing out that the spiritual disease of bad habits can be dried up at its application. When fire is harmless and loses its power to burn before Mary's Habit, so too can the raging fires of temptation be rendered harmless by a mere kiss placed upon the Scapular or a prayerful thought of it. If sterile heavens have poured down rain when the Scapular was carried in procession, how can we feel that our times of spiritual dryness will long persist if we fervently wave the Scapular above our parched souls by practicing its mystical prayer? If wild animals are mollified by the Scapular, so can the hate of our enemies be turned even to love. Raging torrents of water have subsided before the Scapular; storms have been calmed; so will storms of passion dwindle away to leave that sweet tranquility of soul that is characteristic of Mary's children. *The Scapular is a Sign of victory over our invisible enemies.*

As if not content with inviting us to realize the tremendous power of the Scapular by innumerable physical miracles, it seems as though Our Lady took the occasion of Saint John Vianney's unusual vision into that invisible spiritual world that surrounds and penetrates us, to tell us definitely that it is there that we shall find the greatest value of Her Scapular; perhaps too many have not read the outward signs and wonders. A young lady came to the Curé to make a general confession before entering the convent. While she was kneeling before him, the Saint astounded her, and the world, with the following conversation:

"You remember, my child, a certain ball which you attended a short time ago?"

"Yes, Father."

"You met a young man there, a stranger, elegant in appearance and of distinguished bearing, who at once became the hero of the fete? and you wished he would invite you to dance? You were vexed and jealous when he preferred others to you?"

"You are certainly right, Father."

"Do you recollect that when he left the assembly you thought you saw, as he walked, two small bluish flames beneath his feet, but you persuaded yourself that it was an optical illusion?"

"I remember it perfectly."

"Well, my child, that youth was a demon. Those with whom he danced were in a state of serious sin! And do you know why he failed to ask you?

"It was owing to the Scapular which you did well not to lay aside and which *your devotion to Mary impelled you to wear as your safeguard.*" [1]

In his life of Francis Yepès, who died in the odor of sanctity in the year 1617, Father Velasco tells us of most extraordinary encounters with Satan. Once, when the Venerable Francis was at prayer, the demon came, under the form of a black raven, throwing itself upon the holy man and beating him with its wings. But instead of being troubled, Francis took his Scapular, invoked the name of Mary, and put the enemy to flight. At another time, as he was respectfully kissing his Scapular, Satan approached, bearing a golden chain, and said: "Come, wear rather this chain of gold about your neck; throw away that object there which is insupportable to us and serves but to torment us!" [2]

In this twentieth century we have difficulty in appreciating a Marian Sign which torments Satan. One of his greatest conquests is that the modern world disbelieves in him. Today, clergymen as well as laymen often fear to claim acquaintance with such things as violent diabolical possession (rather speaking of "hysteria," or "violent anti-religious complexes") for fear of descending, in the estimation of their hearers, into the category of the overcredulous. One refers frequently to Satan as "Old Nick," divested of his terror, more a myth than a living force and more a joke than the most powerful and horrible enemy we have. When a venerable Brother André is diabolically assaulted in this twentieth century, the incident goes almost unnoticed; when nocturnal noises, unseen blows, curtain fires and the like, attest the hatred of some unseen enemy to the holiness of a Curé of Ars, we believe *but seem to ignore the fact that these same enemies are ours.*

It used to be that Satan did not so completely hide himself as he does today. In the time of Christ the very mention of his name struck fear into human hearts; it was the name of the black prince of this earth who sometimes possessed his victims not only to make them rabid denouncers of God, iconoclasts, fomenters of spiritual and temporal revolution (like the modern demons of Russia) but even to torture them, causing them to throw themselves against obstacles or cruelly to tear themselves.

Not dreaded today as he once was, those whom Satan ensnares to sin do not realize that he is their worst enemy but think him rather one to bring them pleasure, one who is a material friend. Hence, although fallen angels were once forced to cry out after a great public conversion, "O Scapular, how many souls you snatch from us!" [3], it is to be feared that the power of Mary's Garment against spiritual enemies will most probably be underestimated today. Even though the Venerable Francis Yepès was given to understand that Satan fears three things most, the invocation of the names of Jesus and Mary, and the wearing of the Scapular, still, in these days of Satan's victory of silence, the great value of a practice most dreaded by him is liable to go unnoticed. If we happen to perceive little things that would indicate the presence of the spiritual wolves in sheep's clothing, like the favored young woman who interviewed the Curé of Ars, we most likely convince ourselves that they are but delusions. If we refuse to recognize our enemies, how can we possibly appreciate our safeguard?

But the power of the Scapular is a reality whether we are ready to appreciate it or not. In making a promise of Salvation the Blessed Virgin has given us a Sign of Victory—a Sign before which Hell trembles!

Those who do appreciate the power of Mary in the Scapular against Satan have often, through the mere pressing of the Scapular to their lips, been able to cause the most violent temptations to melt away. They know that due to their devout wearing of the Scapular with its presence of Mary, Satan dare not come near them. We discover traces of fright in the words uttered by Pope Leo XI as the Scapular was accidentally being removed from his shoulders at the papal investiture: "Leave me Mary, lest Mary leave me!"

When learned writers apply the following passage of Scripture to Mary: "Her bands are a binding of salvation," Saint Lawrence Justinian asks: "Why bands except it be that She binds Her servants and thus prevents them from straying into the paths of vice?" [4] And Saint Alphonsus remarks: "Truly this is the reason for which Mary binds Her servants." [5] She has affiliated us to Herself by the bonds of a dual, Scapular contract, and why?—that the powers of Hell may be rendered impotent before us.

It must not be believed, however, that one will never sin if he does nothing more than simply wear the Scapular. As Father Lejeune points out, wearing the Scapular is the wearing of Mary only in the degree to which we wear the Scapular piously.[6] *Ordinary state of investiture,* the passive wearing of the Scapular, is a pious act in which perseverance will be ultimately rewarded with victory. But it is not the state in which Satan cannot frequently vanquish us. *An active realization of the Scapular* is a state in which we fervently think of the fact that we are affiliated to Mary in moments of temptation and instinctively fly to Her at the first sign of the enemy. This is a state wherein one will never even fall into sin; Hell is utterly impotent when a Scapular-wearer, besides his silent devotion, faces temptation with a devout invocation of His Mother. No one who calls upon Mary is abandoned by Her [7] and a Scapular wearer, who calls upon Her, can almost feel Her flying to his aid. "Who ever faithfully implored thy all-powerful aid," asks Blessed Eutychean, "and was abandoned by thee?" [8] "Indeed, no one," is the reply of Saint Alphonsus, "for thou canst relieve the most wretched and save the most abandoned; such a case never did occur and never will." [9] How much more, therefore, is not *the Scapular wearer* secure against Hell if he is devout in the Scapular devotion—in the wearing of that sign which devotion impels him to consider "his safeguard"?

Blessed Alan, who knew the value of the Scapular from Mary Herself, was one day assaulted by a violent temptation. Just as he was on the verge of yielding to it, *Our Lady appeared to him*. Another time he heard Mary saying: "If thou hadst recommended thyself to Me, thou wouldst not have run such a danger." [10] Hence we should realize the great value of the Scapular as a Sign of Victory over Satan; it should inspire us with confidence and, by its continual presence, cause us to develop the most desirable habit imaginable: of invoking our Queen Mother at every moment of trial.

When we arise in the morning, would it not be well to realize, as it was once commonly realized, that the day is to be a day of battle? That *some temptation is sure to assault us?* Hell does not rest and there are seven sins into which we easily fall because of our wounded nature: pride, covetousness, lust, anger, gluttony, envy and sloth. Each is a link that Satan would forge upon us as he schemes continually to wrap us in the complete chain of a vicious habit, upon which he would need but jerk to tumble us into the abyss of the most abominable sins.

But Mary has bound us first! She has allied us to Herself with *chains of love* that are an assurance of victory. There are enmities between devils and Mary, the seed of Satan and Her seed; but Mary has marked Her seed with a Sign of Victory. It is a Sign that Satan dreads for did God not say: "And She shall crush thy head"? Yes, and that is what Mary repeats in the words of Her Promise! With Herself, Our Lady has given us in the Scapular a Sign of Victory.

> "No one, unless the irrevocable sentence has been pronounced against him, is so cast off by God that he will not return, and enjoy His mercy, if he invokes My aid. I am called by all the Mother of Mercy, and truly has the mercy of My Son towards all men made Me thus merciful towards them; and therefore, miserable will he be for all eternity who, in this life, having it in his power to invoke Me, who am so compassionate to all, and so desirous to assist sinners, is miserable enough not to invoke Me and so is damned." [9]

OUR LADY TO SAINT BRIDGET

"Men do not fear a hostile and powerful army as much as the powers of Hell fear the name and protection of Mary." [10]

ST. BONAVENTURE

"The Singular Protection which Mary exercises towards those who wear Her holy Scapular consists in three things: (1) She keeps at a distance, from those who wear Her Scapular, whatever might cause their ruin, such as violent temptations, perilous occasions, pernicious counsels, wicked companions; (2) She communicates to them Her living enlightenments and powerful attractions for their well being; She prepares occasions for them and places them in a sort of necessity of working out their salvation; (3) She becomes an aid to them especially in the last moments of their mortal life, repelling the attacks of the demon, inspiring them with a thousand good sentiments, and assuring their final perseverance." [11]

REV. Z. C. JOURDAIN.

"When Father Emmanuel Padial, S. J., was at the point of death, Mary appeared to him. At the same moment an army of demons was seen taking flight and crying out in despair: 'Alas! We can do naught for She who is without stain defends him!'" [12]

ST. ALPHONSUS

"On this day (July 16th) Mary took to Herself, by means of the Holy Scapular, sons of love." [13]— Preface of Mass of the Scapular Feast.

"Who would ever dare to snatch these children from the bosom of Mary, when they have taken refuge there? What power of hell, what temptation can overcome them if they place their confidence in this great Mother, the Mother of God and of them?" [14]

ST. ROBERT BELLARMINE

CHAPTER TWELVE

Mary, Our Way

DOWN IN the hills at the foot of Carmel, the unrecognized Queen of the Universe hastened to the home of Her cousin, Elizabeth, whom She knew—by a messenger from Her Royal Consort—to be with child. When She entered Her cousin's home, Saint Elizabeth did not know how to thank Her and, filled with humility, burst forth in the exclamation: "And whence is this to me that the Mother of My Lord should visit me?" (Luke I, 32.)

"But how could this be?" asks a Doctor of the Church. "Did not Saint Elizabeth already know that not only *Mary,* but also *Jesus* had entered her house? Why then does she say that she is unworthy to receive the Mother and not, rather, that she is unworthy to receive the Son, Who had come to visit her? Ah, yes, it is because the saint knew full well that when Mary comes She brings Jesus, and therefore it was sufficient to thank the Mother without naming the Son." [1]

And so, too, when Our Lady visited this vale of tears with an assurance of salvation, She brought Salvation with Her. As formerly She had "contained Christ as manna in the ark of Her womb, and brought Him forth to be the Food and Salvation of

the world" (C. à Lapide),[2] so in giving Herself to
us in the Scapular She wills to give us the Food of
Angels.

In the days of prophecy, Saint Elias saw a cloud
appear over Mount Carmel, foot-shaped. It was a
vision of Her who was to arise immaculate from the
sea of humankind and to crush Satan beneath Her
heel, as She brought forth the Salvation of the
world. It is traditional that Elias founded the family
of Carmel for Her. But after he had beheld this
prophetical vision of Our Lady of Mount Carmel,
he went down into the desert and there he partook
of another mystery, a prefigurement of *the Holy
Eucharist.*

He had fled to the desert because he feared the
wrath of the wicked Queen Jezabel, whose false
prophets he had slain on Mount Carmel. He sat
heavily beneath a juniper tree and begged God to
take away his soul. Instead, an angel came and fed
him a piece of bread. In the strength of that bread,
the prophet walked for forty days. The Fathers of
the Church interpret it as a prophetical symbol of
the Eucharist.

"Now, if the bread given under the juniper tree
and ministered by an angel is a type of the Holy
Eucharist," asks the Scriptural commentator, Sylveira, "why, indeed, was not that bread which angels
ministered to Elias at Carith a foreshadow of the
Eucharist? Or why should not the bread given by
Divine Power in the house of the widow of Sareptha
obtain this great honor? I answer that this bread
given under the juniper has been so greatly subli-

mated because Elias came to the juniper from Mount Carmel where he had seen, in a small cloud, the Immaculate Queen of Heaven whom he had thereupon loved and wholeheartedly venerated. From this apparition and veneration he had disposed himself to partake, in type and figure, of such an ineffable mystery as the Eucharist." [3]

Although it may sound simply like a play on words, it is true that when we go to Mary in the Scapular we go to Jesus in the Eucharist. Father Faber says: "In the devout life, it is almost the same thing to say of a man that he has a great devotion to Our Blessed Lady or that he has a great devotion to the Blessed Sacrament." [4]

The whole meaning of Our Lady, the whole meaning of any gesture on Her part to assure our salvation, is to be found in the thirst of the Sacred Heart for love. This is as true as the fact that a bridge derives its whole meaning from the banks which it joins. Mary has but one desire, a desire born at the foot of the Cross: to see resound from pole to pole the one cry, "Praise be to the Divine Heart of Jesus!" When She comes to this vale of tears with a Sign of Salvation, She does not come to answer only in part that rending cry of thirst, which quivered into Her heart from the parched lips of Her dying Son. His Sacred Heart rests the world over, motionlessly pulsating in powerless omnipotence behind the doors of tabernacles constructed by human hands. Hence, when Mary comes to us making a promise of Salvation, bearing the Child Jesus on Her arm, whither does She intend to turn our hearts? What means of salvation would this Blessed Mother impart to us other than a share in Her own deep love for the Sacred Heart?

Once while Saint Gertrude was reciting the *Salve Regina,* Our Lady appeared with the Infant Jesus on Her arm. Just as Saint Gertrude said: "Turn thine eyes of mercy towards us," Mary pointed to the eyes of Her Divine Son and said: "These are the most compassionate eyes that I can turn for their salvation towards all who call upon me." [5] Those who enter the Scapular Devotion, in the manner about to be described, will surely feel an attraction to the tabernacle. Our Mother has instituted an easy yet perfect devotion to Herself because She knows full well that God has made Her the perfect way to Him; She knows that where there is devotion to *Her,* there will soon be devotion to that *unsoundable Heart* which is cached under the wafer-species in order to join and love-inflame all human hearts.

In the *Glories of Mary,* the reader is reminded of a vision recounted in the Franciscan Chronicles in which Brother Leo saw a red ladder, on the summit of which was the Son of God, and a white one, on the top of which was His most holy Mother. He saw some who tried to ascend the red ladder and, mounting a few steps, fell. They tried again, and again fell. They were then advised to try the white ladder, and by that one they easily ascended, for Our Blessed Lady stretched out Her hand and helped them. [6] This vision, which of course cannot mean that Mary is a greater aid to Heaven than Our Lord, does indicate that *Our Lord gave His Mother to us that we might have an easy and secure way of climbing to Him.* Blessed Grignion de Montfort says: "There is not anything which makes devotion to Mary more necessary to us than that it is the WAY OF FINDING JESUS PERFECTLY, of loving Him tenderly, and of serving Him faithfully." [7]

At once this opens to us a new appreciation of that perfect devotion which Mary instituted by a Promise. When Blessed Angela of Arena was hesitating about her vocation, she also had a vision of a ladder to Heaven: two saints appeared to her and said that if she wished to ascend that ladder, she should take the Habit of Mary, the Scapular.[8] For, in the Scapular, Mary has given us Herself, the true ladder to Heaven. She has pledged Herself to us and has become continually present to us in a moral and effective manner. She has thus given us God's own way to Himself.

As was mentioned in our treatment of "Mary's sacrament," to merely wear the Scapular is but to obtain a minimum of Marian treasure and to ignore the very best aspect of Our Lady's gift—namely, that She is present to us and that we need but deepen our union with Her to obtain union with Our Lord. From the tabernacle, where He dwells hidden as during the first nine months He spent on earth in Mary's womb, Our Lord seems to ask us to come to Him through Mary: "Can anyone fail to see," asked Pius X, "that there is no surer or more direct road than by Mary to unite all mankind in Christ, that we may be holy and immaculate in the sight of God?" [9] And in the Scapular Promise, it seems that Mary, who first brought us that delightful Food of Angels, has come to clothe us with Herself that we may approach that Blessed Eucharist immaculately, to be consumed by Its divinizing power and flaming love. From Mount Carmel, from the vision of the Immaculate crushing Satan, we are drawn to the tabernacle.

Jesus and Mary are one. If we find Mary, we find Jesus. If we become united to Mary, we become united to Jesus and in a way most pleasing to Him; it was He Who first came to us through Her.

Now, the Scapular Devotion is one that renders union with Mary natural and easy. And by "union," we do not mean here merely the fundamental moral union that actually constitutes the Scapular Devotion but that deeper union with Mary which causes the likeness of Christ to appear in souls and brings about a new and undreamed of intimacy with Him.

Elsewhere we have seen that the wearing of the Scapular imports the practice of a true devotion to Mary: a devotion of homage, confidence and love. In this true devotion we necessarily give Mary our minds (homage), our wills (confidence), and our hearts (love). A moral union results, but it is a union not deep enough to cause us to live in Jesus, through Her. This deeper union results only from the practice of a PERFECT devotion, a devotion not only of mind and heart and will, but of the whole being. This devotion requires that we add to our homage, confidence, and love, the element of IMITATION. And it is here that the Scapular, besides laying the foundation of a lesser union, becomes a great aid.

Sacred Scripture says: "The Queen stands at Thy right hand clothed in gold, surrounded by variety." The Queen *stands* because She did not ascend to Heaven to rest, but to watch over Her children and to constantly aid them to union with Her Glorified Son by Her prayers and melting love; She stands at the right hand of Her Son, watching and praying over us—*being* a Mother. But why has She clothed us in a dark garment while, in Heaven, She is *clothed in gold, surrounded by many various colors?* Is it not that we are to do as She did on earth: make it a garment golden with love and surrounded by the variety of all the virtues that flow from love?

Mary, in the Scapular we wear, seems constantly to say to us: "Love God! and here is my heart with which to love!" For, as Our Lord in procuring our salvation left nothing undone to win our love, Mary has left nothing undone to win our love to Her Son in assuring our salvation. She not only assures us of Her mediation in giving us the Scapular but, like Jesus Who gave not only salvation but Himself entirely, She gives Herself to us during life, at death, and even in purgatory. For almost seven centuries, by more miracles than have been wrought through any other sign, She has given the Scapular such a redundancy of Herself that, as one writer puts it, "It seems that the bounteousness of Mary has crystallized into this Scapular that it might find itself in more intimate contact with the hearts of Her dearest children." [10] *One who wears it devoutly has Mary at his side, sweetly guiding him to fully consecrate himself to Her by imitation of Her love of God.*

It would be impossible to show in how many ways the Scapular is a symbol of love and of consecration of oneself to Jesus through Mary. Its mysteries are bound into the one unsoundable, love-compelling fact that it is an assurance from the Mother of Sorrows, who stood as the High Priestess at Calvary's altar, that through Her mediation the Precious Blood shed there will be our infallible salvation. Just as the garment which She made for Jesus became a symbol of the complete Passion in being stripped from Him on Calvary, so, too, in being an assurance of the Blood shed that day, this garment is the symbol of all those motives of love.

Mary seems to teach us in the Scapular that we should so love Our Lord that we desire nothing more than to give Him the joy of finding Her in us—of seeing us approach Him with the immaculate love that once drew Him from the bosom of His Eternal Father. When Saint John of the Cross received the Scapular he said: "I desire to practice with fervor all the virtues of Mary which this Holy Habit signifies." When he had made that resolution, he says: *"Our Lord made me understand all the tenderness of His Heart. Never would I have believed that there could be so much compassion for men in this Divine Heart!"* [11]

Why did Our Lord make known to the Saint all the tenderness of His Heart when Saint John resolved to practice the virtues of Mary symbolized by his Scapular? Why, indeed, except that to imitate Mary is to go directly and perfectly to Him? Saint Conrad, before entering the Capuchian Order, walked to the nearest town and had himself enrolled in the Scapular. He wore it devoutly all through his religious life with the resolution: "I will always strive to have a deep devotion to Mary, and especially strive to imitate Her virtues." [12] He soon united himself to Jesus through Mary (*die Grignionische Andacht*), attaining perfection in an astoundingly short time. He spoke of the Divine Hearts of Jesus and Mary as One, a truth he had learned rapidly by sweet experience.

The great and rapid triumphs of these two Marian saints—John of the Cross and Conrad of Altotten—are far from unique. Such triumphs have been the reward of all who have known the secret of "to Jesus through Mary." Saint Therese of Lisieux is an example worthy of special attention because she is like a messenger to this century, announcing that the blissful state of union with Jesus through the Scapular Queen is not an unrealizable utopia.

Saint Therese astounded the world by giving Jesus a love that has almost been unparalleled in the whole history of the Church and then saying: "All little souls can imitate me!" [13] She declared that everyone could achieve her perfection and from the age of three she never refused God anything! What is the explanation? Ah, what indeed but union with Mary? This is the secret Therese began to keep from the moment of her miraculous cure, in her infancy, by Our Blessed Lady. She made herself a living reproduction of the Immaculate Conception and did not fear to approach our Lord with the disarming, child-like love that arose from her union with Mary.

Although the Little Flower never read of this devotion as the "Secret of the Enclosed Garden" preached by Blessed Grignion de Montfort, she was inwardly instructed by Mary to practice it; [14] she made her act of consecration to the merciful love of God through the hands of Mary. Many, thinking that her secret stopped at confidence and love, not knowing that the secret of her confidence and love was union with Our Lady of the Scapular, have come to wonder, in their spiritual failures, if Our Lady's "Little Flower of Carmel" had not made some mistake in saying that she did nothing which all little souls could not imitate. But her little way was that of the Scapular—a way in which Mary offers Her Heart to us that we may make it, as it were, our heart. St. John Eudes heard Our Lord saying: "I have given you this admirable Heart of My dearest Mother, which is but One with Mine, to be truly your Heart also, in order that the children may have but one Heart with their Mother, and the members have no other Heart but that of their Head, that so you may adore, serve and love God with a Heart worthy of His infinite greatness." [15] And while Therese says: "He thirsts for our love," Lisieux assures us that Therese "loved the Blessed Virgin as much as is possible on this earth, and she loved her Holy Scapular which is Mary's Habit." [16]

One might show how the Scapular is not only an invitation to love but is an invitation to practice all the virtues of Mary. Like the Little Flower, however, let us but obey the law of love and our garment will not only turn to gold but will soon be "surrounded by variety." Vermeersch says that the Scapular is a devotion by which we practice the homage of respectful affection, of filial confidence, and of continual supplication but, above all, we should enter into it *by love*.[17] Chaignon further points out that the Scapular invites us to imitate all Mary's virtues by the one fact that it constitutes Her assurance that one day, through Her intercession, we shall be saints: "We ought therefore to act as saints. When we are invested in the Scapular *we ought to invest ourselves also in love*." [18]

Hence we say that Mary, in the Scapular, presents Herself as our way to the Sacred Heart. She invites us to Her perfection, which fructifies in union with the Sacred Heart. Father Faber says that: "All our life is nothing but a succession of visitations, visitations from Mary bringing Jesus with Her, but nowhere is this similitude so faithful as it is in the Eucharist." [19] In giving us a true devotion to Herself, Mary gives us, little by little, a true devotion to Our Lord in the Blessed Sacrament. In uniting us to Herself, She is drawing us into the paradise of the Sacred Heart. Our Communions will take on a new significance: "Jesus," says Blessed Grignion de Montfort, "is always and everywhere the fruit of Mary and Mary is everywhere the veritable tree that bears the Fruit of Life and the true Mother who produces It." [20] "To Mary alone," this same saint declares, "God has given the keys to the cellars of Divine Love with the power of entering into the most sublime and secret ways of perfection and the power of causing others to enter in also." [21] And by the Scapular, Mary has declared that we shall be saints in Heaven. Therefore She is desirous of making us saints on earth. She desires to present Herself to us that we may become closely united to Her, the Immaculate, and thus be wholly pleasing to Jesus. She invites us, presenting to us an assurance of salvation that is also a symbol of Her virtues, to come to Her by imitation.

Thus when Our Lady came to make the Scapular Promise, folding the Mystical Body to Her bosom with those powerful words, "Shall not suffer eternal fire," She made a gesture towards the fulfillment of Her mission. It is Her mission to give the Incarnate Word to mankind, and She has taken us under Her Mantle where we can easily partake of Her immaculate purity and be worthy, as little children, to receive Her Son.

> *"O Mary! You were filled with Grace that you might be the way of our salvation, the means of ascent to the heavenly kingdom."* [22]
>
> SAINT FULGENTIUS.

> *"Whoever desires the fruit must go to the tree; whosoever desires Jesus must go to Mary; and whoever finds Mary will most certainly find Jesus."* [23]
>
> ST. ALPHONSUS.

> *"All our perfection consists in being conformed, united, and consecrated to Jesus Christ; and therefore the most perfect of all devotions is, without any doubt, that which most perfectly conforms, unites, and consecrates us to Jesus. Now, Mary being*

*the most conformed of all creatures to Jesus, it fol-
lows that of all devotions, that which most consecrates and conforms the soul to Our Lord is
devotion to His Holy Mother, and that the more a
soul is consecrated to Mary the more the soul is
consecrated to Jesus. Hence it comes to pass that
the most perfect consecration to Jesus is nothing else
but a perfect and entire consecration of ourselves
to the Blessed Virgin."* [24]

BLESSED GRIGNION.

*"In presenting to you a garment of mean material
and color, the Blessed Virgin seems to cry out to
you: 'Love not the world nor the things which are
of the world . . . For the world and the concupiscence
thereof passeth away.' "* [25]

VENERABLE LANICIUS, S. J.

*"Nothing is easier than the exercise of this devo-
tion. I ought to try to enter into the spirit of it
. . . to be docile to the silent lessons this Holy Habit
teaches me."* [26]

FATHER CHAIGNON, S. J.

St. Therese,

the "Little Flower".

Saint Joseph, Father and Model

A TRUE parent begets children, nourishes them, clothes them, educates them, and gives them their identity in society by giving them a family name. Mary has done all these things to show how really She is a mother to those whom She has adopted by Her Scapular contract. "The Most Glorious Virgin Mary, who by virtue of the Holy Spirit brought forth Jesus Christ, is the same Virgin who *produced the family* of the Blessed Virgin Mary of Mount Carmel" (Pope Sixtus IV).[1] She then nourished this family; "She brought forth the Order of Carmel and *nourished* it at Her breasts," says Gregory XIII.[2] And She *clothed* it in a garment of Salvation, saying: "Whosoever dies clothed in this shall not suffer the fires of Hell." She then gave it Her *name*, on account of which five successive Popes have indulgenced the title of Her family so that by designating the Carmelites or their confreres as "Brothers of the Blessed Virgin Mary of Count Carmel," one might gain thirteen years and thirteen quarantines indulgence! And finally, as the reader has just seen, Mary *teaches* Her Scapular children. Saint John of the

148

Cross said: "I wish to practice with fervor *all the virtues of Mary* which this Holy Habit *signifies,*" and not only does Our Lady's Habit signify Her virtues but, as we have also seen, She actively inculcates them in its wearers.

Now, when either husband or wife adopts children, as Mary has adopted us by Her Scapular contract, those children are naturally also those of the spouse. Hence, Saint Joseph is especially the father of the Scapular family. There was never a marital union more purely intense than that which was divinely contracted by Providence between Mary and Joseph. It was a union of two hearts for the greatest work of all time, intensified by a common love for a Divine Infant, Our Salvation. Hence, that children adopted by Mary *in an assurance of salvation* should become the special children of Saint Joseph is even more certain than that adopted children in general should become the children of the foster father as well as of the mother.

We are not surprised, therefore, to find history showing the Carmelite Order to be *among the first to institute the public cult of Saint Joseph* in the Church.[3] Nor are we surprised that Carmel seems to be the Order of Saint Joseph as it is the Order of the Blessed Virgin. It seems that the Feast of Saint Joseph, March 19, was merely extended to the Universal Church from where it already existed in the Order of Carmel. As the Carmelites enjoy the tradition of having erected the first chapel on earth to the Blessed Virgin, so the first church in Europe dedicated to Saint Joseph was erected to his honor by them. "The Carmelites brought the public cult of Saint Joseph from the Orient when they emigrated to the West," was the conclusion of that great papal savant, Benedict XIV, "and that is the opinion commonly held by all learned men." [4] Being the special family of Mary and hence of Saint Joseph, Divine Providence has willed that the present devotion to Saint Joseph in the Church should come to it through Carmel. And that the present world-wide devotion to him did arise from Mary's family is true if for no other reason than that, as Father Faber says, "the great Patriarch is indebted especially to Saint Teresa for his glory on earth." [5]

Indeed, being special children of Mary the Scapular-wearers are all special children of Saint Joseph, Her spouse. Even though the Mother came alone to adopt special children from the orphanage of the world, Saint Joseph took part by his hidden union with Her and by his own deep desire to have intimate children from the legion of the redeemed.

Of all the benefits that flow from the Scapular, this benefit of being the special children of Saint Joseph is one of the greatest. After an assurance of Mary's presence in life, at death and after death, what could be more desirable than the continual love and special protection of the greatest Saint in Heaven? Moreover, during those years at Nazareth Jesus filled the heart of Saint Joseph with a more tender love than has ever been felt by any created father before or since, "not only that Joseph might love Him as a Son," as Father Huguet says, "but that he might love all men as his sons, for as we are all the children of Mary so also is Joseph our father." [6] Hence, here is another fathomless benefit which Mary confers upon us in being Our Mother in a special way: She thereby renders us the special children of Her spouse, the most loving of fathers. "And after devotion to Our Blessed Lord and His Immaculate Mother, there is nothing more pleasing to God or more beneficial to our souls than devotion to the holy Patriarch, Saint Joseph." [7]

Our Lady seems to indicate that it was Her express intention to make us special children of Saint Joseph when She contracted the Scapular alliance. Not only were the Carmelites the special envoys of devotion to Saint Joseph, but Our Lady actually expressed Her desire to have them consecrated to him.

When Saint Teresa founded the first monastery of a reformed Carmel, Our Lord said: "I wish it to be dedicated under the name of Saint Joseph. This Saint will be your guard at one of the doors, the Blessed Virgin at the other, while I shall be in your midst." [8] At another time Saint Teresa found herself in the church of the Dominican Fathers and she felt someone place a beautiful white cloak upon her shoulders. For a few moments she did not see who placed it there, but very soon she saw the Blessed Virgin and Her holy spouse, Saint Joseph. The saint felt a great joy within her heart. Mary spoke, and while Saint Teresa listened to that heavenly voice, she thought that she pressed Our Lady's hand in her own. "I am so pleased that you have consecrated yourself to Saint Joseph," Our Lady told

Carmel's daughter, "that you may ask anything for your convent with perfect certainty that you shall receive it." The two holy spouses then placed a precious stone of great value in Saint Teresa's hands, and left the saint inundated with the purest joy and the most ardent desire to be consumed entirely with the violence of divine love.[9]

If Joseph was so close to Mary on that journey to Bethlehem; at the birth of the Saviour in a cattle-shelter; on their flight to Egypt; at the Presentation, the Offertory of the Bloody Sacrifice of Calvary; during the three-days loss, and at the finding of Jesus in the Temple; when the Saviour of the world went back to Nazareth "And was subject to them"; then can we possibly believe that he was not with Her, in spirit, when She came down from the heights of Heaven to give us a Sign of salvation?

Under no other title is Our Lady so like Saint Joseph as under the title, "Our Lady of the Scapular." In no other way has Mary made *us* so like Saint Joseph, as by the Scapular.

Saint Joseph is the "Patron of a Happy Death." And by the Scapular, are we not assured of a peaceful death? The statue of the Scapular Queen is very frequently seen in the cemeteries of Latin countries. But not only has Mary made Herself like Saint Joseph, the Patron of a Happy Death, but in making a promise of salvation and extending the promise to purgatory, Our Lady goes as far as possible to make us like our foster father, Her spouse, who had the great joy of dying in the arms of Jesus and Mary.

"Preserver of Virgins!" the Church salutes Saint

Joseph. And while a Saint declares there would be no hell were there no sixth commandment, the Scapular is its wearer's assurance that there will be no hell for him if he perseveringly wears it. Hence the Scapular has almost come to be known as a sign of chastity. Was that not the one virtue Our Lady specified in making the conditions for the gaining of the Sabbatine Privilege?

Saint Joseph is the Patron of the Universal Church. Pope Pius X reasoned that he must be the special protector of the Family of the Church now, even as he was appointed by God to be the protector of the Family at Nazareth. But what does Mary do with the Scapular but render Herself, and Saint Joseph, particularly our protectors and our patrons, to the extent that we cannot be lost? By the Scapular, which constitutes a true devotion to his most pure spouse, St. Joseph exercises this patronage in a very special way.

A certain Carmelite used fervently to kiss his Scapular on passing a statue of Saint Joseph, and each time he felt the sweetness of spiritual consolation and the satisfactory peace of soul that accompanies a fitting spiritual duty. One day he decided to analyze just why he always kissed his *Scapular* to honor *Saint Joseph,* and with such profit. It appeared to him immediately that, since by the Scapular he was a special child of Mary, that devotion also made him the special child of Saint Joseph. Our Lady of Mount Carmel is the Mother of all and our special Mother, having adopted us by the Scapular, "and as we are all children of this august Virgin, we may expect to be protected by Her most holy spouse." [10]

The Mother of God and the foster father of God have adopted special children. These children are *clothed, nourished, named and educated in heavenly virtue,* in such a glorious way that their lineage is unmistakable. They are a family of predestined ones. Anyone may join them and enjoy the special love of those parents whom God moulded to the greatest possible perfection.[11] Such is the significance of Mary and Joseph in the Scapular.

But Mary and Joseph have not adopted special children by the Scapular Promise simply that these children may increase the number of their devotees in the Church. Their reasons for the establishment of that vast family—united by a perfect, wordless devotion—are deep and, in their fulness, almost unsoundable. But of one reason we can be certain. They have wrought this work of centuries, from days of prophecy down to the present day, because *they wish to establish the Reign of their Infant God,* the Eucharistic King. That reign is to come about through Mary. Since Jesus dwells here on earth in our tabernacles, He can come to reign in the manner most pleasing to Him if Mary's children imitate Saint Joseph and establish the reign of the Sacred Heart in their hearts, by uniting themselves to Mary.

From Saint Joseph's point of view, the Scapular Confraternity is a great family which he is to protect and for which he is spiritually to provide. From Mary's point of view, it is a legion of hearts wherein She wills to bring forth the King of Kings by making them, like Saint Joseph, one with Her; She clothes them in a wedding garment of Salvation, as it were, espousing them as once She was espoused to Joseph, that they may be like him. And from Our Lord's point of view, the Promise of Salvation is an assurance of His Precious Blood being infallibly applied to us by Her into whose hands He has willed to entrust It, and through whom He desires to come to us, so that we, in imitation of Saint Joseph, should take the same way to Him.

For our sanctification through the Scapular, therefore, there is indeed much to consider in the exclamation of the devout Gerson: "O beautiful, amiable, and adorable Trinity: Jesus, Mary and Joseph! United by such bonds of love and charity, you are truly worthy of the love and adoration of the children of God!" What more could the ordinary man aspire to but a trinity of his heart with the Hearts of Jesus and Mary, like Saint Joseph? And yet it is just to such a glory that Mary, in making the Scapular alliance, invites us. She gives us Herself, Joseph as a model and foster father, and all but to unite us to Jesus. Seeing our ideal realized in the Holy Family we cannot but exclaim: "Great Saint Joseph! fill me with the virtues that will unite me to the Immaculate Heart of Mary, whose garment of espousals I wear, that through Her I may be holy and immaculate in the sight of God! Can so loving a father refuse this to his chosen child?"

But why should Mary and Joseph work together? *What particular value is hidden in the fact that the Garment of Salvation which Our Lady gave to Saint*

Simon, and which constitutes the most perfect devotion to Her, so insistently recalls to us the meaning of the Holy Family?

The family is *the foundation of society.* As no chain is stronger than its links, society is no stronger than the permanent unity of the families of which it is composed. Every irreligious force in the world that seeks to destroy society directs its attacks *against the Christian home.*

Our present society, with its high degree of civilization, is the result of the value of the family having been proclaimed at Nazareth. Before Nazareth, the family was almost universally barbaric: woman was a slave, and the life of the child was at the disposition of the father. As a result, society was barbaric. However, *God*—obedient to a human father and a human mother at Nazareth—changed the status of woman and raised the family to its proper place of glory. The moral conquests of the Church which then rose out of Nazareth were conquests for a firm family and they brought forth a strong society.

Today, the Christian family totters. Thousands of divorces rend the bonds of matrimony and defile the sacredness of the home. Many children find themselves bewildered by having parents other than those who begot them, or, as in Russia, without parents. In the countries where the Christian family has actually ceased to exist, Christian society has disintegrated. Day by day, in other countries, court separations wreak havoc upon the family. These are advances of Satan to a world revolution . . .

"Back to Nazareth" is, and must be, our cry.

Where God Himself—under Mary and Joseph—set an example to the world, we can acquire the force to come forth over the entire world to defend our Christian families with the arms of humility, prayer, chastity and fidelity. God will render us victorious.

However, how can we all return to Nazareth? How can we all enter into the mysteries of *the Holy Family* and bathe ourselves *in the sweet presence of Mary,* who works there with Saint Joseph to give us Salvation?

We carry the lessons of the Holy Family, and Its living strength, in the Scapular.

Since by the Scapular both husband and wife are united to Mary and Joseph, the father of the family is drawn to chaste union with the mother, to fidelity and to a love more lasting than life itself. The mother is drawn to return that love in the thousand little ways to which only a woman's heart contains the secret keys. From this follows a permanent union in the family whose core of love will be a staff with which the children may learn to walk in the spirit of Christ.

Entering into the Scapular devotion by imitating the humble carpenter in his union with Mary, we can achieve not only the personal perfection described in the last chapter, but we can perfect society. Thus may we effectively work to establish a universal reign of peace, a reign of the Sacred Heart. "If we are to believe the revelations of the saints," says Father Faber, "God is pressing for a deeper, quite another devotion to His holy Mother." [12] And since this "quite another devotion to Mary" is but that modelled by Saint Joseph[13] and realized in the Holy Family, it is no wonder that the Church is beginning, the world over, to resound the cry of Scripture: *"Ite ad Joseph!"* "Go to Joseph!" No wonder, too, Mary and Joseph have a Scapular Family.

In the apparitions of Fatima, Our Blessed Lady told the children that on October 13, 1917, She would reveal Her identity, and that She would appear with Saint Joseph, then as Our Lady of Sorrows, and finally as Our Lady of Mount Carmel.

Approximately a hundred thousand people had gathered at Fatima on that day . . . to see the "proof" which the Heavenly vision had promised to give "so that everyone might believe." It had been raining for many hours. The rain seemed to intensify as the hour of the apparition neared. Suddenly the rain stopped. A great shout rang up from the crowd: "Look at the sun! Look at the sun!"

During the time of the great phenomenon which then followed (the "Sun Miracle of Fatima"), Our Lady, who had appeared to the children as usual on top of a small tree, swept up in the sight of the children into a great light in the sky and there, transfigured in the light, Saint Joseph appeared at Her side holding on his arm the Divine Infant.

Slowly both Saint Joseph and the Infant Jesus raised their hands in blessing over the great crowd below.

After this apparition, the light remained, but the figures disappeared in the light, and Our Lady came back simply dressed in blue. Again a figure appeared in the light beside Her . . . and this time it was Our Lord, in all His glorious manhood, and once again He raised His hand as if to bless the crowd. As He did so, Our Lady faded back into the light and then reappeared as Our Lady of Mount Carmel, holding the Scapular in Her hands. Then Our Lord finished raising His hand and blessed the crowd below.

Finally, as the figures of Our Lady of the Scapular and of Her Divine Son (which had been seen only by the children) faded into the light, the great mass of light itself (which the crowd saw and took to be the sun) seemed to loosen itself from the sky and began to hurtle earthwards. Great cries of fear began to rend the air. Many of the crowd fell to their knees, some shouted their sins aloud and pleaded with God for mercy.

When it seemed as though the mass of light was about to burn and consume them . . . suddenly it gathered back and whirled up again into the air. The people began to blink as they then found themselves suddenly staring into the full brilliance of the sun. Only twelve minutes had passed, the rain was gone, and the great Portuguese sun burned once again from its usual place in the noon sky.

Since that day, great changes have come over the world. First Portugal was converted, and then, as prophecies made by Our Lady began, one by one, to come true, beginning with the second World War and the spread of atheism from Russia throughout the world, the message of Fatima became at once the great hope and the great crusade of our generation. "If My requests are heard," Our Lady had said,

"Russia will be converted, and there will be peace."

This book was written before the author had heard of Fatima . . . and would it not seem that the appearance of Our Lady with the Scapular in the final vision of Fatima, together with Her earlier appearance with Saint Joseph, confirms much of what has been said in these pages and, in particular, in this chapter?

Today the "Scapular Family," because of the apparitions of Fatima . . . and most especially because of the Blue Army of Our Lady of Fatima, of which the wearing of the Scapular as a sign of consecration to the Immaculate Heart of Mary is an essential condition . . . numbers not only its passive members but also its active members in the many millions. And do we not expect this vast family, now united in nations all over the world, to practice in themselves and in nations those lessons of spiritual union seen in the trinity of the Holy Family?

The greatest sins in the world today are sins against family. They are the sins against parenthood, against indissoluble marriage. And they are also the national sins against the spiritual family of humanity.

Is it not above all for those deeply consecrated to Our Lady by the Scapular to leaven the settling paste of a society from which Satan would feign filter its only elevating force, the sanctity of the family?

Often in the pages of this book we speak of the great benefits of the Scapular . . . benefits so numerous as to seem almost incredible.

With these benefits, and as an integral part of them, are the responsibilities. The symbolism of the Scapular is the voice of Our Lady speaking to us, constantly exhorting us to the imitation of Her virtues even as it is a constant token of Her moral presence and aid in living up to those lessons.

And the Scapular is not only a symbol of the Josephine formula—"To Jesus through Mary"—but it is a symbol, too, of the humble magnificence of a Nazareth where the world was conquered *without a word*. The silent homage, confidence and love (faith, hope and charity) of the Scapular devotion are but the foundations of the deeper value: the complete gift of ourselves to Mary for Jesus. And when the millions of members of the Scapular family make this consecration, will not Jesus have been born to the world a second time, through the Blessed Virgin aided by Saint Joseph?

After Joseph had learned that his spouse bore the Son of the Eternal God, how he must have sought Mary's company and longed to talk with Her about Jesus, about how they would teach the Son of God to walk, embrace Him, how they would care for Him. These must have been moments of great, great joy as well as of love and understanding—for Mary and Joseph.

Today, when the Son of God is being born again, born in the hearts of His redeemed, can we believe that Joseph is not discussing, in Heaven, "the coming of Jesus a second time through Her"? Is it not also Joseph's work, Joseph's task? Most certainly! Joseph stands as the model for the modern man: in

poverty, in industry, in temperance, in union with
Mary. And not only is he a model, but he actually
engenders in us these virtues which are so hard to
discover in the rush of modern "civilization." It was
at the so-called Reformation, started by Luther, that
our present troubles originated in defection from the
Church. And when Our Lord then appeared to the
great Saint Teresa and said, "My daughter, the ruse
of the demon is to remove from the defectors all that
would awake in them the love of God and more
than ever My faithful ones must follow the direct
opposite way," Saint Teresa says: "I suddenly understood how much *I was obliged to honor the Blessed
Virgin and Saint Joseph!*" [16] And when another of
the most glorious saints of Our Lady of the Scapular,
Mary Magdalen de Pazzi, was given to see the glory
of Saint Joseph in an ecstasy, she cried out: "Joseph,
united as he is to Jesus and Mary. is like a bright
shining star that *protects those souls who fight the
battle of life under Mary's standard!*" [17]

Before such manifestations of Saint Joseph as those
at Montreal and of such wonders of Mary as those
of Lourdes, all of which are witnesses of an unprec-
edented universalization of devotion to the Immaculate Conception and to Her spouse, it would seem
that it has taken twenty centuries for men to understand the lessons of Nazareth. Should we not praise
God if the devotion to Jesus through Mary, as
modelled by Saint Joseph, has been learned by the
world even in its old age? It is to be hoped that the
whole world will soon discover that both Mary and
Joseph are hidden in a humble Marian garment

worn by millions. That Sign of Salvation, a stumbling block to all the vast armies of Hell, seems to cry out an assurance to the saintly Pius IX who exclaimed—half in wonder, half in awe—"If Joseph and Mary regain the place they should never have lost, the world will again be saved!" [18]

"If Joseph is the father of those of whom Mary is the Mother, he is necessarily the special father of those who wear the Scapular." [19]

P. Joseph Andres, S. J.

"As all that belongs to a woman belongs also to her husband, we may believe that Joseph may bestow as he chooses the rich treasures of Grace which God has confided to Mary, his chaste spouse." [20]

Saint Bernard.

"There are three things that God cannot make greater than He has made them: the Humanity of Our Lord, the glory of the elect, and the incomparable Mother of God, of whom it is said that God can make no Mother greater than the Mother of God. You may add a fourth in honor of Saint Joseph. God cannot make a greater father than the father of God." [21]

Saint Thomas Aquinas.

"Mary directed Joseph. She enlightened him and animated him by Her example. Docile and attentive to the lessons given by his immaculate spouse, he learned to see things as She saw them, to despise what She despised, to love what She loved, to act as She acted. This was his perfection." [22]

Father Huguet.

"Happy is the soul who can say LIKE SAINT JOSEPH that Mary lives in her, and that she lives in Mary! For she has Mary constantly before her

*eyes, she studies Her virtues, and so becomes more
and more like her divine model, more and more
united to God."* [23]

FATHER HUGUET.

*"Two Carmelite religious, on leaving their monas-
tery one day, met a venerable old man advancing
toward them. He placed himself between them, and
asked whence they came. The elder of the two replied that they were Carmelites. 'Fathers,' then asked
the stranger, 'why do you Carmelites have such great
devotion to Saint Joseph?' The religious gave several reasons, chiefly stating that Saint Teresa had
had that devotion and instilled it in her followers.
'Look at me,' said the stranger when the priest had
finished speaking, 'and have the same devotion to
Saint Joseph as did Saint Teresa: whatever you ask
of him, you shall obtain.' Saying which, he disappeared."* [24]—*Chronicles of Carmel.*

*"The Church, which at first consisted of the Holy
Family, was in the beginning protected, guided and
directed by Saint Joseph. Thus, is it not right that
the guardian of the early days of Jesus and Christianity should be our protector in these latter days
of the Church?"* [25]

FATHER HUGUET.

CHAPTER FOURTEEN

"All Good Things Have Come to Me Together With Her"

WE MUST not be too greatly astonished at finding the little Scapular so very important. It is not really *the Scapular* that is so important but *Mary in the Scapular Promise,* a promise that was formulated only after centuries of preparation and that has since permeated much of the fibre of history with its Marian color.

If we look on the Scapular, two pieces of cloth and strings, we shall be disposed to quarrel with the fact that eternal salvation, shortened purgatory, Saint Joseph, union with Jesus through Mary, are all related in that badge. It is only a common little sign, and are we to compare it to the Eucharist? to attribute to it dependent omnipotence? to look upon *it* as a source of eternal salvation? Absolutely not.

By now we should realize that the cloth sign of membership in Mary's Confraternity is something incidental even as the material chalice which holds the Precious Blood. It is *Mary* who brings us all those great "Scapular" values. She has chosen to affiliate us to Herself by a sign that constitutes a true devotion to Her.

When we say "Scapular," therefore, we should have a composite view of vast Marian relations. Since the Blessed Virgin communicates Herself to us in a special way through that Sign, it follows that She communicates other incomprehensible values. The Church applies to Her the words of Scripture, *"All good things have come to me together with Her,"* because when Mary communciates Herself to us She brings us all spiritual good. *God* has chosen to come to us through Her.

Our astonishment at the greatness of Mary's Sign of Alliance might therefore give way to self-reproach. How much have we thought of Mary? What have we done to return Her love? Or again our astonishment at this Scapular message might take the form of awakened zeal. We have loved Mary but it has never occurred to us how really all good things come to us with Her. Perhaps we never sought to investigate the fact that She made the most astounding promise this world has ever heard.

As was just said above, the word *Scapular* should take on a deep meaning for us. It does not merely signify two pieces of cloth, given on a certain day of July, in a certain year, to a certain person. It signifies the prayers of the Mother of God, promised to anyone who comes beneath Her Mantle. It signifies values that have no date but eternity, no personage but Mary.

Since Saint Joseph was Mary's partner in procuring the Salvation of the world, naturally he enters vitally into the assurance of Salvation that Mary has attached to the Scapular. And since Salvation is "eternal union with God," union with Jesus is the whole meaning of the Scapular; it is the end towards which the prayers of Mary draw the Scapular child. Thus, Jesus, Mary and Joseph take their places in the Scapular Promise. But there are some other relations to the Blessed Virgin which also manifest themselves in the Scapular. In general, whatever is closely allied to Mary is communicated by the Scapular Promise for the simple reason that Her presence and prayers are communicated to us by it. In particular, there are certain values to which Divine Providence calls our attention in history.

Before citing the more salient values that have come through the Scapular with Mary and have found divine corroboration in history, one might remark that books have been written on each of those Marian values apart from the Scapular. Is it not to be hoped that more will be written from that synthetic point of view, Mary's Sign of Salvation? Satan fears Mary and he especially fears Her in Her Promise of Salvation. How could we better practice an apostolate against him, at the present stage, than by dispelling the clouds of ignorance which hide Her there? *Qui me elucidant vitam aeternam habebunt:* "They who explain me shall have life everlasting" is a passage of Scripture that has caused many men to write about the Blessed Virgin. She has already promised us life everlasting but if we explain Her, spreading books written about Her, may we not hope that so bountiful a Mother will give us life everlasting more abundantly? Not only is She never outdone in generosity but today, more than ever, She

wants to be known that She may draw men to Her
Son. The following facts are a slight indication of
that desire.

THE SACRED HEART

In a revelation to Saint Bridget, Our Lady based
a beautful analogy on the fact that Eve ate part of
the forbidden fruit and then, completing the ruin of
man, Adam ate the other part. "As Adam and Eve
sold the world for one apple," thus runs the words of
the revelation, "so My Son and I redeemed the
world, as it were, with *One Heart*." [1] And Our Lord,
having made His heart one with the Immaculate
Heart of Mary and then having given Her to us as a
Mother, Saint John Eudes would hear Him saying:
"I have given you this admirable Heart of My
dearest Mother *which is but One with Mine,* to be
truly your Heart also, in order that *the children may
have but one Heart with their Mother* . . . that so
you may adore, serve and love God with a Heart
worthy of His infinite greatness." [2]

The modern revelations of the Sacred Heart were
made to the sainted Margaret Mary Alacoque, a
cloistered nun who was a special devotee of the
Scapular Queen. She is a Saint who modelled her
life on that of a Carmelite lay-brother, Francis of
the Infant Jesus, and who was instructed by Our
Lord to come to His Heart through Mary. [3]

The preacher of the revelations made to Saint
Margaret Mary was her confessor, the Blessed
Claude de la Colombière, S. J. Our Lord instructed
Saint Margaret Mary to confide her revelations to

this holy Jesuit that the world might thus receive them. And this Blessed Claude, rightly known as "The Apostle of the Sacred Heart," has been given another title by his admirers. He has also become known as "The Apostle of the Scapular." [4]

So ardently did Blessed Claude love our Lady's livery that he declared it to constitute the greatest of devotions to Mary with values beyond our comprehension. "Because all forms of our love for the Blessed Virgin cannot be equally agreeable to Her," he declared, "I aver without a moment's hesitation that the Scapular is most favored of all. I maintain that there is no devotion which renders our Salvation so certain and none to which we ought to attach ourselves with more confidence and zeal . . . I would reproach myself were I to weaken your confidence in those other practices of devotion to Mary . . . for they are all salutary and cannot fail to touch Her maternal heart. But if She graciously accords Her favors to them, how much *more* propitious will She not be to all who wear Her holy livery!" [5] And at Paray le Monial, while confessor to Saint Margaret Mary, he established the Confraternity as a means perhaps of further propagating, together with devotion to the Divine Heart, devotion to the Scapular. [6]

Both Jesus and Mary have made promises of Salvation: Mary for wearing the Scapular and Jesus for receiving Holy Communion on nine consecutive "first Fridays." Both draw us to the same end: consummation in the fires of the Sacred Heart. "Come to Me through Mary," Our Lord instructed us in the person of Saint Margaret Mary; and Our Lady comes with the Scapular to give us an invaluable means of entering the Sacred Heart through Her.

At Fatima today, pilgrims from distant lands are sometimes surprised to see that the great golden statue in the heart of the Cova da Iria, where Our Lady appeared, is not a statue of Our Lady of Fatima, but a statue of the Sacred Heart. By contrast, the statue of Our Lady of Fatima is a much smaller, wooden statue in an almost insignificant little chapel, off to one side.

Pilgrims are sometimes even further surprised to see that the great demonstrations of faith at Fatima are centered primarily in the Blessed Sacrament.

When pilgrims come to Fatima they think at once of the spot where Our Lady appeared . . . and they flock to that little chapel and realize with awe that they are on sacred, visited ground.

But when the ceremonies begin, the statue is taken from that little chapel and carried in procession . . . attracting the attention and devotion of all to Our Lady . . . and then it leads to the great altar in front of the Basilica, is put to one side, and the *real* devotion of Fatima begins . . . with Mass, Communion, and Benediction of the Blessed Sacrament.

Here one *sees and feels* the true place and purpose of Our Lady. It is as though Her whole presence were merely to attract attention, even of the most hardened sinners, and lead them to the Fountain of Grace. And then She fades into the background.

In this book we are treating of Our Lady's Scapular devotion. Naturally when we look at one particular devotion it assumes tremendous importance

. . . and if this were the only book the reader ever took in hand he or she might go away with the feeling that the Scapular devotion is more important than any other.

Actually, of course, it is only part of a program. It is only ONE of the facets of devotion to Our Lady, as Bishop Sheen so beautifully describes in our foreword. But even more, Our Lady Herself . . . with all Her beauty and power . . . is merely part of a program. When She says at Fatima, "Only the Blessed Virgin can save you," it is only because God has appointed Her to lead men, through Her Immaculate Heart, to the Sacred Heart of Jesus.

In 1689, Our Lord told Saint Margaret Mary Alacoque: "It will take time, but I will reign despite Satan and his supporters."

And today more than ever we are mindful of the words of God spoken to Satan in the Garden of Eden: "Satan, I shall place enmities between thee and the Woman, thy seed and Her seed . . . and thou shalt lie in wait for Her heel and She shall crush thy head."

It is to establish this reign of the Sacred Heart in the world, despite Satan and his supporters who have organized militant atheism in Russia, that Our Lady came to Fatima . . . and that we must awaken to what She can do for us as She reaches out to touch our hands and our hearts with Her Rosary and Scapular.

COMMUNISM

This book was written and first published during the time of the Spanish civil war. A few paragraphs have been added to the book but hardly anything written at that time has been changed. The present edition (1953) looks back on Stalin's death and on the following paragraphs with the satisfaction that during the fifteen years since they were written the great climax of which they speak has been coming ever closer. There is hope now . . . with millions upon millions of members of the Blue Army using the Scapular and the Rosary in almost every nation on earth . . . that victory may be soon, and some readers of these lines will actually be looking back from a world at peace upon this crisis between the West and the East. When they do, they should remember how it was that God delivered them . . . through the humble Virgin Mother.

Satan, through international Communism, has now organized his forces on the whole earth to wipe out the Kingdom of Christ. In the Middle Ages, bloody bearers of the crescent knocked at the eastern gates of Europe. Today, the hammer and sickle are found on the very table of government in very many capitols of the world, while, at the gates of Europe, a vast nation is arming to bring about World Revolution. Russia has fought eleven aggressive wars since 1918 and her dictator, Stalin, has already murdered over seven million people in his own country. The *Posener Zeitungsdienst* reported in 1938 that since the results of the Russian Godless campaign had not been commensurate with the money expended, that year was to be a decisive one; instead of 840,000 rubles expended before, now 1,300,000 are spent for foreign atheistic organization; 1,500 speakers were prepared to deliver addresses in cities and villages. The League of Fighting Godless numbers over 2,000,000 members. They have even succeeded in making Catholic France their ally . . .

"It will take time, but despite Satan and his supporters, I will reign" . . . Despite all the efforts of Atheism with its millions of machine-armed soldiers and vast corps of serpent-tongued propagandists, Jesus will come through Mary.

The union of Communism seeks to destroy the Reign of Christ from the earth; Mary's Confraternity is a union to establish that Reign. The "League of Fighting Godless" in Russia has 2,000,000 men armed with modernity's best materials and driven by a satanic hatred; Mary's Confraternity numbers millions of members and they are armed with true devotion to Mary and can be driven by the love of the Sacred Heart. And if the enemy does have a World Revolution, its mockery will be but the prelude to our final victory.

Anti-religious forces gathered in sanguine confusion throughout Europe today are much like that Red Menace of Mohammedanism, which also once threatened Christianity. For eight centuries a vast, anti-Christian force, it threatened to wipe out Catholicity and to establish the harem in place of the Christian home. Father Lord remarks its similarity to Communism in that "it had pledged itself to wipe out the memory of Christ and to stable its horses in Christian Cathedrals from which it had dragged the Cross of Christ. It was a completely dictatorial government; it regarded itself as international, extending beyond the bond of race or tribe; its banner was almost prophetic: a red field on which was a crescent not at all unlike the curve of the sickle which today is the symbol of another red flag." [10]

The first Red Menace got its primary hold in Spain. There the Turks actually turned the Catholic Churches into Mosques, put Christian women into harems, reduced Christian men to slavery.

What drove the Turks out of Spain? What destroyed their overwhelming power and made their formidable threats vanish like a sultry cloud of black smoke caught in the sudden swirl of a strong wind? The answer is, simply, Mary. When the outlook was blackest, the Church had unanimous recourse to the Queen of Victory, to Her who invariably crushes Satan, and since Mary but awaits our prayers to strike down our enemies, the red peril was driven back to safe distances. At Lepanto, the victory wrought visibly through Mary gave rise to the Feast of *Our Lady of the Rosary* and in Spain to two feasts: that of *Our Lady of Mercy* (or, often, Our Lady of Ransom) and that of the *Patronage of Mary*.

When the Mohammedans were driven from Spain and the Iberian Peninsula, their last holdings were in Portugal. And among the last preparing to leave was a maiden named Fatima, a descendant of Mohammed. She was in love with a Christian, and was attracted to the Christian faith.

When her countrymen finally left Portugal, Fatima remained. She became a Christian, married, and the village of Fatima to this day bears her name

. . . because it was there that she and her husband settled.

In 1917, at the very time of the first bloodshed of the Communist revolution in Moscow, Our Blessed Lady appeared in that village of Fatima, subsequently asked for consecration to Her Immaculate Heart (holding out Her Scapular) and for meditative recitation of the Rosary, while promising the ultimate conversion of the Communists and world peace.

Today She is known as "Our Lady of Fatima." Statues to her under this title may be found in churches and chapels all over the world. "And why?" asks Bishop Sheen. "Why should Our Lady be known by the same name as a converted descendant of Mohammed?"

And the Bishop answered (in his address at the International Congress preparatory to the closing of the Holy Year at Fatima, in October, 1951, at which the present writer also spoke on a similar subject): It is because Our Lady came for the conversion not merely of the carriers of the hammer and the sickle, but also the carriers of the crescent and star. And in the defeats of the two great "Red Forces" of history which we have seen already on the Iberian Peninsula . . . we may now hope to see something better and greater than defeat: Conversion.

Again, the modern Red Menace got its first hold, west of Russia, in Spain. But *under the banner of Our Lady of Mount Carmel and the Sacred Heart,* Catholicity has defeated it there! Yes, despite the cooperation of the great bear, despite the advantage of holding the reins of government, Communism has gone down into the dust before the meager armies struggling for religious independence and for the reign of Christ. Generalissimo Franco, in a dispatch to the newly-elected Pius XII, could say: "Filial congratulations *from a Catholic Spain* which fights against the enemies of the Faith." Ramon Franco, after he had made the first non-stop flight from Palos to Buenos Aires, telegraphed to his family that he owed the success of his flight *"to the special patronage of Our Lady of Mount Carmel."* During the war against Communism, the Generalissimo dedicated his fleet to Our Lady of Mount Carmel. In the first year of the war, a correspondent informed us that whole regiments of the Christian forces "went into battle *with the badge of the Sacred Heart and the Scapular of Our Lady of Mount Carmel worn openly on their breasts."* [11] So much did Spanish soldiers clamor for Scapulars that all the makers could barely meet the demand with bursting activity! In that first year of the war (1936), over half a million Scapulars were bought from the Burgos convent alone. And the Carmelite Fathers of Spain tell us that letters constantly poured in from the front describing Scapular miracles. A Carmelite Father showed the present author a letter from a classmate who was directly fired upon by *four machine guns,* from a distance of 700 or 800 metres for a period of fifteen minutes, and who wrote in a token of gratitude to Our Lady of the Scapular, saying simply: "And here I am." These are partial explanations of the one great fact: *Communism has been unseated in Spain.* When the

Catholic troops marched triumphantly into Madrid, under orders they immediately repaired to the church of Our Lady of the Scapular to thank the Scapular Queen for their victory over Communism.

Never has history so repeated itself. Divine Providence seems to speak a message through these bloody events.

The final battle against the first Red Menace, Mohammedanism, took place at Lepanto. During the battle, the Pope and all the people in Rome prayed the Rosary. Our Lady of Mount Carmel revealed to a hidden Carmelite nun that since members of the Christian armies were not worthy of winning the battle, she should offer herself as a victim.[12] The victory came and Saint Pius V, in Rome, knew of it miraculously. The red peril vanished; Mary had borne down with Her heel. The world was saved.

Communism, the second Red Menace, was recently driven from Spain. What about the rest of the world? What about the Lepanto struggle?

Almost every nation on earth is in unbelievable turmoil. Dictatorships are throttling the Church in their mad march to self-aggrandizement. A short time ago, Catholics in Poland, in Spain, in Holland, in Belgium, or in almost any country except Germany and Russia, were somewhat secure in the practice and furthering of their faith. How many are secure now? At the side of blood and carnage, paganism streaks across Europe from Spain to Finland, from England to Rome, wreaking devastation and seizing power. At the unexpected spiritual battle that must now be fought, at this new Lepanto, what about Mary's Scapular allies? Are they not going to consecrate themselves wholly to Her, victims for the salvation of the world, instruments in the hands of Mary that She may bring about the Reign of Her Son? The vast Third International and its pagan allies may effect their world revolution. But will not that revolution be but a prelude to our final victory under the banner of the Sacred Heart, through Mary in the Scapular? God said in Paradise: "I shall place enmities between thee and the Woman, thy seed and Her seed, and She shall crush thy head!" Mary has placed Her sign of battle and victory upon us; Saint Joseph protects those who fight under that Sign. *Against Satan in his Red threats, we have Mary in Her Scapular Promise.*

> *"With what arms and with what army are we going to resist seventy thousand men?" asked a Captain, expressing the thought of all.*
> *"This is the hope of our victory," replied the Governor (Jerome Hurruitinet) earnestly, taking his Scapular and lifting it up on his sword. And then they met and defeated the overwhelming army of Turks sent by the famous General Zigala to conquer their province, Calabria. (Revista Carmelitana, Volume XI, No. 11.)*

PEACE THROUGH THE SCAPULAR

Just before the Spanish war, the Carmelite who founded an "Apostolate of the Scapular" in Spain penned significant words: "No mother," he remarked, "can take delight in seeing her sons at war;

on the contrary, She longs that they may ever live in holy peace and harmony; if something should arise among them to keep them apart, She intervenes as arbitratrix to make peace among her children. Indeed, she holds secrets for doing this which only a mother knows. And in order to preserve peace among Her children, brothers of the Blessed Virgin, the Virgin of Carmel, our Mother, gave us all the same garment: such is the Holy Scapular which Mary wished to be, besides an alliance of peace, a sign of Her Confraternity." [13]

Saint Peter Damian says of Mary that She is "The Mother of True Peace." [14] For centuries the whole Church has designated Her Scapular the *Signum Pacis,* Sign of Peace. Hence, in our days when peace among nations is so precarious, the Scapular takes on a fresh value in our eyes, i.e., a value Mary has placed there appears in new brilliance. That Sign commandeers the prayers of the Mediatrix of All Grace and since peace is effected solely by the disposition of hearts, something Grace alone can effect, the Scapular can be said to be indeed a most powerful Sign of Peace.

It is to be remembered that absence of conflict is not a state of peace. When a strong man bullies a weak one to quiet submission, although there is no conflict there is no peace. *Only one thing* can bring about world peace, and that is *prayer.* World conferences which are convened to forestall the crazed thirst of a dictator only feed his ego. Only God, Who alone has power over human wills, can prevent war. It is only prayer that will release the graces "stored

in all their fulness in the bosom of Mary." [15] The
Scapular is a *Promise* of Mary's Prayer!

GRIGNION DE MONTFORT

At the time of the Sacred Heart revelations to
Saint Margaret Mary, in a Carmelite Church where
a miraculous picture of the Madonna was venerated,
a certain Grignion de Montfort received a most remarkable mission. He felt called by Our Lady to
become the apostle of a perfect devotion to Her and
set out to preach "Mary and the Cross" up and down
the hills of France.

Blessed Grignion's inspirations on a perfect devotion to Mary, contained in his world-famous book,
"True Devotion to the Blessed Virgin," seems to be
a Marian Gospel. As he had himself prophesied,
Satan tried to prevent the appearance of the book
by concealing it for over a hundred years. But despite a looseness of style and a haphazard organization, revealing its great truths in anything but an
unquestionably clear light, this little book has spread
through the world and awakened a new appreciation
of Mary. The formula of the book is: "To Jesus
through Mary," and its battle-cry: "The Reign of
Jesus through Mary!" Both have become the
formula and battle-cry of thousands of Marian souls.

Grignion de Montfort received his vocation from
the Queen of the Scapular and, two years before his
birth, a most holy Carmelite had published a Latin
book in which the very devotion which Blessed Grignion was called to popularize had been explained in
its more advanced aspects.[16] Nor was "To Jesus

through Mary" a new formula to Carmel even then; the Brothers of Mary had appreciated their Scapular union for centuries. Saint Peter Thomas had completely practiced this devotion in the century after the Scapular Vision.

But Blessed Grignion was chosen to be the apostle and the prophet of only a True Devotion, apart from Mary's perfect aid to that devotion, Her Scapular. Even though he knew the value of Mary's Scapular alliance (Scapular, Rosary and Little Chapelet seem to have been his favorite means of devotion) [17] he suggested the wearing of a chain as an exterior reminder and material aid for realizing the formula, "To Jesus through Mary." If we ask why, perhaps we are like the saintly Carmelite of Grignion's time who asked Mary why She did not make known Her Immaculate Conception and received the answer: "It is saved for the latter days of the Church." [18]

The little chains of Grignion de Montfort are almost indicative of the somewhat pessimistic spirituality of the eighteenth century. Today, the optimism of Saint Francis de Sales characterizes spirituality and instead of the *Miserere* we hear the *Magnificat,* instead of material chains to remind us of Marian slavery, we would prefer the cords of the Scapular to remind us of the arms of Mary embracing Her children.[19]

The Scapular alliance is a True Devotion to Mary and is furthermore the best, the child-like means of perfecting that devotion in ourselves. These facts have always been patent to a few. Now that thousands more deeply appreciate union with the Sacred

Heart (largely from Saint Margaret Mary) and alliance with Mary as the easiest and best way to this union (mostly from Bl. Grignion) they are more likely to appreciate Mary's Scapular union. The reason why the Scapular devotion has been almost hidden until modern days beneath a barrage of controversy is probably the same as the reason why Blessed Grignion's exposé of True Devotion to Mary lay silent, for over a century, in an unsearched coffer. "Devotion to Mary is not the prominent characteristic of our religion which it ought to be," says Father Faber; *"Jesus is not known because Mary is forgotten."* [20] Hence we can understand why Satan has fought to hide Mary from us, to drown the gospel of perfect devotion to Her and to obscure the beauties of Her great gift, the Scapular; we can also understand why there is now hope that soon not only will these things become better known but that the use of the Scapular to go to Jesus through Mary will become intimately woven into our Catholic lives and a daily realization of its inner secrets of sanctification will come to be taken as a very matter of course.

LOURDES

We may wonder that France should be the recipient of such great favors as the revelation of the *Sacred Heart,* the possession of the first church in Europe dedicated to *Saint Joseph,* and of being the scene of *Mary's great apparitions* at Lourdes. However, God works in a single place only because we men are localized. The effects go out through the whole world. In former days, Palestine was the scene of all His wonders. France being the "first daughter of the Church" (i.e., the first country converted to the Church in the West), we should not be surprised that it is there that we witness great wonders.

The victory of Loigny over the enemies of France, paralleled by the victory of Spain over the enemies of the world, seems prophetic. In the setting of the French Revolution followed by the mysterious consecration of a nation to the Sacred Heart, the words "It will take time but I will reign despite Satan and his supporters" seem to be directed at Russia. The World Revolution which Russia has pledged herself to unloose will not be permanent. It will be followed by a Lepanto struggle and the turn of events in Spain is a warning to the Reds; they have allied themselves with Satan and it is not man whom they attack, but GOD. We pity them because they have been misled by the slogan, "We have only our chains to lose!" and in reality they are forging eternal ones. The world is bearing rapidly towards a crucial, uncompromising choice. "We are about to pass over into the hinterland of darkness and ruin," is the opinion of Monsignor Fulton Sheen; "as a matter of fact, there has been a greater de-Christianization in the last one hundred years than in any other given period of Christian history." [21] Nicholas Berdyaev said: "Christianity is entering upon an entirely new era. Henceforth it will be impossible to live the Faith only exteriorly, to stop short at a ceremonial devotion. Believers will have to make their beliefs real on weekdays as well as on Sunday mornings. They will have to defend their religion by the example of their lives, by their personalities, by their faithfulness to Christ and His principles." [22]

Almost anywhere we turn, idolatry is rampant. Growing millions bow down minute after minute before the altars of Baal. Will not the crucial moment be a forced choice between God or Baal, Christ or Materialism? The growing force of a new literature from deeply spiritual men seems to cry from the pinnacle of the world with Elian fire: "If God be God, follow Him!" Do we not expect a prophetical appearance of Mary Immaculate from the sea of chaos, rising above the world in a manifestation of Her might, Her invincible power to crush Materialism beneath Her heel and to pour down rains of saving grace?

Mary *has* thus appeared, at Lourdes, in southern France.

Lourdes is the New Carmel where the cloud of a hidden Virgin takes form and the Immaculate declares Herself. This new Mount Carmel, of the West, symbolizes a Virgin whom God no longer chooses to keep hidden. Its spring of miraculous waters is a symbol of the might of Heaven's Queen, of the gentleness of a perfect human Mother, of the desire of Mary, born in Her heart on Calvary, to be more known and more loved in these latter days. In the numerous cures of bodies and souls, in the prayerful atmosphere, one senses at Lourdes the whole mission of the Immaculate: *to draw souls to Christ*.

But who is this Virgin of Lourdes? Is there any

other title under which She appears and leaves a Symbol of Her *might,* of Her *gentleness* as the sweetest of Mothers, and of *Her desire to be more loved?* Father Petitot, O. P., gives us the answer in his *Apparitions de Notre-Dame à Bernadette:* "Before the institution of pilgrimages to Lourdes there was no invocation more honored in all Christianity than that of *Our Lady of Mount Carmel.* At the time in which Bernadette lived, in all Christian families most children bore the *Brown Scapular* on their breasts." [23]

On the Silver Jubilee of "Our Lady of Lourdes," twenty-five years to the day after Mary's last appearance to Saint Bernadette, representatives from every part of the Catholic World gathered at the grotto in the Pyrenees to honor the Virgin who had appeared there to declare that She was the Immaculate Conception. The Bishop of Nimes, a learned and saintly man, was the preacher. Addressing that great concourse, inspired to the occasion, he said: "Lourdes is the new Carmel where Mary has deigned to appear. Mary Immaculate appeared to the prophet upon the lofty heights of Carmel, raising Herself from the midst of the waves under the image of a light cloud. But at Lourdes the cloud assumes color, it is transfigured, Mary is arrayed in light and splendor. She speaks and reveals Her name, She designates Herself, She declares: *'I am the Immaculate Conception.'* O! Sacred mountain of the Orient! great though thy glory, thou hast beheld but the shadow of what here today we possess in reality!" [24]

To the prelates, ecclesiastics of all ranks, and thousands of devout pilgrims from every corner of the world, standing at the grotto Monseigneur Besson explained Mary's great Scapular Promise in detail. He then recalled the words of Our Lady to Saint Cyril, spoken as Her Carmelites were about to come to the West: "It is the will of My Divine Son, and Mine also, that the family of Carmel be not a light for Syria and Palestine alone; its rays must illumine the entire world!" [25] For on July 16th, 1251, She had given us the Scapular, and on the same day, in 1858, Saint Bernadette felt within her the summons to the grotto at Lourdes. Just as the evening angelus was about to sound from the parish belfry on the Feast of Our Lady of Mount Carmel, she started and cried: "There She is! There She is! She is saluting us! She is smiling across the boarding!" And Bernadette said that though Mary but glanced and smiled, full of tenderness, *She had never been so beautiful.*[26] After the apparitions, Bernadette wished to become a Carmelite. Since tuberculosis prevented her and since she had no other desire, she became indifferent as to what happened to her.

Mary disappeared only from the gaze of Bernadette. She has mystically left Herself in a Sign by which, as the Immaculate, She illumines not Carmel alone, but the whole world. And the world needs to be illumined by Her! She is the Morning Star whose rising heralds the Sun. By the power of Lourdes, are we not again forcibly reminded of the foot-shaped cloud that gave birth to the first of all Mary's titles? In these troublous times, pressing the Scapular to our hearts we repeat in an active sense: "Thou shalt lie in wait for Her heel, and She shall crush thy head."

Lourdes in France is to us as Carmel in Palestine was to the Israelites. They saw a prophecy and received material salvation; we see a fulfillment and receive spiritual salvation. Saving rain-water flowed after the prophetic vision of the Virgin who crushes Satan with Her heel; at Lourdes, a fountain is opened whose waters are again a miraculous symbol.

Be it accurate or not, probably the vision of the Venerable Catherine Emmerick casts some light upon the mysterious connection between the prophetic vision on Carmel and the speaking vision at Lourdes. Long before Bernadette saw Mary on that mountain in the Pyrenees, Catherine had the following vision:

"I then saw another vision. I saw, after the hermits began to live in community, a monk on his knees in his cell. The Mother of God appeared to him with the Infant Jesus on Her arm. *She looked exactly like the statue that I had seen by the spring of the mountain.* She gave him an article of dress in which was a square opening for the head to pass through. It fell in front over the breast. It was shining with light, the colors brown and white intermingling, *as in the vestment* of the High-Priest that Zacharias *showed to Saint Joseph.* On the straps that went over the shoulders were letters inscribed. Mary spoke long to the monk. When She vanished and he returned to himself, he was filled with emotion on seeing himself clothed with the Scapular. I saw him assemble his brethren and show it to them.

"Then I had a vision of a Church festival on Mount Carmel. I saw in the choirs of the Church Triumphant as the first of the ancient hermits, and yet separated from them, Elias. Under his feet were the words, 'Elias, Prophet.' I did not see these pictures one after another, and I felt that a great number of years lay between them, especially between the vision of the reception of the Scapular and the feast, for the latter seemed to me to belong to our own day. *Over the spring where once stood Mary's statue, now arose a convent and its church.* The spring was in the middle of the latter and above the altar was the Mother of God with the Infant Jesus just as She appeared to the hermit, living and moving in dazzling splendor. Innumerable little silken pictures hung at Her sides attached in pairs by two cords and glancing like leaves of a tree in the sunshine, in the splendor which radiated from Mary. The holy Virgin was surrounded by the angelic choirs and at Her feet, *above the tabernacle* wherein reposed the Blessed Sacrament, *hung the large Scapular* She had given the hermit in vision. On all sides were ranged choirs of holy Carmelites, men and women, the most ancient in white and brown striped habits, the others in such as are now worn. I saw, too, the Carmelite Order, monks and nuns of the present day celebrating the feast in their several convents, either in choir or elsewhere, but all upon earth." [27]

Mary has given Herself to us in life and death with a Heavenly Garment, She has given us Saint Joseph to be our special father and model, and all that She may draw us, through Herself, to Jesus in the tabernacle. Since She is now to bring about the reign of Christ by rendering us holy in His sight and hence causing Him to find His joy in our hearts, She no longer hides the fact that She is our way to Him: "My beloved children, I who have taken you under My mantle, *I am the Immaculate Conception.*"

> "*A great sign appeared in Heaven: a woman clothed with the sun, and the moon under her feet, and on Her head a crown of twelve stars: and being with child, She cried travailing in birth, and was in pain to be delivered. And there was seen another sign in Heaven: and behold a great red dragon, having seven heads, and ten horns: and on his heads seven diadems: and his tail drew the third part of the stars from Heaven and cast them to the earth. And the dragon stood before the woman who was ready to be delivered that, when She should be delivered, he might devour Her son: and She brought forth a man child who was to rule all nations with an iron rod: and Her son was taken up to God, and to His throne.*"—The Apocalypse.

CHAPTER FIFTEEN

Fatima and an Important Explanation

IN THE very beginning of this book, when we first treated of the meaning of the Scapular Promise (page 15), we stressed that the whole meaning of the Scapular Promise "derives from the fact that the wearing of the Scapular is a true devotion to Mary and that hence *merely to be enrolled in the Scapular is not enough to obtain the benefits of the Scapular.*"

A century ago Blessed Claude de la Colombiere, S. J., the coadjutor to Saint Margaret Mary Alacoque in making known the revelations of the Sacred Heart, made known something about the Immaculate Heart of Mary of which we are today being happily reminded:

"*In that celebrated Promise* (of the Scapular)," said Blessed Claude, "*Mary reveals all the tenderness of Her Heart.*"

That is why we gave this book its phrased, even unwieldy, title: MARY in Her Scapular Promise.

The promises attached to the Scapular are in themselves very wonderful, but they are not as wonderful as the *lessons* which Our Lady, through the Scapular Devotion, holds out to us: The great value of the promise is only a consequence to the Scapular's value as *an instrument of true devotion to Mary.*

In 1950, commemorating the seventh centennial of the apparition of Our Lady to Saint Simon Stock, Pope Pius XII wrote an apostolic letter on the Scapular devotion in which His Holiness referred to the Scapular as: *"Sign of Consecration to the Immaculate Heart of Mary,* which we are particularly recommending in these perilous times."

His Holiness referred hardly at all to the promise which rewards this consecration.

It is possible for us to be blinded by the Scapular Promise in itself and perhaps fail to see that this great promise is merely a reward and "Seal of Approval" to the devotion which the wearing of the Scapular opens to us.

While we would expect most readers to be sensible enough to realize that the Scapular . . . as we say often in these pages . . . is not a talisman or charm, still there may be some who would be so impressed by the Sabbatine Privilege and the Promise of Salvation that they would mistake the *sign* of the reward for *the devotion which is to be rewarded.*

In Her great gift of the Scapular, Our Lady has given us a sign of a happy death. But what is far more important: She has given us the sign of a Marian way of life . . . of consecration to Her Immaculate Heart, and all that living up to such a consecration implies. And because it is FIRST a sign of consecration . . . the Scapular is, in the second place, a sign of predestination.

In stressing this so earnestly here, we do not imply

that the great promise is not attached to the wearing of the sign.

The promise is explicit: *"Whosoever dies clothed in this Scapular shall not suffer the fires of hell."*

If the promise were not explicit . . . if it were not that those dying in the Scapular had Our Lady's solemn assurance of the Grace of a happy death . . . the whole seven centuries of tradition and teaching on the subject would be a mockery. Furthermore, in all these seven hundred years, it has never been known that a single person dying in the Scapular has died impenitently, and many papal pronouncements and celestial favors, as we have cited elsewhere, bear testimony to this.

However, two very important truths must ever be in our minds as we consider this great promise:

(1) The Scapular bears Our Lady's promise of a Happy Death *only because it is a sign of consecration to Her Immaculate Heart.* It is a sign of salvation because it is an instrument of sanctification through Mary who always and necessarily leads us to Our Lord;

(2) Even as it is a great grace to *have* this gift of Our Lady, *it is an even greater grace* to understand it, to use it, *and to persevere in it.* And those of us who mistake *the sign* of the reward for *the devotion* which is rewarded, those who wear the Scapular without entering into the way of life of which it is the symbol and aid, *should not anticipate dying in it.*

Experience of seven hundred years in this devotion has borne out these facts again and again. In addition to some of the instances cited in this book, consider the "decline" of the Scapular Devotion in the early part of the twentieth century. Although one or two secondary causes can be cited, would Our Lord and His Blessed Mother have permitted this decline if people had not come to forget the meaning of the Scapular Devotion? Was it not true that after many centuries we had begun to think of the Scapular Promise . . . rather than of *Mary* in Her Scapular Promise?

When Our Lady held the Scapular in Her hands seven hundred years ago, appearing to Saint Simon Stock, She was . . . in a manner of speaking . . . *holding in Her hands the devotion of consecration to Her.* When She made Her promise . . . She was making the promise, as we have explained in Chapter Two, for the devotion of affiliation to Her.

A look back at the state of Marian devotion in those days will explain this. Today there are many Marian Orders in the Church, but seven hundred years ago there was only one: the Carmelites. And the Scapular was a part of their habit. It was, therefore, a symbol of the highest form of dedication to the Blessed Virgin at that time: Total consecration and imitation.

It was this *consecration* which Our Lady was encouraging and extending to all the faithful when She appeared to St. Simon with the most reducible part of the Carmelite habit, promising a Happy Death to *anyone* ("Whosoever") who would persevere in it until death.

We repeat that those who read this book, especially if they really understand the last few chapters, will hardly need this important reminder. They will be, by their present knowledge of the devotion, in a better position to use the Scapular intelligently. But those to whom we zealously give the Scapular, that we may put them beneath Our Lady's protecting Mantle, may not understand if we tell them just about the promise . . . without sufficiently emphasizing the consecration. In giving the Scapular alone without the proper explanation we will not be doing them a complete service because, as cannot be stressed too earnestly: To *persevere* in wearing the Scapular *is a grace* . . . and *only those who wear the Scapular properly can be expected to obtain this grace.*

We can think of all the thousands of people who are enrolled in the Scapular at First Communion, who wear it for awhile, but who are without it in later years . . . and at the hour of death. There may even be some persons near and dear to the reader who do not have the Scapular on at this moment . . . even though enrolled at First Communion or during a Mission.

Therefore, if we esteem the Scapular Promise . . . if we value the great consolation we may have at the hour of death because of this pledge from Our Heavenly Mother . . . then we should do all in our power to make sure that neither we nor our loved ones mistake the sign of the reward for the devotion rewarded.

Perhaps this is more important today . . . when the world needs Our Lady so much . . . more than ever before in history. At Fatima Our Lady asked for con-

secration to Her Immaculate Heart. She also asked
for the Rosary, for Communions of Reparation. But
above all, She asked for the fulfillment of daily
spiritual duty. She asked us . . . promising the conversion of Russia and world peace as a reward . . .
to lead a good life, keep the Commandments of God
and of the Church, and She explained that *it was to
HELP us* in this that She asked us to be consecrated
to Her Immaculate Heart and to say the Rosary.

In the final apparition of Fatima She appeared in
the sky holding in Her hands the Brown Scapular . . .
the sign of that consecration which She asked of us
. . . the sign which is one of the aids to a devout
Christian life. It is an aid which, if used in the sense
we have described, can bring the sinner back to the
Sacraments. It is an aid which can help us, during
the day, to be faithful to Our Lord by remaining
close to His Mother.

It is an *important* aid. It is very important. Otherwise Our Lady would not have held it in Her hands
in the final apparition of Fatima. It would not be
the most privileged and indulgenced sacramental in
the Church, together with the Rosary, and com-
memorated by a Universal Feast. It would not be all
the things we know it to be.

But it is important only because, together with the
Rosary, it is one of the hands which Our Lady holds
out to bring us, in this modern age, back and closer
to God. As Our Blessed Lord hangs upon the cross,
where He has been nailed by twentieth century sins
(nails driven home gleefully by militant atheism
organized through the world by International Com-

munism) Our Blessed Mother comes from the foot of
the cross with extended hands . . . the hands of the
Scapular and the Rosary . . . to draw the world back
to Calvary . . . that we may help Her to draw out the
nails, weather the brief crisis of the atomic age, and
survive to hail the risen Christ and to proclaim His
Reign throughout the earth.

Unless the world appreciates this inner meaning
of the devotions of the Scapular and the Rosary, the
coming of Our Lady of Fatima is in vain.

Unless we understand that the Rosary is important
because (as Pope Leo XIII said) "The mysteries of
the Rosary comprise all the essential mysteries of
Christianity" . . . unless we are sincere in pleading
through the Rosary *for the grace and inspiration to
live up to those mysteries* . . . then we have mistaken
the symbol for the essence, figure for reality.

Likewise, unless we understand that the Scapular
is a sign of consecration to Our Lady and the sign of
"Mary, Our Way," then once again we have mistaken shadow for substance.

In a word . . . unless we really understand these
devotions, Our Lady will have held out Her hands to
us from the skies of Fatima, to help us save the world,
and we will have reached for the shadow of Her
hands and missed.

We can conclude this important thought in no
better way than by considering the explanation of
the latest appearance of Our Lady of the Scapular
. . . on October 13, 1917, at Fatima . . . as given by
"Lucia," the one who talked to Our Lady in the
Fatima apparitions and to whom Our Lady said:

"You are to remain on earth because through you I will make known the fullness of My message."

On August 15th, 1950, this only living survivor of the three children of Fatima, Sister Mary of the Immaculate Heart, in the Carmelite Cloister in Coimbra, Portugal (formerly Lucia dos Santos), was asked *why* Our Lady held the Scapular in Her hands in the final apparition of Fatima, and she answered: *"Because Our Lady wants all to wear the Scapular."*

When asked for a further explanation, she explained: *"The reason* for this is that the Scapular is *our sign of consecration to the Immaculate Heart of Mary."*

Asked if the Scapular is as necessary in fulfillment of the requests of Our Lady of Fatima as the Rosary, Sister replied: "The Scapular and the Rosary are inseparable."

(This is a phase of the Scapular which we have emphasized in Chapter Six: "Scapular Prayer." For as the Scapular is an aid to prayer because it enables us to speak more intimately to Our Lady . . . it is most especially an aid to the devout and proper recitation of the Rosary . . . the form of prayer to Our Lady most desired by Her in these days because of its simplicity and power to inspire and lead us to a devout Christian life.)

The Rosary, like the Scapular, bears many rich promises of Our Lady. Also, as in the case of the Scapular, this is only because the Rosary is a great aid from Our Lady *to a devout way of life.* It is a way She has provided to help us find Our Lord. It is one of Her extended hands to lead us to Him.

Only in as far as we understand this fundamental fact can we hope to grasp these blessed hands . . . the Rosary and the Scapular . . . which Our Blessed Mother holds out to us from the skies of Fatima and from the corridors of seven hundred years of use in the Church, now a promise of salvation not only for ourselves, but for the world.*

* We speak very little of the apparitions of Fatima here, and throughout this book, for two reasons. One is cited in the last chapter and the other is that the present writer has subsequently written another book on this subject titled: "Russia Will Be Converted."

Above, Lucia (with whose help the Blue Army pledge was written) with Pope Paul VI at Fatima, May 13, 1967.

And She Shall Crush Thy Head

CALL ALL *Israel to Mount Carmel.* Yes, all the vast Israel of Mary that is marked by Her Sign of Salvation, summon each of its members to the Mount of Prayer. "God wishes to give rain to the face of the earth"—a face that has mostly turned from Him and is being weaned by tremendous anti-Christian forces to the sole contemplation of its earthly self. Jesus is to come a second time through Mary. And this glorious "Woman" of earliest prophecy and ultimate fulfillment rises over that mount to make Herself available to us in a Sign of Salvation.

"Receive, My beloved son, this Scapular of thy Order; whosoever dies clothed in this shall not suffer eternal fires." Mary seems to say: "Receive this garment which I make the sign of membership in My family and now, let everyone enter this family because I promise that there I shall not see them lost; I open My mantle to My children that they may come under it and be saved; beneath it, by their homage, confidence and love, may they silently show themselves to be, before all the powers of the world, My most beloved children. Saint Gertrude saw a vision of leopards and tigers being turned into lambs beneath My mantle, for My Scapular is not a Sign of Salvation merely because I made a promise but also because I keep a promise; it is My will to make My

199

children saints. If only they would give Me their hearts! I but need their cooperation to release all the graces which God has enclosed in My heart and how I long for them but to say the word that I may shower the world with such rains of grace that Satan will be swept from human souls by the very force of its torrent. Even as My prayer has been made necessary for the flow of Grace, so has the prayer of My children been made the one condition for its dispensation through Me. I have given the Scapular that, gathered 'neath My mantle of their own will, My children might thereby show that they *willed* to be saved; and that is the only prayer I need to save them. O that now they should express the will to see all the world saved! If only they would enter more closely into their union with Me that they, too, might become mediators and complete the work of salvation. My son thirsts; since He has made Me Mediatrix, I thirst! Behold a Sign of Salvation. This Sign of union and of love which I place upon you, My beloved, is a proclamation of My thirst. By it I assure your Salvation and as much as it is a Sign of your great victory is it a sign of My great thirst."

Eight hundred and sixty years before Christ, after the little foot-shaped cloud had arisen over Mount Carmel, the whole sky was soon overcast and there fell a great rain. God had not said of the Immaculate, who was to rise pure out of the human sea which Satan had tainted at its very source in Paradise, that there would be enmities between Her alone and Satan alone; He also said: "Between thy seed and Her seed." So, upon the appearance of the Sign

of the Immaculate crushing Satan with Her heel—
his pride by Her humility—we naturally expect to
see Her bring forth Her seed to fight and conquer
with Her. And She has. That Virgin of Mount Carmel has clothed us in the Scapular, a Sign of Her:
the humble Mother, the Victorious Queen. For is it
not at once the Sign of Her seed and a Sign of Victory? Does not Satan hate us with every bit of hatred
he has for Her? Yes, and he hates this Sign which
at once proclaims us to be the seed of Mary and
crushes his pride by its simplicity and invincible
power. Father Faber remarks that it seems to be
that by it God brings to nought the things that are
by things that almost, as it were, are not; [1] He places
the head of the black prince of the world beneath
the heel of that humble Virgin who started his defeat
with Her simple words: "Behold the handmaid of
the Lord."

Today it is no longer a prophecy of the Immaculate that appears over Mount Carmel, but a proclamation of the Immaculate from Rome that is
confirmed at Lourdes. Although prefigured to
Elias as almost its first revelation, the Immaculate
Conception was a mystery destined, like devotion to
the Sacred Heart, "for the latter days." And why
has Our Blessed Lady come to identify Herself as
the Virgin of that ancient prophecy, declaring: "I
am the Immaculate Conception"?

It is not a coincidence that a final appeal for the
love of men be made by Our Lord showing forth His
Sacred Heart while at the same time the Immaculate Conception appears. It is no more a coincidence

than that Jesus was found the first time, on earth, with Mary: "And seeing the star they rejoiced, and entering in they found the Infant with Mary His Mother." . . . The easiest and most perfect way to find the Sacred Heart is to follow a miraculous sign that will lead us to Mary. On finding Her, we find Her divine Child. It is easiest because Mary is our Mother, given to us by Jesus just to bring us to Him; it is most perfect because, realizing our imperfections, we clothe ourselves with perfection, with Mary Immaculate, and approach Jesus in personal humility and Marian purity. Is it any wonder that the Pope who declared Mary's Immaculate Conception a dogma should have wondered if "anyone can fail to see that there is no more perfect and no surer way to unite all mankind in Christ, than Mary"?

When Jesus was first found on earth with Mary, Joseph was there. Two creatures assisted at His first coming. And Joseph appears today, too. It was through the Immaculate that Jesus came to us and it is through Her that He wills that we should come to Him. He makes Joseph our assistant. This great Saint, who on earth was the third person of the trinity between Mary, Jesus and himself, is the perfect model of "To Jesus through Mary," a living explanation of the fact that *the Infant* was found *with Mary,* His Mother. He also works with Mary to assist us by his powerful prayer.

It should excite our deepest gratitude that God has dipped the Scapular into the golden mysteries of Jesus, Mary and Joseph, to be a star-resplendent, beckoning sign of union with the Immaculate, of the victory of the Sacred Heart, and of modelling after Saint Joseph. How true it is that He has left nothing undone to win our love. Not only has He made us the seed of a Victorious Virgin while painfully opening for us the gates of Heaven, but through Mary He has rendered Satan practically powerless before us! He has made an exception to tainted nature that we might become allied to that exception and partake in its invincibility.

But there are millions of souls who are not allied to Mary. There are those who do not choose to be born in love of Mary, but have given themselves to Satan that this serpent might bring them forth in sin and nurse them with his hatred. They are fellow-men whose fists are clenched by wills that know not God. *But they also have been redeemed by the Blood of Christ!* They are the lost sheep while we, beneath Mary's Mantle, are the secure flock. Our Lord would more rejoice over having one of them join us, one of them freed from the thorns of hatred, than over any other good deeds we might do for Him. And what is necessary to the Mediatrix of all Grace that the hearts of those men be lighted by Grace? What is lacking to Her that She cannot crush the head of the serpent as it rises to sting and poison them unto eternal death? *She needs our prayer.*

"Pray for one another that you may be saved," Saint James wrote in his Epistle. Because for a reason of love, Jesus demands our cooperation in order to save others who do not pray. It is because He chooses to act only with us that He did not redeem the human race alone; He made the Immaculate

Conception, the Mother of the living as Eve is the mother of the dead, to be "Co-Redemptrix." It is because He desires that the Head should not operate except through the body that, although the efficient and formal Cause of grace, He does not dispense grace alone but has raised the Immaculate Representative of man to be His "Mediatrix." And "He awaits the prayer of one little soul," says Saint Therese to our wonder, "to save a multitude of others."[2] Is it any wonder, then, that the Co-Redemptrix, the Mediatrix, the Mother of the living, should have marked us for Her seed with a Sign of Salvation that constitutes a continual prayer?

In Marian Prayer lies not only our victory but the complete victory of the Sacred Heart. Willing to make those who have received Him through Mary like unto Himself even in the most sublime work of coming through Her to be the Salvation of the World, Our Lord has made our prayers necessary for the release of the graces that He has enclosed in Her bosom. He wants the children to share even in the very greatest glory of their Mother: to enter into Her Apostolate. Before crying: "I thirst!" He had also said: "Behold thy Mother!"

When we enter into Mary's Scapular alliance we can almost feel that best of mothers folding us to Her breast to guard us in life, at death, and even until She has completely brought us to eternal happiness. As we stop to consider it, do we not feel a burning desire welling up in our hearts, a longing to respond to such a love? Do we not feel, as it is only human for a child to feel, a spiritual thirst to answer Mary's motherly action of fighting the serpent which lunges at us, to take Her very sign of our salvation and, with it, to enter into the fray? She protects us, conquers Satan for us, by Her prayer. Since She thirsts for souls who have not turned to Her, what can we do to conquer Satan for Her?

Burning with the knowledge of Mary's thirst for souls, many Catholics, by word and deed, continually pursue the quest of would-be lost souls and joyfully present to Her the sheep which they find. God is infinitely pleased for He has created Mary that men might have salvation through Her, and Mary's love for those apostolic children is boundless.

Thus many great Marian organizations have sprung up in less than eighty years. Thousands are responding to a growing realization in the Church that Jesus is to come a second time through Mary. We hear such active societies as the Children of Mary, or the Legion of Mary, professing their firm conviction that within twenty-five years they can bring the world to the Sacred Heart through Mary.

Although wearing the Scapular, these glorious men and women may have overlooked the fact that Mary has therein given them the sacrament of their apostolate! Like Francis Yepés, they may capitalize on the assurance of Salvation which Mary has attached to the Scapular devotion and become apostles authorized by Mary in words that are even an assurance of complete success: "Receive, My beloved children, this Scapular; whosoever dies clothed in it shall not suffer the fires of hell."

But of all the modern organizations under the banner of the Immaculate, one has spread with a rapidity and universality that would even rival the most ancient confraternity of the Scapular. What is its purpose? "To release," says one of its founders, the Reverend Father Ramière, S. J., "to cause a downpour of the graces which have been placed in all their fulness in the bosom of Mary *by the humility of our prayers.*" [3] Thus, this society has not so much taken for its model the Virgin physically crushing Satan beneath Her heel (as, for example, has the Legion of Mary), but its office is to imitate the Blessed Virgin at prayer. It is the most Marian of all the recent societies; it imitates Mary in Her seclusion at Nazareth and at Her throne in Heaven. And thus taking to itself Our Lady's essential mission it calls itself THE APOSTLESHIP OF PRAYER.

There are millions who cannot preach sermons, or rescue ensnared sinners from the slavery of vice, or pursue some of the other practices of the active apostolate to which they apparently are not called. But they are far from being deprived of the chance of making the gift of souls to their Mother. On the contrary, we have the assurance of "God's messenger to the Twentieth Century" that God awaits but *one prayer,* from a Marian heart, *to save a multitude of souls!* Saint Alphonsus tells us of a holy religious who made *a* novena to Mary in order to save *one thousand* souls, and when towards the end of the novena she concluded that she was asking too much and would lessen the number, Mary appeared to her chidingly and told her that *already* one thousand souls had entered Heaven that would otherwise have died in the state of sin![4] If the Scapular Promise is invaluable in the active apostolate, what shall we say of it, what words can describe the value of Mary in the Scapular Promise to the Apostolate of Prayer!

"O Jesus, through the Most Pure Heart of Mary, I offer Thee my prayers, works, and sufferings of this day for all the intentions of Thy Sacred Heart." Such is, in brief, the morning offering which constitutes the main feature of the Apostleship of Prayer. It is an offering, a consecration of one's thoughts, words, actions and sufferings to Mary that She may best apply them to the interest of the Sacred Heart. "Through the Most Pure Heart of Mary" means "in union with the Most Pure Heart of Mary." We give *everything* to God through Mary, when we unite ourselves to Her. If our union is constant, this perfect prayer, this apostolate of prayer, is thereby constantly practiced.

The Scapular is the Sign of a constant union with Mary. *Only our intention is necessary* to make that union a consecration to Her of everything we do. If we make that intention, especially if we frequently renew it, *everything we do shall be done, in God's eyes, by Mary.* Will this save the world? Will this bring about the Reign of Christ quickly? For our answer we have only to look at the effects wrought in souls by *one* person who thus did everything through Mary, ever deepening the Scapular union to give Jesus a pure and childlike love. We have only to look at the spiritual victories of Saint Therese of Lisieux.

The Bishop of Besançon said that if the Morning

Offering of the Apostleship of Prayer were extended
through the day, the Reign of Christ would appear
very, very soon.[5] That is just what the Scapular can
do: it can enable us to extend that glorious Offering
through the whole day. And since "through Mary"
means "in union with Mary," the one who uses his
continual Scapular-union with Mary to extend the
Morning Offering through the day, causes his most
ordinary actions to take on great spiritual value. A
bricklayer, laying bricks all his life and doing little
else, may thus attain the missionary power and glory
of a Saint Therese! All God asks from us in requir-
ing us to "pray always" is that we perform the actions *that our station in life requires of us,* with the
intention of pleasing Him. And in order that our
daily actions become, through Mary, this prayer of
little things done in a way most pleasing to Jesus, we
need but unite ourselves to Mary. One with Her, our
actions become those of *other Marys.* We thus do all
things in the way most pleasing to God: we do them
in and *by* Mary. At the same time we become
apostles *for* our Mother, because that intention to
make our daily actions a prayer by union with Her
is all that She requires to save the world.

Therefore, to frequently recall our Scapular union
with Mary is to extend the Offering of the Apostleship of Prayer through the day. It is to actually
live it.

This, then, is the most excellent way to return love
for love. A life of union with Mary, so that everything one does is applied by Mary to the best interests of the Sacred Heart of Her Son, is not only a

state of personal perfection but a supreme apostolate. For Saint Therese says: "Is not the apostolate of prayer higher, as one might say, than that of preaching? How beautiful is our vocation! It is for us, it is for Carmel to preserve the 'salt of the earth' . . . The Creator of the universe awaits the prayer of one poor little soul to save a multitude of others, redeemed like her at the price of His Blood." Can we refuse this?

Using the Scapular to make frequent acts of mystical union with the Blessed Virgin (morally present to us through it), "we become like sharp arrows in the hand of the powerful Mary to pierce Her enemies." [6] *Although we never do more than our ordinary actions,* says Blessed Grignion de Montfort, "we storm against the world, strike the devil with his crew, and strike further and further, for life or for death, with the two-edged sword of the word of God." [7] For what was the word spoken by God against Satan in Paradise? "I shall place enmities between thee and the Woman, thy seed and Her seed, and She shall crush thy head." Later, at an inspired moment a great Prophet saw a foot-shaped cloud rise purely from the sea "and the heavens were filled and there fell a great rain." Even as the rainfall was the salvation of Israel after the prophetic sign of the Immaculate, so may we cause another humble Sign of Victory to become truly the salvation of the world through Her.

In instituting a devotion that is a continual prayer, the Blessed Virgin made a promise. She has marked us for Her seed, making the appreciative wearing of

Her Sign an efficacious victory over all the schemed and diabolically complicated programs of the great mind of Lucifer. Thus the greatest pride is crushed by those two pieces of cloth like the head of a serpent ground beneath the heel. Although Satan lies in wait here on earth to sink the fangs of cunning temptations into our hearts, Mary, through a devotion so simple, bears us up to an eternal paradise from which he can never cause us to fall.

Yes, Saint Augustine is right. Mary does mystically bear us in Her womb to bring us forth to Eternal Salvation. Saint Bernardine explained that when the Blessed Virgin gave the consent which was expected by the Eternal Word before becoming Her Son, "She from that moment *asked our salvation of God with intense ardor,* and took it to heart in such a way that, from that moment, She bore us in Her womb." [8] And the saintly Pope Pius X, referring to the Great Woman whom Saint John describes in the Apocalypse as travailing in childbirth, remarks: "John saw the Most Holy Mother of God, *already in eternal happiness,* yet travailing in a mysterious childbirth. What birth was it? Surely it was the birth of us who, still in exile, are yet to be generated to perfect charity of God and to eternal happiness. And the birth-pains show the love and desire with which the Virgin from Heaven above watches over us and strives with unwearying prayer to bring about the completion of the number of the elect." [9]

The present reader surely needs no urging to clothe himself in Mary's Scapular. He knows its greatness too well. But what about that aid which

Mary needs to save the millions in danger of eternal perdition—an aid that only Her children can give Her? What about the fact that Our Lord said to Saint Mary Magdalen de Pazzi: "O, see how most men are within the grasp of the demon! See how his jaw is open to devour them! Far from avoiding it, they go and cast themselves in, and there is no one who will escape *if My elect do not save them by their prayers.*" [10]

"So many souls are lost," Our Lady said at Fatima, "because there is no one to pray and to make sacrifice for them."

Mary has marked us for Her elect, members of Her family in which Saint Mary Magdalen de Pazzi is a leader. Our Heavenly Mother thirsts for souls because Jesus thirsts and has given the mission of assuaging that thirst to Her and to us through Her. Being the Head of that divine Body, the living Church, He has made His Mother the neck and us the members. His Sacred Heart is the Driving Power. Mary's Immaculate Heart is one with It so that we, Her children, may be one with It by simply being united to Her. That is *our* vocation, *our* apostolate, *our* purpose.

When the Little Flower cast about in the theatre of her longing to save souls, anxiously searching the meaning of a life of ordinary actions, she concluded that she wanted to be the heart of the Mystical Body by her Marian prayer.

Saint Therese's choice shows us the way: the Mystical Body needs a Heart. Only our daily actions, performed through Mary, can complete that Heart.

Chapter Sixteen

A heart receives its meaning from all the members of the body whose life-stream it receives and circulates. The Heart of the Mystical Body is not complete until the Redeemer, the Redemptrix and the redeemed give full meaning to It. Hence the Church continually asks us to turn to Mary that the life of the Church may be more intense in us. Saint Therese is a model. The life of the Church became so intense in her by union with Mary that veritably did she alone save thousands of souls! And she said: "I will do nothing which all little souls cannot imitate . . ." [11]

With the thirst of Her Divine Son for souls, imparted to Her on Calvary, Mary's Immaculate Heart burns with a longing to save them. But not only Her prayer has been made necessary, but our prayer is needed too. And in the Scapular Promise does Mary not beg us for our cooperative prayer? Can we not hear Her saying: "In order to save you, I only needed your will to the extent that you voluntarily took this Scapular. O, that you should now will to see all the world saved and make this Sign a constant expression of that will! My Son thirsts. Since He has made Me Mediatrix, I thirst! Behold a Sign of Salvation! This Sign of Union and Love which I place upon you, My beloved, is a proclamation of My thirst. By it I assure your Salvation and as much as it is a Sign of your great victory, it is a sign of My great thirst."

Victory? Yes, by the Scapular Mary renders Satan impotent against us. By our entering into our union with Mary during the day, we release the graces which God has enclosed in Her Heart.

Saint Grignion de Montfort, the apostle of the Scapular's silent lesson of "To Jesus through Mary," made a prophecy. He said:

> ". . . But the power of Mary over all the devils will especially break out in the latter times, when Satan will lay his snares against Her poor children, whom She will raise up to make war against him. They shall be little and poor in the world's esteem, and abased before all, like the heel, trodden underfoot and persecuted as the heel is by the other members of the body. But in return for this they shall be rich in the Grace of God, which Mary will distribute to them abundantly. They shall be great and exalted before God in sanctity, superior to all other creatures by their animated zeal, and leaning so strongly on the divine succor, that, with the humility of their heel, IN UNION WITH MARY, they shall crush the head of the devil and cause Jesus Christ to triumph." [12]

In union with Mary, how could they fail to cause Jesus to triumph? Mary but wants to be united to our hearts to give us Her strength, Her "oneness" with the Sacred Heart which is hypostatically united to God.

Saint Teresa of Avila, Carmel's great reformer, was enabled to do more than make the prophecy which Saint Grignon proclaimed. She had an actual vision of the latter days of the Church. If we are wondering who those great Saints of Mary are, whom Grignon describes as united to Mary and forming Her heel, shall we be surprised to learn that they will be wearers of Mary's Scapular, the members of that great family of Mary which is marked by Her Sign of Salvation? Saint Teresa says:

> *"Once, in prayer, with much recollection, sweetness and repose, I saw myself, as it seemed to me, surrounded with angels and was close to God. I* began to intercede with His Majesty on behalf of the Church, *and I was given to understand the great services* which the Scapular family would render in the latter days.
>
> *"On another occasion, when I was at Matins in choir, six or seven persons who seemed to me to be of this Family appeared and stood before me with swords in their hands. The meaning of that, as I think, is that they are to be defenders of the faith; for at another time, when I was in prayer, I fell into a trance and stood in spirit on a wide plain, where many persons were fighting with great zeal. Their faces were beautiful and, as it were, on fire. Many they laid. low on the ground and defeated, others they killed. It seemed to me a battle with heretics."* [13]

Yes, a battle with the atheist forces who can be universally defeated and laid to the ground by Mary. It is Her office to crush them by the humility of Her prayer.

As Christ has placed all His merits in Her hands to be distributed by Her to us, we children of that Immaculate Virgin of Mount Carmel may place all our satisfactions in Her hands to be distributed by Her for Him. What joy this will give to the best of Mothers! It will mean the assuaging, through Her, of a thirst which called us along with Her to an apostolate on Calvary. Yes, our prayers of union with Mary can cause that rain of Grace from the Mediatrix which will slake, with thousands upon thousands of souls, the thirst of an Infinite Heart.

The modern appearances of Our Lady, the revelations of present day saints, the Marian literature, the awakening giant of a new and tremendous Marian devotion throughout the Church, are all indications that God is asking us to come to Him through our Mediatrix. It is sure that we shall not answer this call with the victorious Sign of membership in Mary's family without opposition. Mary's great Scapular Promise is hated in itself and if ever Satan and his crew fought against Mary, and against that Promise, what will be their efforts against that crushing foot—that humbly invincible family of Mary—turned into an Apostolate!

It is by Mary that the Salvation of the world was begun and it is by Mary that it must be consummated.

In the days when the world sighed for a Saviour it ignorantly reveled in material pleasures while He was born at their very doorsteps in a stable. So in these troublesome times the Marian Apostolate is producing Salvation where men see days of ordinary actions, but where God reaps multitudes of souls.

Just as a humble Nazarene Virgin, in the dim brightness of a stable, stooped down to draw swaddling clothes protectingly about the precious Body of the Incarnate God, so She stooped from Heaven, in the dim brightness of repressed glory, to draw spiritual clothes protectingly around the Mystical Body. When She stooped over the manger this most glorious Mother spoke (to Him Who knew Her inmost thought) an ineffable word of melting love and adoration. When She stooped from Heaven to clothe the Mystical Body of this Son, where It lay in the manger of the world and bathed in the light of the universe, as She wrapped Her double garment about It, She spoke Her word of love: *"Behold a Sign of Salvation!"*

> *"I know well that the Saints have spoken most encouragingly on the powerful protection of Mary, but enlightened and holy as they have been they are, after all, only men; only servitors of the Queen. Here it is the Queen Herself, who, in that celebrated revelation, reveals all the tenderness of Her Heart to Saint Simon Stock! Those great Saints have assured me that with Mary to protect my interests I need fear nothing. That does not suffice me. I wish to know if She does protect my interests. Yes! She gives me proof unequivocal. I have but to glance at my Scapular, TANGIBLE PROOF BEFORE MY EYES, and recall the Promise attached to its devout wearing: 'Whosoever dies clothed in this shall not suffer eternal fire.'"* [14]

BL. CLAUDE, S. J.

Although the Blue Army began in 1947, it was not formally organized until 1950. In that year the Most Rev. Joseph Correia da Silva, Bishop of Fatima, sent the statue below as his personal gift to the U.S. Centre of the Blue Army with the prayer: "Through it may the Blessed Mother grant... to the Blue Army and to all those associated with it... a flood of graces and favors." During the ensuing years, the mantle of the statue changed to blue, although the tunic... with the same pigment... remained white. The Bishop's secretary said of the aged Bishop: "It seemed that he clung to life until the Blue Army was established in the world."

CHAPTER SEVENTEEN

Saint Dominic's Prophecy

SEVERAL TIMES we have suggested that the reader might be surprised at the great emphasis given to a devotion as apparently simple as the Brown Scapular. But one of the most interesting testimonies to the importance of the Scapular devotion today has so far been scarcely mentioned.

In the pages of an ancient history of the Carmelite Order (written in mediaeval Latin by a forgotten writer named Ventimiglia) the author of this book found the following account:

Three famous men of God met on a street corner in Rome. They were Friar Dominic, busy gathering recruits to a new Religious Order of Preachers; Brother Francis, the friend of birds and beasts and especially dear to the poor; and Angelus, who had been invited to Rome from Mount Carmel, in Palestine, because of his fame as a preacher.

At their chance meeting, by the light of the Holy Spirit each of the three men recognized each other and, in the course of their conversation (as recorded by various followers who were present), they made prophecies to each other. Saint Angelus foretold the stigmata of Saint Francis, and Saint Dominic said:

"One day, Brother Angelus, to your Order of Carmel the Most Blessed Virgin Mary will give a devotion to be known as the Brown Scapular, and to my Order of Preachers She will give a devotion to be known as the Rosary. AND ONE DAY, THROUGH THE ROSARY AND THE SCAPULAR, SHE WILL SAVE THE WORLD."

Since he was gathering material for a book on the Scapular Devotion, the present writer was deeply impressed on finding this story in Ventimiglia's History . . . and he was especially impressed by the prophecy of St. Dominic.

Yet that prophecy appears nowhere in the past sixteen chapters which (with the exception of Chapter Fifteen and a few paragraphs referring to Fatima) were for thirteen years the total of this book . . . unchanged through several printings totaling more than 70,000 copies.

St. Dominic's "prophecy" was omitted repeatedly, through all those printings and years, despite the fact that the author came later to know that today a Chapel, on that very street corner in Rome, commemorates the meeting of St. Dominic, St. Francis of Assisi, and St. Angelus as described by Ventimiglia.

Therefore, why the omission?

Why were not the words *"Through the Rosary and the Scapular She will save the world"* blazoned across the pages and even perhaps included in the title of this book?

There are two reasons.

First, the writer was not sure that Ventimiglia was

a reliable historian. But that would not have been sufficient reason to omit any reference whatever to a story of such importance. The second and graver reason is that, even though he was himself convinced that the Scapular Devotion is important, the writer was by no means convinced that the Scapular could be one of two instruments to SAVE THE WORLD. He did not believe that the Scapular, or *any* sacramental, could be *that* important.

Thus in the year of Our Lord 1940, *Mary in Her Scapular Promise* was published without the "finding" in Ventimiglia's history mentioned. And it was omitted through one reprinting after another.

In 1941, following the first success of the book, the author told the story of how it had all come about in a sequel titled *From a Morning Prayer*.

This second book told how a saintly Carmelite lay-brother, after what he thought was a vision, commissioned the author to make the Scapular devotion better known, and especially the practice of using the Scapular while making the Morning Offering (to emphasize the offering through the Immaculate Heart of Mary) . . . carrying the offering through the day, in all our sacrifices, thoughts and deeds . . . walking always under the mantle of Mary and thus doing all, as She did on earth, for God and for the Reign of Christ in all hearts.

A few months after this second book was published Archbishop Finbar Ryan, of Trinidad, wrote a letter to the writer, congratulating him, and adding: "While I congratulate you on this book, *From a Morning Prayer*, I cannot help wondering why you have made no mention of OUR LADY OF FATIMA . . . since in the last apparition at Fatima Our Lady held the Brown Scapular in Her hands."

The author, like most people in the United States at that time, had heard only vague rumors about Our Lady of Fatima.

It happened that Archbishop Ryan had written the first book in the English language on the Fatima apparitions. It had just come off the press in Dublin and the copy which he then sent to the present writer opened a whole new view of Our Lady's role in the modern world.

Therein . . . for the first time . . . the author read of Our Lady's words at Fatima: *"Only the Blessed Virgin can save you"* . . . and of Her final appearances during the miracle of the sun: First, dressed in white and *holding the Rosary,* while Saint Joseph, holding the Infant, stood at Her side; second, dressed in blue, while Our Lord appeared at Her side; third and finally, dressed in the brown of Carmel, *holding the Brown Scapular* in Her hands . . . while Our Lord, who had not changed from the second apparition, slowly raised His hand and blessed the great crowd in the Cova below.

With feelings he can hardly describe the author realized that, at Fatima, Our Lady had confirmed this prophecy recorded by Ventimiglia. Holding the Rosary and the Scapular, She had come to say: "Only the Blessed Virgin can save you." *And She promised the conversion of Russia and world peace if Her requests would be heard.*

Although the previous chapter . . . and, indeed,

most of this book . . . was completed in 1939, *before* the author had heard about Fatima, it would seem actually to have been based on the Fatima message.

Perhaps the explanation of this, as well as of many other events which have contributed to a sudden "bursting forth" of the Fatima Apostolate all over the world in this second half of the twentieth century, will be found solely in the designs and powers of Our Lady Herself.

If only the Blessed Virgin can save the world today, naturally it is because God wills that we establish *the Reign of Christ* only *through Mary*.

And for that reason her two most privileged, most indulgenced, most universal, most ancient and most valued sacramentals . . . *the Rosary and the Brown Scapular* . . . assume a greater importance than ever before in history.

The strongest evidence of this cannot be measured in words confirmed by footnotes and references. *It is confirmed by the action of Our Lady in the world,* now, all about us. Each one has the evidence he sees daily in many conversions and in the apostolates of the hour.

In 1940, following the first publication of this book, the V. Rev. Gabriel N. Pausbach, Assistant General of the Carmelite Order, founded a *Scapular Apostolate* at the Church of Our Lady of the Scapular of Mount Carmel, at 338 East 29th Street, in New York City. (It is now the National Shrine of Our Lady of the Scapular.)

Within three years, the morning offering dictated by the lay-brother (as described in "From a Morning

Prayer") was printed three million times. Year after year, month after month, the devotion of the Scapular began to flourish more and more throughout the United States. Units of the *Scapular Apostolate* sprang up in most major cities. In 1953, the unit in Detroit was making and distributing over 400,000 Scapulars in one year . . . a number in that one city which was equal to almost half of the number of Scapulars used annually in the entire nation before 1940. The unit in Cleveland, Ohio, was making and distributing over 100,000 a year. The total number of Scapulars produced annually now in the entire country is in the many millions.

Although the children of Fatima had said, in 1917, that Our Lady appeared in the final vision with the Scapular (as Archbishop Ryan published in his book, *Our Lady of Fatima*), attention of early writers focused rather on the prophecies of Our Lady of Fatima, on authenticity of the apparitions, on the miracle of the sun, cures at Fatima, etc. . . . and very little authoritative work was done on the meaning of the message, particularly as regarded the multiple apparitions on the day of the miracle of the sun.

In 1946, in an interview lasting several hours, the present writer asked "Lucia," sole survivor of the three children who saw Our Lady of Fatima, about that last apparition on October 13 of Our Lady of the Scapular.

She confirmed what Archbishop Ryan and a few other early writers on the subject had said. But we found, especially among some of the "authorities" on Fatima in the United States, an inexplicable hostility to the inclusion of the Scapular in the Fatima message. We feel today that this was in the Providence of God because it led to an incontrovertible statement on the subject from "Lucia" on the Feast of the Assumption, August 15, 1950.

It was in an interview which two Carmelite Fathers had with "Lucia," who had herself become a Carmelite nun with the name, Sister Mary of the Immaculate Heart, in the Carmel of Coimbra, Portugal. The interrogator in the interview was the V. Rev. Howard Rafferty, O. Carm., Provincial Director of the Third Order Secular of the Carmelite Province of the Most Pure Heart of Mary in the United States. He began by remarking that most of the recent writers on Fatima (up to 1950) made no mention of the Scapular, and some even denied that the Scapular Devotion was a part of the Fatima message.

"Oh, they are wrong!" Lucia exclaimed

Shortly after the apparitions in 1917, Lucia told interrogators that the vision of Our Lady of the Scapular on October 17, "Looked just like the picture of Our Lady of Mount Carmel in the parish church."

This picture is the very old, universally-used portrayal of Our Lady in the Carmelite Habit, with the Infant Jesus holding the little Scapular in His Hands and angels descending into Purgatory . . . apparently at Our Lady's bidding . . . freeing souls from the flames. From an explanation which Lucia gave to the present writer in 1946 it is apparent that reference in 1917 to this picture referred only to the

Habit and general appearance of Our Lady. In the Fatima vision Our Lady Herself held the Scapular in Her hands and, instead of the Infant in Her arms, Our Lord stood at Her side, in the fulness of manhood, blessing the crowd below.

"Why do you think Our Lady appeared with the Scapular in this last vision?" Lucia was asked in 1950.

"Because," Lucia replied, *"She wants everyone to wear the Scapular."*

One Fatima apostolate, known as "The Blue Army" . . . which spread farthest in the world . . . insisted on the wearing of the Brown Scapular as a sign of Consecration to the Immaculate Heart of Mary.

In France, leaders of this apostolate met great opposition to the wearing of the Scapular. Some said: "Cannot we just as well wear the Miraculous Medal or any sign of devotion to Our Lady to show our consecration to Her?"

Therefore they sent a petition to the Bishop of Fatima, asking His Excellency to settle this matter once and for all. They wrote: "On this question we cannot have a sufficient and practical certainty unless through the intervention of Holy Church. If, Your Excellency, you could let us know your thought, it would help us to adopt a line of conduct and to work on public opinion for the better understanding of Our Lady's desires."

In the July, 1953, issue of the VOICE OF FATIMA, published as the official voice of the Bishop of Fatima, simultaneously in five languages, on the front page, in bold type, the Bishop of Fatima gave a detailed answer. It is only fitting that that answer, in its entirety, be quoted here because . . . in the first definitive statement on this subject by the Bishop of Fatima . . . His Excellency pierced the three most controversial points of the Scapular Devotion:

STATEMENT OF THE BISHOP OF FATIMA

(1) **Substitution of a medal for the Scapular.** This was authorized by a decree of the Holy Office, December 16, 1910. According to this decree "in wearing the medal one participates, as with the Scapular proper, in all the Indulgences and in all the privileges, not excepting that called the Sabbatine Privilege of the Scapular of Mount Carmel."

But the same decree begins with the following words: "As the holy Scapular contributes efficaciously to the progress of the spiritual life among the faithful and is in great favor amongst them, the Holy Father desires that the habitual form be maintained." (Act. Ap. Sedis, III, 22.)

Therefore, the use of the medal instead of the Scapular is permitted. But it was the wish of Blessed Pius X, who granted the permission, and of the Pontiffs who succeeded him, that preference should be given to the use of the Scapular. Our Lady's wishes cannot be different from the wishes of the Vicar of Her Son.

Try then to use the Scapular (even with the medal as many people do in Portugal). You will find that in practice it is not so inconvenient to use as might at first appear. And besides, if on occasions it is necessary to make a little sacrifice and win a battle over human respect . . . so much the better.

(II) **The Scapular of Mount Carmel or another?** There is no doubt that, in Portugal at least, the Scapular of Mount Carmel is the Scapular par excellence. When we speak of the Scapular we have only one in mind. Very probably it is the oldest of all and is a model and example to all others. In the minds of the faithful it is the one which best symbolizes participation in a religious Order and subordination to Mary.

His Holiness Pope Pius XII, happily reigning, in a letter which he wrote to the Generals of the Carmelite Order, on the occasion of the seventh centenary of the Scapular of Mount Carmel on February 11, 1950, said explicitly that we should all recognize that the Scapular is the sign of our "consecration to the most holy Heart of the Immaculate Virgin." His Holiness on this occasion is most certainly referring to the Scapular of Mount Carmel and to no other. The Blue Army then was right in choosing, proposing and propagating the Scapular of Carmel—and not one of the many others which exist in the Church—as a sign of the consecration of its members to the Immaculate Heart of Mary.

(III) **The Apparition of Our Lady of Mount Carmel.** The fact that Lucia, on October 13, 1917, saw the Blessed Virgin as She is generally represented under the invocation of Our Lady of Mount Carmel, lends itself to many interpretations. There is nothing to prevent people seeing in this fact the desire of Our Lady to be better known, loved and invoked as Queen of Mount Carmel, or that the use of Her Scapular, with all its obligations, be considered one of the points of Her message, as a very efficacious means of salvation of souls and of the world.

The "Blue Army," which we mentioned above, and to which the Bishop of Fatima refers in his statement on the Scapular, has caused *millions* of people, all over the world, to promise to wear the Scapular always as their sign of consecration to the Immaculate Heart of Mary. The "pledge" used by the Blue Army was first used in a "March of Pledges" which the present author inaugurated in the Scapular Apostolate in New York, in the fall of 1947.

Even as the "March of Pledges" was beginning (netting one and three-quarter million pledges in the United States in twelve months), Our Lady Herself was "founding" the *Blue Army* elsewhere in America . . . the Army which would, by the use of the Rosary and Scapular and fulfillment of daily duty . . . extend Her power over the earth even into the very heart of the Communist empire.

It began in the last weeks of 1946 when a devout priest, worn by years of intense labor in the Lord's Vineyard, was dying of a serious heart ailment. Five heart specialists had decided that he had but a few months to live.

In this extremity, the good priest . . . Father Harold V. Colgan, of Saint Mary's Church, in Plainfield, N. J. . . . had recourse to Our Lady. He had ever loved Her with a simple, childlike devotion, and he had been one of the best promoters of Our Lady's Sodality among the secular clergy in America. *"If you cure me,"* he said to Her, *"I will give you the rest of my life . . . to do your work."*

And he was cured.

At once he began to do three things in his parish:

He resolved that not one of his parishioners would die without the Scapular. He strove to establish the daily Rosary in every home. And he asked everyone in his parish to thus form for Our Lady, by their devotion and above all by their good daily lives, a small Marian army against the red armies of Communism. He asked them to wear some little outward

sign of blue as a token that they had pledged themselves to this . . . that they were saying the Rosary,
wearing the Scapular, and offering up their daily
duties in a spirit of reparation for the sins of the
world.

The number of daily Communions in the parish
doubled in one year. Masses on the first Saturday
filled the Church (which seats 1,000) to capacity.
Everyone in the parish could see and could feel the
spiritual light this Marian devotion had brought to
them. They could see it above all in the greatly
increased number of people at the Communion rail.

Other pastors in the area heard of it and took up
the idea of the "Blue Army." And coincidentally
there was a growing friendship between the author
of this book and Father Colgan while the idea of the
Blue Army . . . as though by magic . . . began to
spread far and wide.

In January, 1950, he and Father Colgan published
the first issue of SOUL Magazine, official organ of
the Blue Army.

In May, Father had a private audience with His
Holiness, Pope Pius XII, and presented the Holy
Father with the first three issues of SOUL. After
perusing them the Holy Father said (on May 8,
1950):

"As the World Leader against Communism . . . I
gladly give my blessing to you, to the Blue Army, and
to all readers of SOUL Magazine."

Within three years the Blue Army leaped to over
two million signed members in the United States,
and more than twice that number in other nations.

On December 8, 1952, the Army sponsored a Fatima demonstration in Paris . . . where the apostolate of Fatima had been slow to get under way . . . and it was the largest Catholic demonstration in Paris since World War II. Subsequently an European Committee of the Blue Army was founded and Father Andrew Fuhs, of Germany, known in Europe as "The Radio Priest of the Saarland," was elected president. One of the best-loved Catholic-Action papers of France, *L'Homme Noveau,* changed its colors from red and black to BLUE and black, and became the official organ of the Blue Army for France.

Books and pamphlets on the Blue Army sprang up all over the world, even in many little-known dialects of Africa and many parts of Asia.

On October 13, 1951, when the Holy Father closed the Holy Year at Fatima for all the world outside of Rome, the Blue Army was the only formal apostolate honored by representation at the International Congress held in Portugal in preparation for the closing of the Holy Year. The following year the Blue Army acquired land immediately adjacent to the Basilica of Fatima for an International Headquarters and, on February 13, 1953, the Most Rev. Jose Correia da Silva, Bishop of Leiria-Fatima, officially became Honorary President of the Blue Army Headquarters at Fatima and *International Spiritual Director of the Blue Army.*

On July 3, 1953, when the Blue Army in France was meeting difficulties, particularly because of its insistence on the use of the Scapular as a means of consecration to the Immaculate Heart of Mary, the

Dean of Cardinals . . . First Prelate of the Church after the Holy Father . . . His Eminence, Eugene Cardinal Tisserant, issued a rather lengthy statement in which he said:

"Today, more than ever, Christ wills that we have everything from Him through His mother, according to the word of Saint Bernard recalled recently by His Holiness, Pope Pius XII. An apostolic movement multiplies its efficacy to the degree that it consecrates itself more expressly to Mary . . . And the Blue Army . . . constitutes a sort of spiritual mobilization for a most precise objective: the conversion of the peoples of the Union of Soviet Socialist Republics and their satellites. The Blue Army is a response to the demands of the Blessed Virgin of Fatima . . . The Blue Army enters into the spirit of the Church in working to bring about a personal living . . . by men and women . . . of the consecration which the Sovereign Pontiff has willed to make of the entire world, and most particularly of the peoples of the Union of Soviet Socialist Republics, to the Immaculate Heart of Mary.

"Is it not *necessary*," (italics our own) the Cardinal continues further on, "that all those Catholics who still enjoy their liberty should arrange themselves like an army around Our Lady, *stronger against evil than an army arranged in battle,* yet tender like the most tender of mothers, *if they wish mercy to be poured forth abundantly upon all sinners?* . . .

"Therefore, with all my strength, I appeal for a more and more widespread and more popular imploration of Our Lady, certain that only the intervention of the most Blessed Virgin Mary will obtain the necessary graces of conversion and re-awaken an authentic sense of unity in Christ and in the Church for a true world peace." (See SOUL Magazine, Vol. 4, No. 5.)

By July 16, 1953, when it closed its first public meeting in the United States (in Plainfield, N. J.), the Blue Army was already one of the largest Marian apostolates in the world, with International Headquarters at Fatima and National Headquarters in twenty-seven other nations.

And what is it that the millions of members of this vast apostolate promise?

Well . . . perhaps if the reader does not already know . . . he or she would enjoy the climactic surprise of reading the exact words of that pledge (as it is used precisely in almost every known corner of the world):

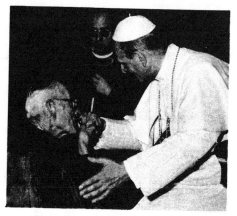

Above: Msgr. Colgan, founder of the Blue Army, greeting Pope Paul VI.

MY BLUE ARMY PLEDGE TO OUR LADY

DEAREST Queen-Mother, who didst appear at Fatima and promise on three conditions to convert Russia and bring peace to all mankind, I hereby solemnly pledge to Thy Immaculate Heart that in reparation for the sins Thou didst so sorrowfully lament, I shall offer up each day the sacrifices necessary for fulfillment of daily duty; I shall say a part of the Rosary each day while pondering the mysteries; I shall wear the Scapular as profession of this pledge and as an act of consecration to Thee. I also promise to renew this pledge especially in moments of temptation.

....

(Signature)

THIS PLEDGE IS NOT A VOW AND DOES NOT BIND UNDER SIN.

Even now the power of the Blue Army . . . a power altogether spiritual, even as it is profoundly Marian . . . is being felt in the world. It is not difficult, in view of the mountainous evidence which it would take many more pages to record, to feel that the power of evil in the world, as it has manifested itself especially in the concentration of military atheism in Moscow, is slowly and inexorably falling back before the greater power of Mary.

"One day,. through the Rosary and the Scapular, She will save the world," Saint Dominic is reported to have said.

And whether the Saint did actually speak those words seven hundred years ago or not, they were recorded in a book at least more than two centuries ago. And from the skies of Fatima Our Blessed Mother today holds down to us . . . *the Rosary and the Scapular* . . . with the promise of great conversions and of world peace.

N. B.: National offices of the Blue Army Apostolate in the United States are at Ave Maria Institute, Washington, New Jersey.

*T*he preacher of the revelations made to Saint Margaret Mary was her confessor, the Blessed Claude de la Colombiere. Our Lord instructed Saint Margaret Mary to confide her revelations to this holy Jesuit that the world might thus receive them. And this Blessed Claude, rightly known as "The Apostle of the Sacred Heart," has been given another title by his admirers. He has also become known as "The Apostle of the Scapular."

So ardently did Blessed Claude love our Lady's livery that he declared it to constitute the greatest of devotions to Mary with values beyond our comprehension. "Because all forms of our love for the Blessed Virgin cannot be equally agreeable to Her," he declared, "I aver without a moment's hesitation that the Scapular is most favored of all. I maintain that there is no devotion which renders our Salvation so certain and none to which we ought to attach ourselves with more confidence and zeal . . ."

SUMMARY

"Without any preliminary reasoning, we see that one never honors the Queen of Heaven in vain; that She rewards Her faithful servants magnificently; and that the cult of Mary is extremely important to our own good and to the good of the entire Church. In the Scapular, this lesson *is* not given to us in any haphazard way, but solemnly. It comes to us in the history of a great religious Order and from the action of that Order in the Church. With what bounty does Mary intervene here! . . . We can well apply to Mary, and to the Order that is Hers, those words of holy Scripture: *She shall be exalted in the midst of Her own people . . . She shall have praise from the multitude of the elect . . I came out of the mouth of the Most High, the firstborn before all creatures . . . I made that in the heavens there should rise light that never faileth, and as a cloud I covered the earth . . . He that made me rested in my tabernacle and He said to me: Let thy dwelling be in Jacob, and thy inheritance in Israel, and take root in my elect . . . And I took root in an honorable people, and in the portion of my God his inheritance, and my abode is in the full assembly of saints . . . As the vine I have brought forth a pleasant perfume, and my flowers are the fruit of glory and abundance . . . In me is all grace of the way and of the truth, in me is all hope of life and of virtue . . . Come over to me, all ye that desire me, and be filled with my fruits . . . He that hearkeneth to me shall not be confounded . . . He that worketh by me shall not sin . . . They that explain me shall have life eternal . . . Like an aqueduct I came out of paradise . . . I said: I will water my garden . . . And behold my brook became a great river . . . For I make doctrine to shine forth to all as the morning light . . . I will penetrate to all the lower parts of the earth, and will behold all that sleep, and will enlighten all that hope in the Lord . . . See ye that I have not labored for myself only, but for all that seek out the truth* (Eccli., xxiv). (From Father Meschler's *L'Année Ecclésiastique*, Vol. II, pg. 173.)

235

BIBLIOGRAPHY

Section One: HISTORICITY

BARTHOLOMEW, A. S. MARIA, O.D.C.: *Origen de la devocion del Escapulario del Carmen.* pp. 223, Barcelona, 1871.

BOSTIUS, O. CARM., ARNOLD: *De Patronatu B. V. Mariae.* 1479 edito. (In chapter ten there is much historical information on the Scapular. Together with Grossi's *"clam* portaverunt," notice his "clandestine." This may be more than a picturesque way of saying "parvum scapulare."

CHERON, O. CARM., JOHN: *Privilegiati Scapularis et Visionis S. Simonis Stockii Vindiciae,* pp. 192, Bordeaux, 1642.

CLARKE, S.J., R. F.: *The Catholic Dictionary and the Brown Scapular.* In *The Month* (of which Fr. Clarke was editor), 1886; *Carmelite Review,* 1894.
Le Scapulaire de N.-D. du Mont-Carmel (tr. by a Discalced Carmelite), Paris, 1895; Nemours, 1900.

DANIEL A VIRGINE MARIA, O. CARM.: *Speculum Carmelitanum,* pp. 2,050. Antwerp, 1680. Reproduces the following:

  a. *Chronicon* of William of Sanvico
  b. *Viridarium* of John Grossi
  c. *Chronicon* of Thomas Scrope (Bradley)
  d. *Fasciculus Tripartitus* of John Paleonydorus
  e. *Tabulare Ordinis,* P. Bruno
  f. *De Patronatu B. V. M.,* Arnold Bostius
  g. *Maria Patrona,* P. J. Bta. Lezana
  h. *Instructio pro fratribus,* by T. Strazius

DE LANTENAY, A.: *Melanges de biographies.* Bordeaux, 1885. (Included life of John Chéron is valuable for discussion of Swaningtonian fragment. Cf. Analecta II, 246, note 2. The author says: "In his (John Chéron's) time, I do not find a man more esteemed, although no affectation appeared in him for all of that. He was accessible and affable to all."

237

EUGENIUS A S. JOSEPH, O.D.C.: *De Sacro Scapulare*. Analecta Ordinis Carmelitarum Discalceatorum (Rome, 1929), Vol. IV, pg. 169. (One of the best historical presentations of the day.)

ELISEE DE LA NATIVITE, O.D.C.: *Le Scapulaire de N.-D. du Mont-Carmel: Etude Historique*. In *Le Carmel* of July, 1938; pp. 306-328. (One of the best historical presentations of the day, adding little, however, to the work of the author's confère, Eug. a S. Joseph.)

FESAYO, O. CARM., PHILIBERT: *Duplex Privilegium Sacri Scapularis Seu Responsio* ad *J. Launoy*. pp. 538. Aquis Sextiis, 1649. (Note the date and object of this work. On pg. 67 the author says: "Our first sound document is that of John Grossi." Should we call the author "a modern"?)

FLORENCIO DEL NINO JESUS, O.D.C.: *El Monte Carmelo*. Madrid, 1924. pp. 610.

FRANCISCO DA CHERASCO: *Vita Generalis Henrici Silvii*, Asti, 1613. (Historical value shown by Fr. Gabriel Wessels in Analecta O. C., Vol. II, pg. 271.)

FALCONE, P. JOSEPH: *La Cronica Carmelitana*. Piacenza, 1595. pp. 776. (Pg. 506: Vita S. Simoni Stock; pg. 771: Bulla Sabbatina. The work is valuable both in itself because of its antiquity, and on account of the author's scholarliness.)

GABRIEL DE STE. MARIE MADELEINE: *Mater Carmeli*, Rome, 1931. (Esp. for Origin of Promise.)

GOASMOAL, O. CARM., IRENAEUS OF ST. JAMES: *Tractatus Theologicus de singulari, Imm. Virginis Protectione*. Paris, 1650.

GROSSI, O. CARM., JOHN: *Viridarium*. 1389 edito; *Analecta Ord. Carm.*, Vol VIII, pg. 124: reproduced from older sources.

JOSEPH DU SACRE-COEUR, O.D.C., R. P. Marie: *Le Scapulaire de Notre Dame du M.-Carmel est authentique:* In *Les Etudes Carmélitaines*, 13 année, 1928.

LEERSIUS, BALDUINUS: *Collectaneum Exemplorum et Miraculorum*. (In Ch. VI is found the famous statement that then, in the author's time (1450) the Sabbatine Bull was in the London archives.)

LEZANA, O. CARM., JOHN BAPTIST: *Annales Sacri Profetici et Eliani Ordinis.* 4 Vol. Rome, 1645, 1650, 1653, 1656. *Maria Patrona* Rome, 1648.

LO GRASSO, DANIELE: *La divozione al Sacro Scapolare Carmelitano in Sicilia.* In *Analecta O. C.,* Vol. II, 617-628. (The author demonstrates, by contemporary documents, the tremendous popularity of the Scapular Devotion in Sicily during the XV and XVI centuries. Valuable in reference to Sabb. Bull.)

MAGENNIS, O. CARM., P. E.: *The Scapular and Some Critics:* Rome, 1914. (The most complete historical study of the Scapular of this century. The presentation is weak but the judgments of the author are mature and scholarly. Arguments are rather too much *ad hominem* for the layman.) *The Sabbatine Privilege:* New York: Connoly, 1923. *Scapulare B. V. M. de Monte Carmelo: Joannes Cheron et Fragmentum Petri Swaningtoni:* Rome, 1915.

MATTEI, O. CARM., P. S.: *Ristretto della Vita di S. Simone Stock:* Rome, 1873. (Against Launoy the author uses several arguments, particularly from art works. Mostly about Sabb. Bull.)

MONSIGNANO, ELISIO: *Bullarium Carmelitarum.* Vols. III and IV, Rome, 1738.

MONBRUN, ALFRED: *Leben des heiligen Simon von Stock; ubersetzung von P. Bernhardt, C. D.* Regensburg, 1888.

PANNETIER, P.: *Vie de St. Simon Stock,* Bordeaux, 1779. *Instructions pour la Confrairie du St. Scapulaire.* Bordeaux, 1834. (Author was martyred in 1794.)

PATRICK DE S. JOSEPH: *Antiquum Ordinis Carmelitarum Ordinale Saeculi XIII*—Appeared in *Etudes Carmélitaines* (1912-13), now in book form, 251 pgs.

PHILLIPE DE LA TRINITE, O.D.C.: *Historia Carmelitana,* Paris, 1656.

PLACIDUS A VIRGINE DE COLUMNA, C. D.: *El Santa Escapulario y la Bula Sabatina.* Burgos, 1913.

POTEL, FRANCIS: *De Origine, Antiquitate et Titulo Ordinis, ac Confraternitatis Scapularis B. V. M. de Monte Carmelo.* Attrebati, 1611.

RAYNAUD, S.J., THEOPHILUS: *Scapulare parthenico-carmelitanum illustratum et defensum.* Lyons, 1665. (Fr. Magennis called it "a classic." It was a work which Launoy not only attacked but libeled.)

RUSHE, O.D.C., JAMES P.: *The Scapular Promise from the Historical Standpoint. Irish Eccl. Record:* Series 4, Vol. 29, pp. 266-288 (Dublin, 1911).

SANVICO, WILLIAM OF: *Chronicon* (Written about 1260.) *Spec. Carm.,* 1 pg. 95. (The authenticity of this work has been questioned by Dr. Clemens Kopp in his *Elias und Christentum auf dem Carmel* (Paderborn, 1929). However, see the brilliant response of Fr. B. Xiberta, O. Carm., in *Analecta O. C.,* Vol. VII, pp. 180-211.

SARACENUS: *Menologium Carmelitanum:* Bononiae, 1628. Pg. 295 he affirms that Swanington was sent with Reginald Scotus to Innocent IV.)

SEINER, PETER: *Maria Carmelitana.* Maguntiae, 1623.

SOLER, O. CARM., LUIS: *Revista Carmelitana,* No. 79, pg. 107 et passim: Proof of Scapular Vision from tradition. (Barcelona, 1867-92.)

SYLVEIRA, O. CARM., R. P.: *Commentaria in Acta Apostolorum; cum quadam apologia Carmelitana,* Lyons, 1681.

THOMAS AQUINAS OF ST. JOSEPH, O.D.C.: *Pro Sodalitio sacri Scapularis, adversus dissertationem J. Launoy:* Tutelae, 1648. (A defense of John Chéron's Vindicae.)

VENTIMIGLIA, FR. MARIANUS: *Historia Chronologica Priorum Generalium Ord. B. M. Virginis de Monte Carmelo:* Naples, 1773; Rome, 1929. (Especially pp. 23-38.) Bulla Sab., pg. 117.

VILLIERS, O. CARM.; COSMAS: *Bibliotheca Carmelitana.* pp. (cols.) 861-1053; Rome, 1927. (New edition by Fr. Gabriel Wessels.) Vol. I, col. 721 seq. contra Launoy; Vol. II, col. 123-124, pro Bulla Sabbatina; Vol. II, 752-765 contra Launoy.

XIBERTA, O. CARM., VERY REV. B. M.: *De Sacro Scapulare:* Analecta Ordinis Carmelitarum, 1939-1940. Also published in pamphlet form (in Latin) at Via Sforza Pallavicini 10, Roma (113). This work on the historicity of the Scapular excels, in thoroughness and exactness, any similar work before it.

ZACHARIAS A S. JOANNE BAPTISTA, O.D.C.: *De Bulla Sabbatina.* Ms. written about 1700. Cf. Villiers, Bibl., t. II, 883.

ZIMMERMAN, O.D.C., BENEDICT MARIA: *The Scapular:* Irish Ecclesiastical Record, Vol. 15 (1904), pp. 142-153; 206-234; 331-352. (This article, although written in the interest of true history, precipitated a debate because of its novelty and contradictions. The author became an antagonist of the Scapular, at least in his writings.) *Historica Carmelitana:* Lirinae, 1907. *Ordinale Ord. B. M. de Monte Carmelo:* Paris, 1910, pp. 402. *De Sacro Scapulare: Analecta Ord. Carmelit. Disc.* (Rome, 1927) Vol. II, pg. 79. (Probably the most significant article in the recent, now closed debate. Fr. Zimmerman became of the opinion that S. Simon "confortavit fratres" with the story of the Vision. The documentary evidence has been found incontrovertible although some minor points need to be settled. History is never a closed book and major events have many sides.)

WEMMERS, PETER: *Chronicon,* Antwerp, 1666.

WESSELS, O. CARM., GABRIEL: *Antiqua Documenta de S. Scapulari: Analecta Ord. Carm.,* Vol. II, pp. 119, 241, 612; Vol. IV, p. 241; Vol. V, p. 406, *Acta Capitulorum Generalium* (1284-1593) Rome, 1912, pp. 654. *Acta Capituli Generalis:* Rome, 1931. *Bibliotheca Carmelitana:* Rome, 1927. (Cites Scapular Mss.)

Section Two: MIRACLES

BERTHELOT DE SENS: *Collectio Miraculorum Scapularis:* Toulouse, 1645; Bruxells, 1652. (Written in French.)

BEWFU, WILLIAM: *De Miraculis Beatae Mariae Virginis.* Cf. Raynaud, pg. 249.

CAPUTO, O. CARM., FILOCALUS: *De Imagine miraculosa Neopolitana B. V. Mariae de Monte Carmelo, et miraculis sacri habitus Scapularis.* Naples, about 1625. Italian.

DE LA FUENTE, O. CARM., VEN. P. MICHAEL: *Compendium historiale gratiarum et beneficiorum per Sacrum Scapulare et ad invocationem B. V. Mariae de M. Carm.* Toledo, 1619.

GRASSI, O. CARM., SIMON: *Miracoli et Grazie della Santissima Vergine Maria del Carmine.* pp. 312, Florence, 1727.

GUARDIUS, O. CARM., A.: *Thesaurus Coelestis.* Brixiae, 1611; Venetiis, 1621. (Italian.)

HUGUET, S. M., R.P.: *Vertu miraculeuse du Scapulaire.* (Chez Haton) Paris, 1879.

HUNNER, R. P.: *Unsere Liebe Frau.* Regensburg, 1882.

KELLER, D.D., REV. DOM JOSEPH: *Maria Sanctissima* (English) : *Mary's Habit—The Holy Scapular*, pgs. 46-65. London, 1930.

LEERSIUS, O. CARM., BALDUINUS: *Collectaneum Exemplorum et Miraculorum.* (Cf. Section I.)

MOLLA, O. CARM., SALVATOR A MATRE DEI: *Ano Mariano-Carmelitano.* (Was in press in 1931. P. Besalduch, in the *Enciclopedia*, says that it contains about two thousand miracles.)

MAGNETUS, O. CARM., JOHN BAPTIST: *Summarium Miraculorum B. V. Mariae de Monte Carmelo*, Naples, about 1612.

N. N.: *Faveurs obtenus et l'Enfer evité par le Scapulaire.* pp. 136. Paris, 1896.

PAULUS AB OMNIBUS SANCTIS, O.D.C.: *Historia Miraculorum Dei-Parae Virginis de M. Carm.* (German) Monachii, 1657.

SERRA, O. CARM., J. A.: *Libre des Miracles del Carme.* pp. 344, Gerundae, 1701.

VIFQUIN, O. CARM., PHILIP OF THE VISITATION: *Des Miracles du St. Scapulaire.* Trèves, 1663.

Section Three: DEVOTION

ALEXIUS A S. ANNA, O.D.C.: *Pia exercitia pro Confratibus Scapularis Carmelitici.* French. Poitiers, 1769.

BESALDUCH, O. CARM., SIMON M.: *Devocionario-Manual de la Virgen del Carmen.* Barcelona, 1925. pp. 551. (Indulgenced by Spanish Episcopacy.) *Ramillete de la Virgen del Carmen.* pp. 318. Barcelona, 1928. *Ante el Altar de la Virgen del Carmen.* pp. 446. *Quince Minutos con la Virgen del Carmen.* Barcelona, 1929.

DIETHER, O. CARM., LAWRENCE: *Imitation of Mary.* Chicago, 1928.

DOWNEY, COLUMBA: *Little Flower Prayer Book.* Chicago. Carmelite Press, 1930. (A prayer manual which enjoys great popularity.)

HERIZ, O.D.C., PASCHASIUS: *Fifteen Minutes at the Feet of Our Lady of Mount Carmel.* pp. 88. Washington.

LEO A S. JOANNE MACE, O. CARM.: *Les Heures de la Sainte Vierge, avec l'exercice de la Journée Chrétienne, particulièrement pour les dévots qui portent le saint Scapulaire.* Paris, Padeloup, 1655.

MAGENNIS, O. CARM., ELIAS: *Carmelite Devotional Handbook.* pp. 172. Rome, 1925.

PLACIDUS A VIRGINE DE COLUMNA: *Cartilla de los Religiosos, Terciarios y Cofrades Carmelitas.* pp. 208. Valentia, 1925. *Aromas del Carmelo.* Valentia, 1905. (Contains pious exercises for each day of July.)

RUBI Y FERRER, MATTHAEUS: *El Carmelo y el Santo Escapulario: Novena Meditada.* Palmo in Maiorica, 1902.

WALTERS, O. CARM., LEO: *Totus Marianus.* Chicago, 1933. (This brochure is an exposition of the Carmelite formula:. "To Jesus through Mary.")

N. N.: *Carmelite Manual.* New York: Benziger, 1934. (Contains the *Little Office* of Our Lady of Mount Carmel in the vernacular.)

Section Four: INSTRUCTIONS

BERINGER, S.J., R. P.: *Les Indulgences,* Paris: *Léthieux,* 1903; Vol. I, pp. 537 sq.

BERTEROS, JOSEPH A JESU: *Sacre Instruzzioni per i divoti del Carmine.* Taurinensis, circa an. 1748.

BESALDUCH, O. CARM., S. M.: *Cofradia de Ntra Senora del Carmen: Cédula de inscripcion, Reglamento e instrucciones sobre el Escapulario.* 4th ed., Barcelona, 1930.

DIETHER, O. CARM., LAWRENCE: *Scapular Booklet,* Chicago, 1928. (For directors and members of Confraternity.)

GRECH, O. C., SPIRIDION: *Carmelite Privileges,* Chicago: The Carmelite Press, 1935.

HERES, O. CARM., P. M.: *Ordenacion de los Capitulos que tienen que observar los Cofrades. Ms. in pergameno,* pp. 38, *Maioricae,* 1618.

JOSEPH-BONAVENTURA, T.O.S.F.: *Los Escapularios.* Barcelona, 1906. (Contains almost all decrees of the Sacred Congregation concerning the Scapular and Confraternity.)

MAGENNIS, O. CARM., E. P.: *The Scapular Devotion.* Dublin, Gill & Son, 1923. pp. 168. (Contains information on all the small Scapulars but is primarily concerned with the Brown Scapular. Written especially for priests.)

NAZIANZENUS A BASILIO, O.D.C., GREGORY: *Instruction familière pour la Conrie du S. Scapulaire.* Paris, S. Huré, 1646.

STRAZIO, O. CARM., THEODORUS: *De modo erigendi Confraternitatem Ord. Carm.* Rome, 1634. *Instructio pro Fratribus*

Carmelitis Antiquae Reg. Observantiae. Rome, 1640; Brussels, 1651; Spec. Carm., p. 472 et seq. (Antwerp, 1680).

N. N.: *Instrucciones para el Devoto Carmelita.* 11th Ed., Barcelona, 1898.

Section Five: GENERAL WORKS

Alfonso Maria, O. C., Frei: *O Escapulario do Carmo e a medalha,* Pernambuco, 1939; pp. 197. (This book, now in its third edition, tries to prove that the Scapular Medal does not carry the Promise attached to the Scapular of Carmel.)

Alphonsus a Matre Dei, O.D.C.: *De Scapulari B. Virginis.* (Spanish) 1630?

Andres, S.J., Joseph: *Decor Carmeli.* Cologne, 1669 (Latin)

Angelus de Summaran, o. carm., Peter: *Thesaurus Carmeliticus.* Cologne, 1621.

Angelus Torrents, o. carm., Joannes: *Glorias del Carmelo.* (Translation of *Decor Carmeli* with notes.) Palmae, 1860.

Archangelus a S. Michaele, C.D.: *De Dei-Parae Virginis de Monte Carmelo Scapularis, Gratiis, beneficiis ac Privilegiis.* (Polish) Cracovia, 1653.

Arsenius a S. Antonio, O.D.C.: *Stimulus devotionis erga Beatissimam Virginem De Monte Carm.* Rome. (Treats of the antiquity, graces, privileges, etc., of Confraternity; author died in 1703.)

Azzarelli, o. carm., Albertus: *Manuale degli ascritti all' Abitino.* Palermo, 1927.

Barrett, O.S.B., Dom Michael: *Our Lady in the Liturgy,* Herder: Saint Louis, 1912, pp. 117-128. (Very highly commendable. This Liturgical study is a Scapularia gem.)

Barry, W. J.: *Sacramentals.* (Under "Scapular.")

Bartholomaeus, a S. Maria, O.D.C.: *Tesoro de gracias que la Virgen otorgo a sus fieles devotos.* Madrid, 1863.

Benedict XIV, Pope: *De festis Domini Nostri Jesu Christi et Beatae Mariae Virginis,* lib. II, c. V, n. 1-10. Also: *De Servorum Dei Beatificatione et Beatorum Canonizatione,* lib. IV, p. 2, c. IX, n. 10. In *Opera Omnia, Pratie, Aldina,* 1831.

Besalduch, o. carm., S.: *Pulpito de la Virgen del Carmen.*

(2 Vols.) Barcelona: Luis Gili, 1928. *Enciclopedia del Escapulario* (pp. 703) Barcelona: Luis Gili, 1931.

BIGOT, O. CARM., TUSSANUS: *l'Institution de la Confrairie du S. Scapulaire.* Paris: Padeloup, 1661.

BLANC, O. CARM., ANGELUS: *De la Confrairie du st. Scapulaire.* Lyons, 1638.

BROCARD, A S. THERESLA, O.D.C.: *Recueil d'instructions sur la dévotion du Saint Scapulaire.* Gand, 1845-1875. *Collecion de Instrucciones sobre la devocion al Santo Escapulario,* pp. 556. Vitoriae, 1895. (Translation of *Recueil d'instructions.* Due to the worth and popularity of this work a new edition is likely to appear very soon.)

CATALDI, O. CARM., RMO. M. G.: *Panegirici di Nostra Signora del Carmine.* Naples, 1840; 4 Vols. (Historicity, Vol. IV, pg. 50.)

CHAIGNON, S.J., R. P.: *Sacerdotal Meditations* (tr.). New York: Benziger, 1916, sub festo.

CHAIX, O. CARM., THOMAS: *L'Excellence de la dévotion du Scapulaire.* Lyons, 1835; Paris, 1835. (Published at both cities in the same year.)

CHAMPECHEVRIEUX, O. CARM., G.: *De Antiquitate et Privilegiis Ord. Carm.* Paris, 1624. (This work revived the Scapular Devotion in France at time of writing.)

CHEAUDEAU A S. CLAUDIO, O. CARM., PHILIP: *Instruction facile ou sont expliqués par abrégé l'establissement, les faveurs et les devoirs du S. Scapulaire.* Lyons: Denis, 1641.

CHRISTOPHER BRENZON, O. CARM.: *Sermones Sexdecim in Canticum IV Salomonis, habiti in Processione S. Scapularis.* Pisis, 1606.

COLGAN, D.D., R. J.: The Scapular. pp. 180. Philadelphia, 1890 (?)

COLONGUE, O. CARM., GEORGE: *De Confraternitate Scapularis.* Toulouse: D'Estey, 1633.

CURTIN, J. C.: *The Catholic Church* (14 Vols., New York, 1906): Vol. III.

CYPRIANO A S. MARIA, O.D.C.: *Thesaurus Carmelitarum, sive Confraternitatis Scapularis.* Cologne, 1627. (One of the earliest Scapular-Confraternity manuals. It is divided into three parts. The first gives hist. of Scapular in 24 chapters;

the second treats of practice in virtue in 11 chapters; the
third enumerates proper devotions in nine chapters.)

DANIEL A VIRGINE MARIA, O. CARM.: *Origo, Privilegia, vera
et solida Devotio Sacri Scapularis.* (Latin) Antwerp, 1673.

DE LA COLOMBIERE, S.J., VEN. CLAUDE: *Sermon du Scapulaire. Oeuvres.* Tom. III, édit. d'Avignon, 1832. (Has been
reproduced in Carmelite periodicals in most countries.)

DE LA FUENTE, VEN. M.: *Compendium historiale gratiarum
et beneficiorum per Sacrum Scapulare et ad invocationem
B. V. Mariae de M. C.* Toledo, 1619.

DE VALENCE DE MARBOT, BARONNE: *Le Scapulaire de N.-D.
du Mont Carmel.* Paris, 1934 (Profusely illustrated).

DOLAN, O. CARM., A. H.: *Scapular Facts* 40 pp. Chicago, 1929.

DRESSEL, O. CARM.: *Scapular Confraternity Devotion* pp. 19.
sine loco, 1933.

D'ARVILLE, R. P.: *The Year of Mary* (tr. by Mrs. Sadlier),
sub festo.

DUMAX, L'ABBE, V.: *N.-D. du Mont Carmel et le Saint
Scapulaire.* Haton-Paris.

ELIAS A S. CATHERINA: *Agricultura Spiritualis, oder Geist-
licher Acker Bau.* 1736. sub festo. (Devotional; shows the
power of the Scapular skillfully and thoroughly.)

ENRICO MARIA DEL SS. SACRAMENTO, O.D.C.: *La Divozione
illustrata dello Scapolare.* 2nd edit. Oneglia, Ghilni, 1876.

ESTRUGOS, O. CARM., J. E.: *Fenix Catala, llibre dels singulars
privilegis, favors, gracias y miracles de Nostra Senyora del
Mont Del Carm.* (Catalan) Perpiniani, 1644.

FORMAU, O. CARM., GERARD: *De Confraternitate Sacri Scapularis Carmelitarum.* Valencennis: Veruli, 1627; German
edit, Cologne: Brachel, 1634. *Compendium Privilegiorum
Confraternitatis Sacri Scap.* (French) Attrebati: G. de
Raismes, 1647.

FRIDERICUS A S. ANTONIO, O.D.C.: *Il Devoto della SS. Vergine Maria del Carmine.* Mediolani, 1882.

GAILLARD, O. CARM., G.: *Conciones aliquot pro Festo Comm.
Solemnis V. M. de Monte Carmelo.* (Latin) Cologne: Bu-
saei, 1660. *Foedus Marianum: Conciones de Scapulari.*
(Latin) ibidem. *Trifoedus Marianum.* pp. ultra 572. Cologne, 1683. (Sermons on the Scapular for every Sunday in
the year, taken from the Gospels.)

GAUME, D.D., MGR.: *The Catechism of Perseverance.* (tr. from 10th French edit.) New York: Benziger, 1882. Vol. IV, pp. 403-415. (Highly recommendable from many points of view.)

GARCIA, O. CARM., E.: *Sermon de la Santisima Virgen del Carmen.* Valentia, 1685.

GEARON, O. CARM., D.D., P. J.: *The Brown Scapular.* Dublin: Anthonian Press, 1928.

GEMMINGER, R. P.: *Marien-Predigten.* 2 Vols. Sub festo, in both volumes. Regensburg, 1864.

GERVASIUS A S. ELIA, O.D.C.: *Irutti d'Elia: Discorsi distributi per ogni Domenica.* (Treats of Scapular.) Bologne, 1684-1686.

GRACIENSIS CONVENTUS (pseudonym), O.D.C.: *Monile Aureum in quo agitur de S. Scapulare.* (German) Graeci: S. Hault, 1643.

GRASSI, O. CARM., SIMON: *Origine, privilegi, etc., del S. Scapolare.* pp. 70.

GUERANGER, DOM P.: *Anné Liturgique; The Liturgical Year,* Eng. tr. Shepherd, Dublin, 1870 sqq., Worcester, Eng., 1895-1903, in 15 vols.; sub festo.

HARDT, O. CARM., T.: *Das hl. Skapulier U. L. Frau vom Berge Karmel ein sicheres Unterpfand der Beharrlichkeit.* Vienna, 1936. pp. 48.

HENRICUS A MONTE CARMELO, O. CARM.: *De Confraternitate sacri Scapularis.* Maguntiae, 1652.

HENRICUS MA. A S. TERESIA, O.D.C.: *Le Scapulaire de N. D. du Mont Carmel.* pp. 214. Paris, 1895.

HOHN, D.D., LL.D., H.: *The Scapular of Our Lady of Mount Carmel.* Salford, 1915. (Preface by the Bishop of Salford; contains extracts from Cardinal Vaughan's pastoral letter on Scapular.)

HOYCIUS, O. CARM., B.: *De Confraternitate Scapularis B. V. M. de Monte Carmelo.* Ms. Polish and Latin. circa 1620.

JOANNES AB ANNUNCIATIONE, O.D.C.: *Prontuario del Carmine per i religiosi.* 2 Vols. Trenti, 1723.

JOURDAIN, Z.-C.: *Somme des Grandeurs de Marie.* Paris: Hyppolyte Walzer, 1903. T. IV, pg. 434 sq.; VI, 534 sq.; IV, 281; V, 423, et passim.

JOUVE, L'ABBE: *La Vie des Saints.* Sub festo S. Simonis Stock, May 16. Paris, 1883.

LAMBING, D.D., LL.D., A. A.: *Sacramentals* under *"Scapular."* Benziger's, 1896.

LANCICIUS, S.J., VEN.: *Select Works.* London, 1884. (Scapular Feast in book of daily Meditations.)

LEO A REGIBUS, O.D.C.: *Monile Aureum.* Graeci, 1643, (German).

LIGOURI, ST. ALPHONSUS: *Glorie di Maria.* Rome: Pia Societa, San Paolo, 1932. Eng. tr. by Rev. E. Grimm, C. SS. R.: *The Glories of Mary,* New York, 1931. (Prompt deliverance from Purgatory, 235; advantages of Scapular, 606; answer to critics, 699.) Germ. tr. by Schmoger: Regensburg, 1928: Ursprung, 535; Nutzen, 223, 535, 611. Special tr. for *Somme des Grandeurs Marie* (Paris, 1902), Vol. X, pg. 428 sqq.

LLOP, O. CARM., ALOYSIUS M.: *La Virgen del Carmen Predicada.* Xeritii Sidoniorum, 1920.

MACE, O. CARM., L.: *L'Alliance de la Vierge touchant les Privilèges du S. Scapulaire.* Paris, 1635. (Reprinted nearly forty times.)

MAILLARD, O. CARM., P.: *De Confraternitate Carmelitana.* Cfr. V. Villiers, Bibl. Carm., t. 2, col. 583.

MARTEAU A S. GRATIANO, O. CARM., MARTIN: *Compendium Privilegiorum, Meritorum et Indulgentiarum, etc.* (French) Paris, 1648.

MATTHIAS DE ST. JEAN: *La Véritable Dévotion du St. Scapulaire,* pp. 502. Paris, 1656. (An often quoted work.)

MAYER, O. CARM., MOST REV. P.: *The Brown Scapular.* New York, 1879, pp. 134.

MESCHLER, S.J., N.: *L'Année Ecclésiastique.* Vol. II, pp. 173-184.

MOLLA, O. CARM., S.: *La Virgen del Carmen.* Hispali, 1916.

NAVARRO, O. CARM., ALPHONSUS: *De la Gracia o Indulgencia que llaman Sabatina.* (Spanish) 1615 (?)

NAZIANZENUS A S. BASILIO, O.D.C., G.: *L'Adoption des Enfants de la Vierge dans l'Ordre et la Confrairie de N. D. du M. Carmel.* pp. 1173. Paris: S. Huré, 1646.

NIDERWILTZ, O. CARM., IOANNES: *De Maria Carmelitana.* Cologne, 1645. *De Origine, Confirmatione et Privilegiis Confraternitatis S. Scapularis* (German). Cologne, 1648.

PATE, O. CARM., T. A.: *Piena Notizia di tutte quelle cose che sono concernenti al sacro habito della Beatissimo Vergine*

Maria del Carmine. Messana: J. Matthaeus, 1655.

PAULUS AB OMNIBUS SANCTIS, O.D.C.: *Clavis Aurea Thesauri Partheno-Carmelitici*. (Latin) Vienna, 1669.

PHILLIPUS A S. PETRO-THOMA, O. CARM.: *Vera Devotio Sacri Scapularis Nostrae Dominae de Monte Carmelo*. pp. 502. Paris: Thierry, 1656.

PUGLIESSE, O. CARM., P.-T.: *Scapularis Partheno-Carmelitici Gazophilacium* (Latin) Naples, n.d. (Author d. 1707).

RAPHAEL A S. JOSEPH, O.D.C.: *Signum Salutis in Periculis*. Lincii, 1718.

REALI, O. CARM., A.: *Cosi parlo la Madonna del Carmine*. Tip. Doglio, Cagliari, 1938. pp. 42. (Brief exposition of the Scapular Devotion.)

RODRIGUEZ, EMMANUEL: *Quaestionum Regularium*. a. 1600 (First edit. 1598.) Extensively treats of Scapular and Sabbatine Bull.

ROIVELA, O. CARM., P.: *Breve Suma de la Antiquedad, gracias e Indulgencias de la Orden del Carmen y de la Cofradia*. Madrid, 1585.

ROSSI, O. CARM., R. P.: *Dal Carmelo alla Gloria*. Ravenna, 1929.

SAIUS, O. CARM., Z.: *De Confraternitate Carmeli*. Circa 1611.

SALART, O. CARM., H.: *La Voye pour passer heureusement de ce monde en l'autre. En faveur des Confrères du S. Scapulaire de la Glorieuse Vierge Marie du Mont-Carmel*, etc. Podii: A. de la Garde, 1659.

SAMBUCY, L'ABBE: *La Dévotion du S. Scapulaire*. Paris, 1842; *Die Andacht zum heiligen Scapulier;* Ubersetzung vom R. P. Sintzel: Regensburg, 1848.

SANVILLIACUS, WILLIAM: *Liber de Patronatu Virginis* (Author died at Paris, 1348.)

SAVARIA, J. T.: *Le Scapulaire de Notre-Dame du Mont-Carmel*. Montréal, 1898, pp. 354. (Clear and simple; highly recomended by Canadian Episcopacy.)

SCHULTINGIUS, O. CARM., G.: *Exegesis Mariana, seu Idea Confraternitatis B. V. M. .de Monte Carmelo*. (German) Cologne, 1629.

SEEBERGER, C.P., P.S.: *Scapular and Confraternity of Our Lady of Mount Carmel*. Collegeville, Ind. 1900. pp. 257.

SEGERUS, O. CARM., PAULUS: *Funiculum triplex viginti qua-*

*tuor beneficiorum modis CARMELITAS obligans ad fes-
tum Commemorationis Solemnis B. V. M. de Monte Carmelo.* (Latin) Cologne, 1643.

SERAFINUS, O. CARM., G.: *De Confraternitate Sacri Scapularis.*
(Italian) Lucca, 1640 and 1664. Latin tr. by P. Angelus
Bucellenius, O. Carm.

SERAPION A S. ANDREA, O.D.C.: *Scapulier-Buchlein.* pp. 204.
Graz, 1892.

SERRADA, O. CARM., GABRIEL: *Escudo triunfante del Carmelo:
su Sto. Escapulario.* pp. 308. Hispali, 1709.

SIMON A SANTO SPIRITU, O.D.C.: Neapolitan, (d. 1656):
De Confraternitate S. Scapularis. Cf. *Enciclopedia* del P.
Besalduch, pg. 670, no. 6.

THEODORUS A S. TERESIA, O.D.C.: *Compendium Privilegiorum, Gratiarum et Indulgentiarum sacrae Confraternitatis
B. V. M. de Monte Carmelo.* Typis M. Formicae. Vienna,
circa an. 1650.

THOMAS A JESU, O.D.C.: *De Privilegiis, Gratiis et Indul-
gentiis Confraternitatis B. V. M. De Monte Carmelo.*
(Spanish) Salmanticae: A. Renaut, 1599.

RICOLO, MONS. PASQUALE: *Il Mese di luglio in onore di
Maria SS. del Carmine.* Pp. 276. Naples, 1937. (History
of Scapular given with Church documents, the consent of
writers and of the universal devotion of Catholics.)

VAN ASSCHEN, O. CARM., R. P.: *Den Schat des H. Scapuliers.*
Antwerp, 1620.

VERMEERSCH, S.J., R. P.: *Meditations on the Blessed Virgin.*
London: Burns and Oates, 1909, pp. 800, 2 Vols.

VERCRUYSSE, S.J., B.: *New Practical Meditations.* New York,
Benziger. Vol. II, sub festo 16 Julii.

VIFQUIN, O. CARM., P.: *Breviarium Confratrum et Consoror-
um S. Scapularis B. V. M. de Monte Carmelo, continens
eorum praecipua privilegia, magnas Indulgentias et parva
debita, cum multis Miraculis.* (Latin) Valencennis, 1659.

WALSH, R. P.: *Apparitions and Shrines of Heaven's Bright
Queen.* New York, 1904.

N. N.: *Origen de la devocion del Escapulario del Carmen.*
pp. 223. Barcelona, 1871.

N. N.: *Petit manuel sur le St. Scapulaire.* pp. 48. Gand, 1875.

N. N.: *El Escapulario del Carmen.* pp. 140. Vitoriae, 1891.

N. N.: *L'Escapulari del Carme: sa excellència i condicions per a valdre.* (Catalan) Barcelona, 1929.

N. N.: *El Privilegi Sabati dels Confrares del Carme.* (Catalan) Barcelona, 1929.

N. N.: *Little Manual for the Scapular Confraternity.* pp. 64. sine loco, 1922.

Section Six: *PERIODICALS*

ANALECTA ORDINIS CARMELITARUM: Rome, sub. P. Gabriel Wessels, O. Carm., from 1909-1937. Now edited by P. Gabriel Pausback, O. Carm. (Fr. Wessels published extracts from many ancient Scapular documents. Under Fr. Pausback there is to be a section of the periodical regularlv devoted to the Scapular.)

ANALECTA ORD. CARM. DISCALCEATORUM: Rome. Begun in 1926. P. Ambrosius, Corso d'Italia 38, Rome 34.

AROMAS DEL CARMELO: Apartade 525, Havana, Cuba.

BOLETIN CARMELITANE: Buenos Aires, 10 Cadiz, Argentina.

CARMELITE REVIEW: Niagara Falls, Ont., Canada, 1893-1902. Director: Very Rev. Anastasius Kreidt, O. Carm.; Washington, 1940-: Director, Rev. Andrew L. Weldon, O. Carm.

CARMELO BALEARS: Edited by Discalced Carmelites in Palma de Mallora.

CARMELROZEN: A Hollandese publication, begun in 1911: under the direction of the Carmelite Fathers. (Numbered 13,000 subscribers in first year.)

CHRONIQUES DU CARMEL: Alost (Belgium), under Fr. Raphael de Saint Joseph, O.D.C., 1889-1893. (One of the best sources for student of Scapularia.)

ECOS DEL CARMELO: Published at Burgos, monthlv.

EL ANGEL DE CARMELO: Chareas 2465, U. T. 44, Juncal 1890, Buenos Aires, Argentina.

EL CARMEN:Pamplona, Spain. Carmelitas Descaizos.

EL MONTE CARMELO: Pub. at Burgos. (Contains much Scap. information; complete set in Discalced Monastery at Washington, D. C.)

EL SANTO ESCAPULARIO: Osuna, Spain. Begun in 1911 (?) (Especially treats of the Scapular and traditions of the Carmelite Order.)

ETUDES CARMELITAINES: Paris: Desclée de Brouwer, 23 anné. (The editorial policy of this famous periodical changed in 1931 when R. P. Bruno de Jésus-Marie became the director. Formerly, under the direction of P. Marie-Joseph du Sacré-Coeur, it contained Scapular material.)

IL MONTE CARMELO: Rome; begun in 1914. Under the direction of R. P. Antoninus Franco, O. Carm. (Contains Scapular information only at rare intervals, except during July. All of Vol. XX is quite full of Scapularia, however, and there is always information about Carmelite activities.)

MOUNT CARMEL: Washington, D. C., under direction of Rev. Thomas M. Kilduff, O. D. C. Begun in 1921.

LA VOIX DE NOTRE DAME DU MONT CARMEL: P. O. B. 22, Haifa, Palestine.

LE CARMEL: Agen; begun in 1915. *Bulletin Mensuel du Carmel de France et de Son Tiers-Ordre.* (The number of July-August, 1938 was solely on the Scapular. This historical article, by R. P. Elisée, O.D.C., is especially good.)

O MENSAGEIRO DO CARMELO: Rio de Janeiro, under direction of Frei Thomaz Jansen.

REVISTA CARMELITANA: Barcelona, 1876-1892; under direction of R. P. Luis Ma. Soler. (Almost every number is of value for Scapular research.)

REVISTA CARMELITANA: (Monthly pub. by Disc. Carm.) Tucson, Ariz. P. O. B. 308.

RUNDSCHAU VOM BERGE KARMEL: Niagara Falls, Ont., Canada, 1897-1899, under the direction of the Very Rev. Anastasius Kreidt, O. Carm.

SKAPULIER: Linz, under direction of R. P. B. Miesbauer, O. Carm. Begun in 1910. (Strangely enough, articles on the Scapular are rather rare in this publication.)

STIMMEN UNSERER LIEBEN FRAU VOM BERGE KARMEL: Bamberg, under P. Thaddeus Ballsieper, O. Carm. Begun in 1924.

SWORD: Englewood, N. J., 1937. This periodical is published by the Carmelite Province of the Most Pure Heart of Mary. It contains a section on the Scapular in each issue (quarterly), and, in 1939, some special articles on the historicity of the Scapular. It is not available to the layman.)

SZENT TERESKA ROZSAKESTJE: (Hungarian pub. of Disc. Carm.) Kiadja. Karmelita, Rendhaz, Huba—Utca 12. Budapest, Hungary.

REFERENCES

Chapter One

1 Bk. of Kings, III, xviii, 19.

2 S. Antoninus in *Summa*, pg. 4 tit. 15, c. 4; St. Albertus Magnus in *Super Missus est;* St. Augustine in his Serm. xxvii, *in Natali Domini*, xix; St. Ambrose, *"De Institutione Virginis,"* xiii; St. John Damascene *in Nativ. B. V. M.*; St. Epiphanius in serm. *De Laud. Virg.* For other Doctors and Fathers see *Revista Carmelitana*, VIII, 102: "La Santisima Virgen y La Nube de Elias" by Mons. de Segur; Jourdain's *Somme des Grandeurs de Marie*, II, 538.

3 Sanvico, a contemporary historian, in *De Multiplicatione Religionis Carmelitarum per Provincias Syriae et Europae: et de perditione Monasteriorum Terrae Sanctae.* Lib. I in Tome I of *Speculum Carmelitanum*, pg. 95, no. 400.

4 Genesis, iii, 15.

5 "Petre, ne timeas, quia durabit in finem Carmeli religio nostra; nam et pro ea supplicavit etiam Filio meo primus Ordinis Patronus Elias in transfiguratione et impetravit." Defensorium, by JOHANNE HILDESHEIMENSI, discipulo Sancti Petri Thomae Patriarche Constantinopolitani. Cap. 5— Speculum Carm., t. I, 149. Cf. Fr. Zimmerman: Monumenta historica carmelitana, pp. 223-431.

6 *La Vie de St. Simon Stock* by Alfred Monbrun: German translation by R. P. Bernhard (Regensburg, 1888), pg. 49.

7 Letter to Mary of St. Joseph, Aug., 1582.

8 Autobiography, ch. iii.

9 The beauty of this prayer lies not only in its mystic power but also in its literary perfection. The Latin text is: Flos Carmeli, Vitis Florigera, Splendor Coeli, Virgo Puerpera, Singularis! Mater Mitis, sed viri nescia, Carmelitis da privilegia, Stella Maris!

10 Viridarium Ordinis B. Virginis Mariae de Monte Carmelo per JOHANNEM GROSSI, reproduced in the Analecta Ordinis Carmelitarum, VIII (1932, Rome) from the Spec., t. I, by Danielis a V. M.

11 *The Liturgical Year*, Eng. tr. Shepherd, Dublin, 1870:

sub festo 16 July: (All such references, to famous meditation books and the like, will be given in this general manner to cover all editions.)

[12] Monbrun, Alfred: *La Vie de St. Simon Stock,* in Preface written by Pius IX. Consult bibliography.

Chapter Two

[1] J. T. Savaria, *Le Scapulaire* (Montréal, 1898), pg. 110. N. B.: This author, an honorary canon of the Cathedral of Montreal, was at once learned and spiritual. His book is prefaced by four Archbishops and eight Bishops.

[2] *Le Scapulaire,* Les Chroniques du Carmel, IV, 105, 246, 284, 287, 421. N. B.: This book-length study dwells largely on the theology of the Scapular and is fully explanatory of the *"pie"* found in the Liturgy.

[3] P. S. Besalduch, O. Carm.: *Enciclopedia del Escapulario del Carmen,* nos. 241 to 253 (Barcelona, 1931).

[4] Ibidem, nos. 281-286; Analecta, X, p. 217.

[5] S. Congregatio S. Officii, Dec. 16th, 1910; cf. Analecta O. Carm., vol. II, pg. 3 and 4.

[6] E. P. Magennis, O. Carm.: *The Scapular Devotion* (Dublin, 1923), pg. 86.

[7] Cum sacra, quae vocant, scapularia ad fidelium devotionem fovendam sanctiorisque vitae proposita in eis excitanda maxime conferre compertum sit, ut pius eis nomen dandi mos in dies magis invalescat, SSmus. D. N. Pius divina providentia PP. X, *etsi vehementer exoptet ut eadem, quo hucusque modo consueverunt, fideles deferre prosequantur, plurium tamen ad Se delatis votis ex animo obsecundans,* praehabito Emorum." cf. Enciclopedia, no. 287.

[8] Per sacrum Scapulare filios delectionis assumpsit . . . In the Missa Votiva of the Carmelites and for the Mass of July 16th. Missale Carmelitarum; Rome, 1935.

[9] Enciclopedia, no. 268.

[10] Ibidem, no. 302.

[11] Vic. Dioces, de Malinas; cf. Encicl., no 299.

[12] Analecta Ord. Carm., II, 65.

[13] Letter of His Holiness PP XI on the occasion of the Sixth Centenary of the Sabbatine Privilege, cf. P. E. Magennis, *The Sabbatine Privilege of the Scapular,* New York, 1923.

[14] P. Huguet: *La Devotion à Marie en exemples*, t. II, 62.

[15] Savaria, op. cit. pg. xviii.

[16] P. S. Besalduch, O. Carm.: *Pulpito de la Virgen del Carmen*, Vol. I, pg. 6 (Barcelona, 1928).

[17] R. P. Chaignon, S.J., *Meditations* (tr.) New York, 1916: sub festo 16 July.

[18] *Die Ablasse* (tr.) Paderborn, 1886. Sub festo.

Chapter Three

[1] *Das. hl. Skapulier*, by P. T. Hardt (Vienna, 1936); Bl. Claude de la Colombière, in *Serm. pour la Fête du Scap.*, Oeuvres, t. III; P. S. Besalduch in *Pulpito*, t. I, pg. 300; M. D'Arville, in *The Year of Mary*, sub festo; P. H. Hohn, D.D., LL.D., in *The Scap. of O. L. of M. C.* (Salford, 1915); Monsignor Gaume, *Catechism of Perseverance*, Vol. IV, pg. 400; et alii.

[2] *Enciclopedia de la Virgen del Carmen:* pg. 335.

[3] *Enciclopedia:* no. 143.

[4] Cf. R. P. Magennis: *Scapulare B. V. M. de Monte Carmelo: Joannes Cheron et Fragmentum Petri Swaningtoni*, pp. 184, Rome, 1915.

[5] R. P. Clarke, S.J.: "The Brown Scapular and the Catholic Dictionary" in *The Month*, 1886.

[6] R. P. Papabroech: *Responsiones, De Rev.* Accusatio II, n. 28: 'It would be wicked to deny that this devotion of the Scapular has been honored by graces and privileges granted by *the Supreme Pontiffs* and approved by *celestial favors.*" N. B.: Father Papebroech was the greatest hagiologist of his day and probably of all time, cf. P. E. Magennis: "The Scapular and Some Critics," pg. 139.

[7] De festis Domini Nostri Jesu Christi et Beatae Mariae Virginis, lib. II, c. V, n. 1-10; Prati, 1831.

[8] Launoy was answered by Father John Chéron, O. Carm., with a letter which the latter claimed to have been written by Swanington, the secretary of Saint Simon Stock. This letter (Fragmentum Vitae S. Simonis Stockii) was taken to be the foundation for the historicity of the Vision, or at least the cornerstone. When it was called into question at the turn of the present century, repercussions were felt in the mightiest

volumes of the day: the Encyclopedias. The two greatest
figures in the modern debate were the R.P. Benedict Zimmerman, O.D.C., and the R. P. Elias P. Magennis, O. Carm.
Both died within a month of each other in 1937. Most writers
of historical note are now agreed that it is best to completely
ignore the Swanington fragment, regardless of its possibili-
ties, together with all doubtful documentation. *See Analecta
Ord. Carm. Disc.*, II, 80; *Les Etudes Carmélitaines*, 13 année,
1928; *Le Carmel*, July-Aug., 1938; *Analecta Ord. Carm.*,
1939-1940.

[9] *Viridarium Ordinis B. Virginis Mariae de Monte Carmelo per Joannem Grossi; Analecta Ord. Carm.*, VIII, pg.
124.

[10] R. P. Benedict Zimmerman, O.C.D., in *Analecta Ord.
Carm. Disc.*, 1927; pg. 79. See also *Enciclopedia*, ch. VI, pg.
122-150.

[11] *The Scapular and Some Critics*, pg. 30.

[12] Henry III, Pat. Roll 37, m. 21, Public Rec. Off. London; cf. *The Scapular and Some Critics*, pg. 33.

[13] Innocent IV, 1252.

[14] MS. Harley 3, 383 (Bale's *Heliades*). In the list of confreres, taken from Nic Cantilupe, we find: ". . . to these must
be added the Popes Gregory X and Benedict XII, who, Cantilupe assures us, wore the scapular before their ascent to the
papal throne." N. B.: Fr. Benedict Zimmerman, O.C.D.,
opines that this list dates from 1348, being first recorded by
William Coventry.

[15] Acta Capitulorum Generalium (Rome, 1912), pg. 253.

[16] All references for these facts will appear in the text.

[17] Bk. of Kings IV, ch. ii, 9.

[18] Ordinamenti della Compagnia di S. Maria del Carmino,
1280: '. . . e trato i *chapucci* dinanzi ai detti capitani e con-
silleri e tutta la compangnia." cf. Analecta Ord. Carm. Disc.,
IV, 174.

[19] *The Scapular and Some Critics*, pg. 57.

[20] Most notably in Italy.

[21] cf. *The Scap. and Some Cr.*, pg. 55.

[22] Ibidem, pg. 50

[23] Ibidem, pg. 56.

[24] Carmelite Review, Vol. I, pg. 104: "A Holy Sister's

Vision"; Very Rev. Anastasius Kreidt, O. Carm. (?)

25 Miracles were largely the occasion of the rapid spread of the Scapular Devotion. John Grossi merely says: "Ratione ergo huius magni privilegii diversi Proceres regni Angliae, utpote Eduardus Rex Angliae secundus post conquestum (qui Fratres praedictos fundavit Axoniis, dans ipsis proprium pala-tium pro Conventu) similiter Dominus Henricus Dux Lan-castriae (qui miraculis multis dictur claruisse) et etiam multi alii nobiles illius regni praedicti, Scapulare Ordinis *clam* portaverunt, in quo postea obierunt." (Viridarium: Analecta, O. C., VIII, 140-141.)

26 "The cloaks shall indeed be with capuche and the upper part closed, by the cape of the capuche, over the breast; from that part lengthwise to the bottom they are to be open in order that the Scapular, which is inside, may be clearly discerned (dilucide discernatur) through the aperture." Cf. Analecta O C. D. IV, 174.

27 The purpose of the meeting was expressed thus: "A rendere laude a Dio e la gloriosa Virgine Madonna Santa Maria: che ne conceda e doni grazia che possiamo perseverare in bene e fare verace e buona fine." See ref. 18.

28 *Analecta Ord. Carm.* II, 612: "In the Bull of Urban IV 1262, there is already word of hearing the confessions of *con-fratres* (confraternity members), while at that time there were no confraternities in other Orders. Therefore, during the life of St. Simon Stock there already existed in our Order, *until this time almost completely contemplative,* secular confra-ternity members." See also: *The Scapular Devotion,* pg. 86.

29 *Analecta Ord. Carm.,* Vol. IV, pg. 241; *Scap. and Some Critics,* pg. 118.

30 *Catechism of Perseverance* is a typical example. Many used to mention the Swanington fragment, however, because that document was briefly treated and seemed convincing. That is probably why it came to be taken as the soul of the tradition.

31 *The Cath. Dict. and the Brown Scap.,* in *The Month,* 1886.

32 *Enciclopedia,* pg. 335.

33 *Catechism of Perseverance,* IV, 411.

34 *Carm. Rev.,* Vol. II, pg. 146.

Chapter Four

[1] Encyclical *Jucunda semper:* "The fact that by our prayer we seek the help of Mary is based on its foundation upon Her function of conciliating Divine grace for us."

[2] Encyclical on the Jubilee of the Immaculate Conception.

[3] R. P. Petitalot: *The Virgin Mother according to Theology* (London, 1889), pp. 409-429.

[4] S. Alphonsus Liguori: *Glorie di Maria* (Rome, 1932), t. I, pg. 317, 349.

[5] Ibidem, t. II, pg. 374.

[6] *Ut Laudes,* Sept. 18, 1577.

[7] *Serm. pour la Fête,* Oeuvres (Lyons, 1702), t. III.

[8] B. Fernandez: *In Gen. c. 3, a. 22.*

[9] R. P. Tanquerey: *The Spiritual Life* (Phila., 1930), pg. 86. N. B.: Reader will profit by starting at pg. 80 and reading through to pg. 95, in this connection.

[10] *Glorie,* t. I, pg. 310.

[11] *Sermon pour la fête du Scapulaire,* Oeuvres (Lyons, 1702), t. III.

[12] *Meditations, sub festo.*

Chapter Five

[1] St. Thomas: *Summa Theologica:* III, Q lxi, a, 1.

[2] R. P. Vermeersch, S.J.: *Meditations.*

[3] R. P. Chaignon, S. J.: *Meditations:* see ref. 18, ch. 2.

[4] Ibidem.

[5] S. Bernard: *In Salv. Reg. Serm. 1:* "Quod divinae pietatis abyssum, cui vult, quando vult et quomodo vult, creditur aperire; et quivis enormis peccator non pereat cui Sancta Sanctorum patrocinii sui suffragia praestat."

[6] See Ref. 7, ch. 4.

[7] Cf. *Sommes des Grandeurs de Marie* by Jourdain (Paris, 1903), t. V, p. 432.

[8] R. P. McGowan, O.S.A., in *Carm. Rev.* VIII, 207.

[9] See ref. 31, ch. 3.

[10] John, ii, 3.

[11] *Enciclopedia,* no. 95.

[12] *Annales du Carmel,* année 1881, pg. 199.

[13] Op. cit., ibidem.

[14] Op. cit. *Avant propos,* pg. 16.

[15] *Glorie,* t. I, pg. 133.

[16] *Pùlpito de la Virgen del Carmen* (Barcelona, 1928), t. II, pg. 117.

[17] See ref. 12, ch. IV.

[18] *Somme des Grandeurs de Marie,* t. V, pg. 407.

Chapter Six

[1] Deschamps: *The New Eve* (Tournai, 1862).

[2] *Sommes des Grandeurs de Marie,* t. V, pg. 433.

[3] S. Luke, i, 48-49.

[4] R. P. Fuhr, O.S.F., in *Carm. Rev.,* II, 201.

[5] Cath. Encycl. IV, 171.

[6] R. P. Schoberl, *Marien Predigten,* Vol. I, pg. 336.

[7] Sr. Agnes of Jesus (The "Little Flower's" eldest sister); Letter to present author, July 27, 1937.

[8] Clement VII, Bull *Ut Laudes,* Orvieto 1528, Rome, Aug. 12, 1530, B. II, 47; Clement X: *Agni Immaculati,* Aug. 11, 1670, B. II, 573, and *Universis,* July 13, 1672, Br. 388.

[9] Op. cit., ibidem.

[10] Cf. *Apologia Carmelitana* (R. P. Sylveira; appendix to *Commentaria in Acta Apostolorum*) Qu. XXIII, 314.

Chapter Seven

[1] See Ref. 16, ch. 2.

[2a] *Analecta O. Carm.,* Vol. IV, pg. 250.

[2b] This letter of Pope Pius XI was written to the Most Rev. Elias Magennis, Prior General of the Order of Carmel, dated in Rome, March 18, 1922. Father Magennis used it to open a book defending the authenticity of the copy of the Sabbatine Bull quoted in note No. 2a above. The book, *The Sabbatine Privilege of the Scapular,* was published by C. F. Connolly, New York, 1923, 141 pages. Although it presents both intrinsic and extrinsic arguments of value in defending the authenticity of this copy of the "Sabbatine Bull," no evidence to date can be said to be altogether conclusive. It can only be said that it is *probable* that the defended copy of the Bull is authentic, but there remains the fact that the copy had been rapidly and carelessly made and the important

word *Sabato* might just as well have been *subito*. Until further documents are discovered, this copy of the Bull cannot be taken as giving an accurate definition of the Sabbatine Privilege. For this our only reliance can be on the six-hundred-year-old tradition, on the decree of Pope Paul V, and on such other papal pronouncements as this one made in 1922 by Pope Pius XI.

²c SOUL Magazine, special issue, *Hope for the World,* Sept., 1952. See also author's book, *Russia Will Be Converted,* AMI Press, Washington, N. J., 1950.

³ Cf. Savaria, pg. 222.

⁴ *Revelations* (Rome, 1628), Bk. V, ch. liii.

⁵ R. P. Louvet, *Le Purgatoire d'après les révélations des Saints,* pg. 119, cf. Savaria, op. cit., pg. 223.

⁶ Louvet, op. cit., pg. 87.

⁷ Treatise on Psalm xxxvii; cf. Savaria, op. cit. 231

⁸ St. Bernardine: Serm. 3, de Nom. Mar. a. 2, c. 3.

⁹ *Glorie,* viii, pg. 305. (N. B.: Novarinus says, in Cit. Exs. 86, "Crediderim omnibus qui in flammis purgantur, Mariae meritis non solum leviores fuisse redditas illas poenas, sed et breviores, adeo ut cruciatum tempus contractum Virginis ope illius sit." Such is the meaning of the Sabbatine Privilege.

¹⁰ St. Dionysius, Cart. Serm. 2, de Ass. N. B.: Note that the Saint says that Mary *descends* and that *on a certain day:* Beatissima Virgo singulis annis in festivitate nativitatis Christi ad purgatorii loca cum multitudine angelorum descendit."

¹¹ Autobiography, ch. xxxviii (near the end): "I was amazed that he had not gone to purgatory. I understood that, having become a friar and carefully kept the rule, the Bulls of the Order had been of use to him, so that he did not pass into purgatory." (N. B.: Fr. Zimmerman opines that this does not refer to the Sabbatine Bull and to the Bulls that confirm it; but since he gives no grounds for his opinion and since he had very "queer" ideas about the Sabbatine Privilege itself, readers of his edition of St. Theresa's autobiography might discredit his opinion.)

¹² R. P. Bauss, *Das Fegfeuer* (Mainz, 1883) ; cf. *Scapulier-Büchlein* (Graz, 1892), pg. 34.

¹³ R. P. Serapion a S. Andrea, *Scapulier-Büchlein der Carmeliten-Bruderschaft* (Graz, 1892), pg. 34.

[14] These communications took place on Nov. 23rd, 1870. Accounts of them appear in current periodicals the world over. For a scholarly book account see Father Serapion's *Scapulier-Büchlein* cited above.

[15] The present copy of the Sabbatine Bull is not quite clear. Definite regulations have been made, however, by the Holy See. Consult *The Sabbatine Privilege* by P. E. Magennis, O. Carm., or any recent book on the Brown Scapular and its privileges.

[16] Ordinarily, however, a confessor will not mutate such a difficult condition as the recitation of office or tri-weekly abstinence into something too simple. The mutation is usually to the daily recitation of seven Our Fathers and Hail Marys. Note that there is a three-hundred-day indulgence attached to abstinence on Wednesdays and Saturdays.

[17] Of the nine Popes who have sanctioned the Sabbatine Privilege, note these words of St. Pius V (*Superna dispositione*, Feb. 8, 1565): "With apostolic authority and by tenor of the present, we approve each of the privileges (of the Carmelite Order) and also the Sabbatine."

[18] Attack on the Privilege was first made by Launoy and nothing has been added to his negative arguments since, except painful discussion; rather they are clearing. *The Sabbatine Privilege,* by the Most Rev. E. P. Magennis, O. Carm., is an excellent work in defense of our present copy of the Sabbatine Bull. However, the layman is to be warned that he will appreciate it only with difficulty, as well as other works of the same illustrious author, because the arguments are not very clearly presented and often they are strictly *ad hominem.*

[19] See note 22 below.

[20] *Carm. Rev.,* Vol. V, pg. 184.

[21] Deposition of witness present at the last moments of Saint John: Barthelemy de Saint Basile; cf. *St. Jean de la Croix,* by R. P. Bruno de Jésus-Marie (Plon. 1929), pp. 360 and 461.

[22] See *Glorie* (San Paolo Ed. pg. 306.)

[23] *Pulpito,* t. I, pg. 7.

[24] *Sommes des Grandeurs de Marie:* t. V, pg. 426.

Chapter Eight

[1] *Enciclopedia,* Chapter XXIX: El Jubileo del Carmen, pgs. 444 to 459.

[2] *Cincinnati Catholic Telegraph,* July, 1892.

[3] Cf. *Cath. Encycl.* III, 785.

[4] R. P. Rossi, *Dal Carmelo alla Gloria* (Ravenna, 1929), pg. 30 and 81. N. B.: Consult this work for the Sabbatine Privilege and in the present connection.

[5] *The Scapular Devotion,* pg. 97.

[6] This catalogue of indulgences is from the *Ritus servandus in receptione ad Confraternitatem B. V. M. de Monte Carmelo,* 1926. Cf. *Le Carmel,* 16 July, 1928, pg. 361.

[7] See No. 5 above.

[8] A. A. Lambing, D.D., LL.D.: *The Sacramentals:* under "Scapular."

Chapter Nine

[1] *Enciclopedia,* pg. 227; *Carm. Rev.,* III, pg. 323.

[2] *Carm. Rev.,* III, pg. 323.

[3] R. P. Hardt, O. Carm., *Das hl. Skapulier;* Wien, 1936.

[4] *Enciclopedia,* pg. 172, no. 92.

[5] Cf. *Carm. Rev.,* V, pg. 184.

[6] S. Catherine of Sienna, *Dial. c. 139:* Ipsa est a me velut esca dulcissima electa pro capiendis hominibus et animabus praecipue peccatorum.

[7] Cf. Savaria, pg. 179.

[8] *Enciclopedia,* pg. 181, no. 96.

[9] *Carm. Rev.,* IV, pg. 70; *Chroniques du Carmel,* July, 1892.

[10] Cf. *Glorie,* t. I, ch. vi, paragraph iii.

[11] *Glorie,* I, iii.

[12] *Marial,* p. 3, s. 1. Cf. *Glorie,* IX, 260.

[13] *Chroniques du Carmel,* 1889, in *Calendrier.*

Chapter Ten

[1] R. P. Garriguet, *La Vierge Marie* (Paris, 1933), pg. 1.

[2] *Pùlpito de la Virgen del Carmen,* Vol. I, pg. 38.

[3] *Apologia Carmelitana,* Quaestio XVII, pg. 304.

[4] See Ref. 1, chp. 3.

[5] R. P. Bayrhamer, *Sommes des Grandeurs de Marie,* t. V, pg. 422.

[6] *Carm. Rev.,* II, 190. N. B.: This type of miracle is not uncommon. It was duplicated at Ballon, in 1789, and was then formally documented at the chancery, signed and sealed by the Bishop himself. See R. P. Brocard: *Instructions sur le Scapulaire,* pg. 262; Savaria: *Le Scapulaire,* pg. 185.

[7] Rev. Dom Joseph A. Keller, D.D., *Marie Sanctissima* (London, 1930), ch. II.

[8] *Carm. Rev.,* Vol. V, pg. 338. The author actually interviewed Mr. James Fisher, two hundred miles from Sydney.

[9] *Il Monte Carmelo,* XXI, Fasc. vii, pg. 147.

[10] Op. cit., ibidem.

[11] *Glorie,* t. I, ch. iii, paragraph 2.·

[12] *L'Année Ecclésiastique,* II, pg. 180.

[13] *The Way of Perfection:* iii, no. 4.

[14] *Les Chroniques du Carmel,* Vol. I, pg. 114.

Chapter Eleven

[1] *Annales du Carmel,* 1881, pg. 199.

[2] Savaria, pg. 177.

[3] Conc. X in Jubil. Carm. monachii habita, anno 1751; cf. *Sommes des Grandeurs,* Vol. V, pg. 421.

[4] *Glorie,* t. I, pg. 104.

[5] *Sommes des Grandeurs,* t. V, pg. 426.

[6] *In Vita S. Theop.,* cf. *Glorie,* t. I, pg. 166.

[7] *Glorie,* t. I, pg. 166.

[8] Cf. *Glorie,* t. I, pg. 103.

[9] *Rev.* I, 6, c. 10.

[10] *Spec. B. V. M.,* lect. 3.

[11] *Sommes des Grandeurs de Marie,* V. 434.

[12] *Glorie,* t. I, ch. ii, 3.

[13] *Missale Carmelitarum* (Rome, 1935).

[14] De Sept. Verb. 1, i. ch. 12. (No specified connection with preceding quotation.)

Chapter Twelve

[1] St. Alphonsus: *Glorie,* t. I, pg. 208.

[2] Cornelius a Lapide: *Pro Fest. V. M.* s. 12, a. 1.

[3] *Apologia.* Quaest. XVII.

[4] *Our Lady in the Blessed Eucharist:* pg. 18.

[5] *Glorie:* I, viii, 1.

[6] Wadding. Ann. 1232, n. 28.

[7] B. Grignion de Montfort: *La Vraie Dévotion à la très Sainte Vierge* (Tours, 1933, nos. 31 and 50).

[8] *Pùlpito:* t. I, pg. 38.

[9] Encyc. on Jubilee of the Immaculate Conception; Cf. R. P. Husslein, S.J., *All Grace Through Mary* (New York, 1934, pamph., pg. 4).

[10] *Pùlpito:* t. II, pg. 269.

[11] *Chroniques du Carmel,* Vol. 1, pg. 100.

[12] R. P. Anton, O.M.Cap., *Im Dienste Gottes und der Menschen,* pg. 48.

[13] R. P. Taylor, *Saint Thérèse of Lisieux: An Autobiography* (New York, 1926), pg. 232.

[14] Letter of Sr. Anne of Jesus to present author (Sept. 6, 1937): "En pratique Sainte Thérèse de l'Enfant Jésus a imité le Bx. Grignion de Montfort puisqu'elle a fait passer son acte d'offrande à l'Amour miséricordieux par les mains de la très Sainte Vierge, mais elle ne connaissait pas la dévotion à Marie dite du Bx. Grignion. Sous un autre pli nous vous envoyons un livre sur la dévotion de Sainte Thérèse à la Sainte Vierge. Vous y verrez ce qu'est la spiritualité mariale de Notre Sainte." N. B.: The book sent was *Pour Aimer la Ste. Vierge comme Ste. Thérèse,* by R. P. Martin (Luçon, 1935). Sr. Anne's letter is quoted here exactly because some recent authors are not quite in agreement.

[15] S. Jean Eudes: *Le Coeur Admirable de la très Sainte Vierge* (Paris: Lethielleux, 1935), pg. 195.

[16] Letter to author: Nov. 5th, 1936.

[17] Op. cit., ibidem.

[18] Op. cit., ibidem.

[19] See ref. 4.

[20] Op. cit., no. 44.

[21] See ref. 24, ch. 3.

[22] Scala coelestis, quia per ipsam Deus descendit ad terras, ut per ipsam homines mereantur ascendere ad coelos. *In Annunt.,* s. 1.

[23] *Glorie:* t. I, ch. v, paragraph 2.

[24] Op. cit., no. 120.

[25] *Meditations* (From *Select Works:* London, 1884) sub festo.

[26] See ref. 18 of ch. 2.

Chapter Thirteen

[1] *Dum Attenta,* Nov. 28th, 1476, B. I. 428.

[2] *Ut Laudes,* Sept. 18th, 1577.

[3] R. P. Léon de St. Joachim, *Le Culte de St. Joseph et L'Ordre du Carmel,* Gand, 1902. 219 pgs.

[4] *De Serv. Dei Beatif.,* Lib. II, p. IV, xx, n. 18.

[5] Cf. *Le Culte de S. J. et L'Ord. du Carm.,* pg. 75.

[6] R. P. Huguet, *The Power of St. Joseph:* 21st Med.

[7] R. P. Huguet, op. cit., pg. 1.

[8] Life, xxxiii; Bonix I, pg. 454.

[9] Foundations, ch. xxxiii.

[10] See ref. 6 above.

[11] According to St. Thomas: see ref. 21.

[12] "Devotion to Mary is not the prominent characteristic of our religion which it ought to be. It has no faith in itself. Hence it is that Jesus is not loved, that heretics are not converted, that the Church is not exalted; that souls, which might be saints, wither and dwindle; that the Sacraments are not rightly frequented, or souls enthusiastically evangelised. Jesus is obscured because Mary is kept in the background. Thousands of souls perish because Mary is withheld from them. It is the miserable unworthy shadow which we call our devotion to the Blessed Virgin that is the cause of all these evils and omissions and declines. Yet, if we are to believe the revelations of the saints, God is pressing for a greater, a wider, a stronger, quite another devotion to His Blessed Mother." (Preface to his translation of Bl. Grig. De Montfort's *La Vraie Dévotion:* London, 1904.)

[13] Naturally Fr. Faber referred to the revelatory devotion preached by Grignion de Montfort, i. e., the consecration of oneself to Mary in order to be united to Her and thus to find Jesus.

[14] Cf. *Apologia Carmelitana,* p. 281: Ita referunt Guillelm. Sanc. de multicit. Ord. c. 3; Arnold, cap. 5; Paleonyd. Lib. 3, cap. 4; Thomas de Jesu, lib. 2 de frat. Carmeli, cap. 11.

[15] R. P. Phillips, *Loretto and the Holy House* (London,

1917), pp. 110-116. N. B.: Blessed Baptist of Mantua, on the Feast of Our Lady of Mount Carmel, 1489, witnessed the following marvel in the Holy House: "I will not pass over a thing which I saw with my own eyes and heard with my own ears. It happened that a French lady of some means and gently birth named Antonia, who had long been possessed by several evil spirits, was brought into the holy place that she might be delivered. Whilst a priest named Stephen, an exemplary man, was reading over her the usual exorcisms, one of the demons, who gave himself the name of Arctus, and who boasted that he had been the instigator of the massacre of all the Innocents, being asked whether this had been so indeed but that he owned it against his will, admitted, to his confusion, that he was *compelled by Mary* to confess the truth. He moreover pointed to the places (in the Holy House) where Gabriel, and where Mary, had each of them been. Being further adjured to say who had had charge of the place itself when it was in Nazareth, after repeated exorcisms he at length unwillingly replied that the ancient Carmelites had had the charge of it."

[16] Letters, Ed. P. Grégoire, III, rel. ix, pg. 402.
[17] Cf. Huguet, op. cit., Med. 25, pg. 130.
[18] Ibidem, Med. 30.
[19] R. P. Joseph Andrés, S. J., *Decor Carmeli*, I, Decor xiv, n. 40.
[20] *The Power of Saint Joseph:* R. P. Huguet; 20me Méd.
[21] Cf. ibidem, 10me Méd.
[22] Ibidem, 16me Méd.
[23] Ibidem, 4me Méd.
[24] *Les Chroniques du Carmel:* II, pg. 210.
[25] Op. cit., *Introduction.*

Chapter Fourteen

[1] *Revelations*, I, i; c. 35; cf. *Glorie*, V. ii.
[2] S. Jean Eudes, *Le Coeur Admirable de la très Sainte Vierge* (Paris: Lethielleux, 1935), pg. 195.
[3] *La Vie du Vénérable Francois de l'Enfant Jésus*, Chroniques du Carmel, 1892-93, pg. 272: "Saints make saints," said the Curé of Ars, a few hours before his death. Saint Margaret Mary Alacoque, that privileged confidante of the

Sacred Heart of Jesus, chose the Ven. Francis for her special protector; she read his life assiduously; she even spread devotion to him through the whole community; the name of the Venerable Brother was invoked every day at the common prayer.

[4] *Carm. Rev.*, Vol. IV, pg. 17.

[5] Op. cit., ibidem.

[6] *Paray le Monial*, Jan. 24, 1937 (letter to author): "Pour plus de précision, nous avons communiqué votre lettre au R. P. Supérieur des P. P. Jésuites d'ici, et il nous a répondu que rien, dans leurs archives et leurs traditions, ne donnait aucune lumière sur ce sujet. On peut seulement présumer que le Bienheureux, s'il avait une grande dévotion au St. Scapulaire, a pu l'inspirer aux confréries dont il s'occupait." N. B.: We only know positively that it was a confraternity of the Blessed Virgin.

[7] *Chroniques*, II, 191; and *Carm. Rev.*, IX, 355. N. B.: In these two sources one will find most of the facts narrated in this paragraph.

[8] *Chroniques*, II, 191.

[9] Ibidem, pg. 171.

[10] Daniel Lord, S.J., *What Is Wrong with Europe?* (pamph.) America Press, 1936.

[11] For other facts on Spain see *Enciclopedia*, pgs. 183-186; *Mount Carmel*, XVIII, no. 5, pg. 15 (Sept., 1938); *Irish Monthly*, Oct., 1936: "Despite the almost unbelievable atrocities being committed against the Faith in Spain, it is the stage for one of the greatest religious revivals in the history of the Church. Many of the soldiers wear on their breasts pictures of the Sacred Heart; others, the Scapular of Our Lady of Mount Carmel. Eyewitnesses say that it is not unusual to see a whole regiment stop to recite the Angelus in unity when the bells peal out."

[12] *Chroniques du Carmel*, I, 196b: The leader of the Christian armies was Prince Don Juan of Austria. The Venerable Catherine, who had been his governess before entering Carmel, "saw the Heavens open while the fleets were grappling with one another: the good angels on one side were interceding for the success of the Christian army; the bad angels were calling to the Divine Justice because of the bad Christians. Ven. Catherine flagellated herself to blood and

finished by appeasing the aroused Justice of the Sovereign Master." See also: *Revista Carmelitana:* VII, 228.

13 *Pùlpito,* II, 91.

14 *Tu Mater Verae Pacis!* Cf. *Glorie,* t. I, XI, iii.

15 R. P. Ramière, S.J., *The Apostleship of Prayer,* Phila., 1893.

16 R. P. Michael of St. Augustine, O.C.C., *Introductio ad Vitam Internam,* Rome, 1926 (Nova editio curante P. Gabriele Wessels) Appendix: *De Vita Mariae-formi et mariana in Maria propter Mariam,* pgs. 363 to 388.

17 *La Vraie Dévotion,* édit. cit., no. 64: Complaining to Our Lord of those who belittle devotion to Mary: "regardant LE ROSAIRE, LE SCAPULAIRE, LE CHAPELET, comme des dévotions de femmelettes, propres aux ignorants, sans lesquelles on peut se sauver."

18 *Chroniques,* I, pg. 226b: Ven. Dominic of Jesus and Mary.

19 There are volumes of revelatory Scapular thoughts in a comparison of ideas expressed in Müller's *Frohe Gottesliebe* (Trans. *St. Francis de Sales,* S & W, 1936) and in the article *Causa Nostrae Laetitiae in Les Etudes Carmélitaines* (19 année, II). Is not the present victory of joy that of the Queen of Carmel, of the Mother who promises Salvation to Her children? The Little Flower's life seems to say "Yes" . . .

20 See ref. II, ch. 6.

21 Msgr. Fulton Sheen. *The Cross and the Crisis,* pg. 217.

22 *The Catholic Student,* Jan. 1, 1937.

23 R. P. Petitot, O.P., *Apparitions de Notre-Dame à Bernadette;* cf. R. P. Elisée de la Nativité, O.C.D., *Etude historique* in *Le Carmel* of July, 1938, pg. 328.

24 Mgr. Besson, *Lourdes and Carmel;* Carm. Rcv., II, pgs. 157, 193, 211; *Chroniques du Carmel,* III, pg. 208, 394.

25 See ref. 13, ch. 13.

26 Nevers, April 3rd, 1937 (letter to author): "Notre Révérende Mère Générale et Monsieur notre Aumônier ayant pris connaissance de votre lettre me chargent de vous dire que nous regrettons vivement de ne pas etre parfaitement informés sur le sujet qui vous intéresse; jamais il n'a été fait d'etudes ici entre les relations de Lourdes et du Mont Carmel . . . Un ouvrage sur cette question pourrait avoir certainement son

intérêt. Bernadette n'a pas décrit la dernière apparition sinon en disant que la Dame était plus belle que toujours et très souriante elle n'a rien dit ce jour-là. Notre chère petite Sainte nous a toujours dit que Marie était vêtue de Blanc une ceinture bleue nouée à la taille et dont les pans tombaient devant . . . Nous tombons parfaitement d'accord dans l'affirmation que l'apparition de Notre Dame tant au Mont Carmel qu'à Lourdes est une manifestation de son amour pour les hommes. Oui, le Signe de la Sainte Vierge est bien nécessaire à l'heure actuelle et c'est en Elle que nous mettons tout notre espoir." N. B.: Although there were no studies made in Saint Bernadette's community, see *Les Chroniques du Carmel*, III, pgs. 208, 394.

[27] See ref. 24, ch. 13.

Chapter Fifteen

[1] R. P. Faber, *Doctrinal Subjects* (London, 1866), II, pg. 40.

[2] Letter to her sister Celine, August 15th, 1892.

[3] See ref. 15, chp. 14.

[4] *Glorie,* VIII, iii: t. I, pg. 317.

[5] Letter to clergy on the Apostleship of Prayer; cf. *Messenger* from Wimbledon, London, Sept., 1932.

[6] Op. cit., no 56.

[7] Op. cit., no. 57. N. B.: This is an allusion to Scripture. The two-edged sword of the Word of God is *the sword of the spirit*. St. Paul says: "Take unto you . . . the sword of the spirit, that is, the word of God." (Eph. VI, 17).

[8] Pro Fest. V. M., s. 8.

[9] See ref. 9, ch. 12.

[10] Serm. de B. M. V. Deiparae; cf. *Glorie,* t. I, p. 95.

[11] *Glorie,* t. I, pg. 95.

[12] *Chroniques,* IV, p. 76.

[13] See ref. 15, ch. 12.

[14] Op. cit., no. 54.

[15] *Autobiography,* cf. *Analecta Ord. Carm.* V, 411: *De Revelatione S. Theresiae quoad futura Ordinis nostri; Speculum Carmelitanum,* IX, pg. 790. N. B.: St. Theresa actually wrote, in her autobiography, "a certain Order." However, a companion of the Saint who was also endowed with mystical

favors (Bl. Anne of St. Bartholomew) tells us that St. Theresa did not mention that it was the Carmelite Order "lest others should be aggrieved". The present author translates it "the Scapular Family", a more meaningful term than "Carmelite Order", yet designating the same thing.

16 Op. cit., no. 57.

17 *Serm. pour la fête du Scapulaire,* (Oeuvres: Lyons, 1702; t. III.)